REFORMED FAITH
AND ECONOMICS

REFORMED FAITH AND ECONOMICS

Robert L. Stivers, Editor

UNIVERSITY
PRESS OF
AMERICA

LANHAM • NEW YORK • LONDON

Copyright © 1989 by

University Press of America,® Inc.

4720 Boston Way
Lanham, MD 20706

3 Henrietta Street
London WC2E 8LU England

British Cataloging in Publication Information Available

Co-published by arrangement with the Advisory Council
on Church and Society of the Presbyterian Church (U.S.A.)

"By What Authority...?" (Matthew 21:23) : An Unscholarly
Foray into Acts 2:44–45; 4:32–35 © 1989 by Jack L. Stotts

"Calvinism, Racism, and Economic Institutions"
© 1989 by Preston N. Williams

Library of Congress Cataloging-in-Publication Data

Reformed faith and economics / edited by Robert L. Stivers.
p.   cm.
"Co-published by arrangement with the Advisory Council on Church
and Society of the Presbyterian Church (U.S.A.)"
T.p. verso.
Includes bibliographies.
1. Economics– –Religious aspects– –Presbyterian Church (U.S.A.)
2. United States– –Economic conditions– –1981–   3. Presbyterian
Church (U.S.A.)– –Doctrines. 4. Presbyterian Church– –United
States– –Doctrines. 5. Reformed Church– –United States– –Doctrines.
I. Stivers, Robert L., 1940–   .
BX8969.5.R44   1989   89–30054 CIP
241'.64– –dc19
ISBN 0–8191–7380–0 (alk. paper).
ISBN 0–8191–7381–9 (pbk. : alk. paper)

To Dean H. Lewis

*Social Witness of the Church
and
Companion in Ministry*

Contents

List of Contributors

Marvin L. Chaney, Nathaniel Gray Professor of Hebrew Exegesis and Old Testament, San Francisco Theological Seminary, San Anselmo, California

Gordon Douglass, Dean of the College, Franklin and Marshall College, Lancaster, Pennsylvania

Jane Dempsey Douglass, Professor of Historical Theology, Princeton Theological Seminary, Princeton, New Jersey

William E. Gibson, Coordinator, Human Prospect Program and Editor of *The Egg*, Eco-Justice Project, Center for Religion, Ethics, and Social Policy, Cornell University, Ithaca, New York

Christian T. Iosso, Ph.D. candidate, Union Theological Seminary, New York, Formerly Associate for Mission Responsibility Through Investment and Special Studies, The United Presbyterian Church

Carol Johnston, Ph.D. candidate, Claremont Graduate School, Claremont, California

Dean H. Lewis, recently retired as Director, The Advisory Council on Church and Society, The Presbyterian Church, U.S.A.

David Little, Professor of Religious Studies, University of Virginia, Charlottesville, Virginia, currently Jennings Randolph Distinguished Fellow at the United States Institute of Peace, Washington, D.C.

Lee C. McDonald, George Erving Thompson Professor of Government, Pomona College, Claremont, California

William L. Raby, Senior Partner Emeritus, Touche Ross & Co.; Visiting Professor, Arizona State University, Tempe, Arizona; and Senior Editor, "The Raby Report on Tax Practice and Management"

Robert L. Stivers, Professor of Religion, Pacific Lutheran University, Tacoma, Washington

Bebb Wheeler Stone, Ph.D. candidate, the Joint Cooperative Program of the University of Pittsburgh, Department of Religious Studies and Pittsburgh Theological Seminary, and Associate Minister, Third Presbyterian Church, Pittsburgh, Pennsylvania

Ronald H. Stone, Professor of Social Ethics, Pittsburgh Theological Seminary, Pittsburgh, Pennsylvania

Jack L. Stotts, President, Austin Presbyterian Theological Seminary, Austin, Texas

Preston N. Williams, Houghton Professor of Theology and Contemporary Change, Harvard Divinity School, Cambridge, Massachusetts

Introduction

Reformed Faith and Economic Justice

Dean H. Lewis and
Robert L. Stivers

Successful navigation requires sturdy ships and savvy sailors. In a like manner economic policies which provide sustainable expansion, full employment, and low rates of inflation depend on an efficient and ethical economic system and wise leadership. In a protected port or on calm seas even a poorly maintained and badly sailed ship can provide an adequate platform and safe passage. In high winds and heavy seas such ships go under, and even the most stoutly built and surest sailed encounter rough going. Prudent sailors prepare for all weather.

Christians in the Reformed tradition want to be like prudent sailors as they look at economic issues. To popular opinion the late 1980's might seem an inappropriate time to address economic issues from a theological perspective. Sitting in its snug North American harbor, buoyed by a flood tide and wafted by light and gentle winds, the United States economic ship looks sound. The Gross National Product is growing, employment is up, and inflation is down. Hard times, according to official reports, are distant memories or vague possibilities. The free enterprise system seems to be in no need of reform. In such times as these, who wants lessons in ship repair and refresher courses in navigation? It is better to hold the analysis for high winds and heavy seas. Perhaps then the message can be heard.

The church, like the prudent sailor, does not always listen to popular opinion or official reports to set its maintenance and education schedules or to assess the conditions of its passengers. It has a prophetic tradition which is constantly ready to sail. To ships at anchor in snug harbors of prosperity and false optimism it speaks out against idolatry, illusion, and neglect. Judgment is the message. To ships at sea in the high winds of recession and the heavy seas of pessimism it talks softly of a God who is still active. Mercy, forgiveness, and hope are the message.

Reformed churches have always taken this tradition seriously. We take our bearings in this tradition from the Reformed religious vision which James Gustafson has summarized in three points: 1) a recognition of the sovereignty of God, 2) the commitment to piety or religious experience in Christian life, and 3) the regulation of personal and social life according to the will of God. This is a rich vision with a variety of well built rafts, skiffs, yachts, workhorse freighters, and luxury liners. It fixes our position. Our course and speed come from the dialogue of this biblically-based vision with new ways of imaging God, scientific analysis, and present experience.

The Reformed tradition has loaded on excellent new ecumenical cargo from several recent economic statements, such as the U.S. Catholic Bishops' Pastoral Letter on the Economy. We are incorporating the insights of feminists and straining to hear the voices of the world's poor who demand justice more than charity and call us to a new vantage point in their rafts.

We are acutely aware that the rising tide of economic expansion has not lifted all boats. Poverty persists, significantly in this country as a whole, enormously in the third world and our own urban ghettos. Unemployment remains high for periods of prosperity. In spite of so-called tax reform, the distribution of income and wealth has shifted in favor of the rich. The number of homeless families, either unable to afford housing or to find it, is a national disgrace. Poor families are breaking down at an alarming rate. Women and minority groups do not receive equal pay for equal work. Trade and budget deficits fuel economic expansion but raise vexing dilemmas for the next administration. Problems with food production, energy, resources, and pollution, which seem like driftwood in the present high tide, will be the flotsam and jetsam of a receding tide and obstacles on the high seas. Finally, third world dependency floats past us in the hull of development, with voices of liberation reporting the hull to be unseaworthy with debt, overcrowded with refugees, and under attack by pirates.

In storm or calm, God's Holy Spirit is at work, recalling us to the creative and personal power that undergirds our life together and to the convenants by which we are related in our human communities. That same power calls us to discern the signs of the times, to show compassion and do justice, and to construct more adequate and sturdy vessels for the future toward which the Spirit moves us. High tides or low, fair winds or foul, it makes no difference in the exercise of Christian prophetic responsibility. The call to speak comes from the Spirit, not from those who chart popular opinion and official courses, nor from those who fear to rock the boat.

Responses to the call of the Holy Spirit are made in this volume by fourteen Presbyterians representing a variety of academic disciplines and ministries related to political economy and economic justice. These Presbyterians participated in a series of week-long seminars held at Ghost Ranch in northern New Mexico in the summers of 1985-86-87. Ghost Ranch is a national adult study center of the Presbyterian Church (U.S.A.).

Each participant was asked to deliver a paper to the invited members of the seminar and to other Ghost Ranch program participants who elected to attend the sessions. The thirteen essays were selected from a much larger number by a committee of four. They were then reworked and put in order by the editor.

The Ghost Ranch seminars and this volume were sponsored by the Advisory Council on Church and Society of the Presbyterian Church (U.S.A.). Both were part of a larger multi-year process designed to produce among Presbyterians a better understanding of appropriate economic policy and structural alternatives in the emerging world society, and to develop a conceptual framework for the operation of the national economy under alternative policies more likely to yield results in accordance with the Christian understanding of justice for all.

The term "political economy" was deliberately applied to the overall exploration to emphasize that production, distribution, and consumption are powerfully determined and continuously affected by human policy decisions. An economic system is not the result of inexorable and immutable economic laws. The values of a society, its judgments about which is important to protect or achieve, are reflected consciously or unconsciously, intentionally or inadvertently, in the policy decisions which shape the economy. Policies can be changed, and within very broad limits the national economy can be designed and operated to serve the values that matter most to us.

These current efforts continue a Presbyterian tradition of vigorous witness for economic justice initiated in the early 1900's with a decade of strong support and active engagement with the movement of rights for organized labor. Through the heady pleasure cruise of the Twenties and the rough seas of the Thirties, the church consistently sought to apply what a 1937 General Assembly called the "Christian idea of God's rule in the world." As American affluence dramatically expanded in the Fifties, the church concentrated policy advocacy and its own resources on the world's poor majority. In the Sixties both church and nation awoke to the "curable moral cancer" of poverty in America and its deplorable connection to racial oppression. The church created special structures for witness and work that would move against the causes of poverty as well as relieve its symptoms. In the Seventies, faced with the unmistakable evidence of a desperately hungry world and structural relationships that prolonged the problems, Presbyterians created a structure for the sustained commitment to feed the hungry and to change structures and policies.

All these efforts, including the Ghost Ranch seminars and this volume, have at least three elements in common. 1) They recognize and address the reality that political policies and economic conditions are intertwined. 2) They define Christian witness and responsibility in terms of both compassionate service to the suffering and attempted reform of the structures and policies that result in suffering or allow it to continue. 3) They proceed from the conviction that Christians, using biblical standards of justice and equity, judge any policy or any order by its effect on people.

John Calvin, the initial systematizer of Reformed theology, was intimately involved with the policy and practice of political economy in the Geneva of his day. His writings and sermons reflect that involvement. Beyond the well-known thesis of a connection between later Calvinist ethics and the rise of entrepreneurial capitalism, there are basic principles in the Reformed tradition which illuminate the contemporary search for economic outcomes which will more faithfully reflect the biblical vision of a just and compassionate society. Those who were invited to prepare papers for the Ghost Ranch seminars were asked to identify these principles as they simultaneously addressed the issues of modern political economy.

The thirteen essays in this volume are arranged under four headings: 1) Biblical Perspectives, 2) The Reformed Tradition on Economic Justice, 3) Contemporary Policy Issues, and 4) Church Responses. Under the first heading are two essays. In the first chapter Jack Stotts looks carefully at passages from the Book of Acts and raises the issue of authority in Christian economic ethics. Stotts is an ethicist rather than a biblical scholar, and is well known to Presbyterians as one of their best teachers. In the second chapter, biblical scholar Marvin Chaney describes a process of land seizure and consolidation for the purpose of increasing the production of cash crops for export in eighth century B.C.E. Israel. The process has striking parallels to similar developments in the third world today.

The Reformed Tradition on Economic Justice is the focus of the second section. Ronald Stone leads off in Chapter Three with an excellent summary of John Calvin's thinking on the subject. He is followed in Chapter Four by Preston Williams who raises disturbing questions about racism in the Reformed tradition, in particular the Presbyterian Church. Williams' questions provide a clear imperative for the Presbyterian Church to reform itself. In Chapter Five David Little continues the discussion of John Calvin and the Reformed tradition. Little successfully builds a foundation in Calvin for progressive taxation, but only after developing Calvin's split personality on the subject.

The third section is oriented to specific issues. Robert Stivers picks up in Chapter Six where David Little left off by developing a contemporary ethical analysis to address tax reform and to advocate progressive taxation. William Raby in Chapter Seven is more specific on taxes, offering a stinging critique of recent tax reform efforts in the United States.

Moving beyond the issue of taxes, Gordon and Jane Dempsey Douglass team up in Chapter Eight to address agricultural issues, specifically sustainability. Their essay is a model of thoroughness and of how theologians and economists should integrate disciplines. William Gibson turns the heat up in Chapter Nine. In prophetic fashion, Gibson takes current economic arrangements to task and envisions a more just future.

Bebb Wheeler Stone brings in both feminist and third world perspectives in Chapter Ten. Her use of third world women's stories is a refreshing and enlightening change to the more abstract reasoning of the other essay. Finally, Lee McDonald looks at the classical concept of virtue in Chapter Eleven from the vantage point of a political scientist. His analysis helps to reform our thinking about social policy to include considerations of character.

The last section turns to the Church. Carol Johnston thoughtfully reflects on the U.S. Catholic Bishops' Pastoral Letter on the Economy. Her appreciative essay draws out significant insights for those in the Reformed tradition. Christian Iosso wraps it up with his historical look at General Assembly statements on economics. His essay is descriptive and critical. Constructively he suggests several new directions for Presbyterian social witness on economic justice.

This volume marks the end of one era in the Presbyterian Church and the beginning of a new. The Advisory Council on Church and Society went out of existence in January 1988 in the major restructuring occasioned by the reunion of the two largest Presbyterian churches in the United States. In the new organization the Committee on Social Witness and Policy and the Social Justice and Peacemaking Unit, both with excellent new leadership, will be responsible for carrying on the policy and program tradition in the social witness of the Presbyterian Church (U.S.A.).

That witness will surely continue to respond to the storms and perils which beset the economic voyage and the problems which plague many of the passengers. And where might the search for a better ship lead? Certainly to an increasing focus on the world as the basic economic unit. Both economic activity and economic problems have escaped the bounds of nation-states and outrun their capacity to manage or control. The great transnational conglomerates must be made accountable to the global community and responsible to global regulation. The search for effective authority and the strictures to ensure accountability is an urgent priority.

The several interlocking and accelerating ecological crises will certainly become ever more prominent. Acid rain and ozone depletion, ocean death and forest loss, land erosion and water degradation, species loss and population growth—the current damage is epidemic and the rate of industrialization and urbanization assures catastrophe in the absence of drastic remedial action. These are not the ordinary high seas and heavy winds of any ocean crossing. The basic patterns and values of the global technological-industrial political economy will undergo fundamental modification in the face of these realities. If the church continues faithful to its prophetic task, it will give high priority to the needed modifications, knowing the consequences of waiting to make repairs until an ecological crisis strikes.

In making this emphasis, ongoing economic issues cannot be ignored. In their efforts at reform, Presbyterians must continue in advocacy and service to meet the specific and immediate needs of those victimized and oppressed by current economic policies and structures. A 1983 report of the Committee on A Just Political Economy provides a telling reminder of that commitment and a fitting conclusion for this introduction.

The biblical authors never gave an abstract definition of justice but keep pointing to the poor, the oppressed, and the vulnerable as those whom God is especially concerned to protect and restore. Justice, we find, means standing with the lowest neighbor, rejecting the worship of wealth or power, and creating structures supportive of all, with public officials acting for the good of all. Justice thus practiced lies at the center of a right relationship between a people and the living God who acts in their own unfolding history.

Part One
Biblical Perspectives

Chapter One

"By What Authority . . . ?" (Matthew 21:23): An Unscholarly Foray into Acts 2:44–45; 4:32–35

Jack L. Stotts

One of the pivotal convictions of our Reformed heritage is that scripture is authoritative for the faithful life, both for individuals and for the church. The Westminster Confession of Faith's initial chapter is entitled, "Of the Holy Scriptures." It includes this affirmation:

> Although the light of nature, and the works of creation and providence, do so far manifest the goodness, wisdom and power of God, as to leave men inexcusable; yet are they not sufficient to give that knowledge of God, and of his will, which is necessary unto salvation; therefore it pleased the Lord, at sundry times, and in diverse manners, to reveal himself, and to declare that his will unto his Church, and afterwards for the better preserving and propagating of the truth, and for the more sure establishment and comfort of the Church against the corruption of the flesh, and the malice of Satan and of the world, to commit the same wholly unto writing; which maketh the Holy Scripture to be most necessary; those former ways of God's revealing his will unto his people being now ceased.

More recently, the Confession of 1967 maintains:

> The one sufficient revelation of God is Jesus Christ, the Word of God incarnate, to whom the Holy Spirit bears unique and authoritative

3

witness through the Holy Scriptures, which are received and obeyed as the word of God written. The scriptures are not a witness among others, but the witness without parallel. The church has received the books of the Old and New Testaments as prophetic and apostolic testimony in which it hears the work of God by which its faith and obedience are nourished and regulated.

While the question of the locus and force of authority itself is disputed,[1] the Reformed churches testify by their confessions that all of life and all of faith—including confessions of faith—are subordinate to scriptures. This notion is related, as Hannah Arendt argues, to the sense of the "sacredness of foundation," the proposal of a tradition that once something has been founded it remains binding for future generations. The Latin root of the word *auctoritas* is *augere*, augment, and the task of those who claim a foundational base is that of augmenting what has been received.[2]

Authority so understood has reference to the documents and experiences from the past that have a claim both upon the here and now and also upon the future of a people. The process by which past becomes present and future may, indeed does, involve theological convictions about *how* past becomes present (doctrines of the spirit, for example). It also involves human interpretations of the central or core meanings reflected or expressed in the "authoritative documents" (hermeneutics).

What I propose to do in this brief and very unscholarly paper is to examine how various interpreters use a particular passage from scripture that refers to the economic life of the early Christian community and then apply it to the current scene. Acts 2:44–45 and 4:32–35 have been chosen because they have been reference points, both historically and currently, for those addressing the economic life of the church and of the society. My goal is twofold: (1) to illustrate how particular religious traditions (Reformed and Roman Catholic, in this instance) shape the way the scriptures are interpreted; and (2) to encourage discussion as to how we legitimately may use scriptures in providing an authority base for our contemporary concerns. Certainly the question addressed to Jesus by the chief priests and elders is one put to General Assemblies, to Councils of General Assemblies, and to each of us who proposes an economic policy and program from a "Christian" perspective, "By what authority are you doing these things and who gave you this authority?" (Matthew 22:23b)

The verses in Acts are as follows:

2:44–46 And all who believed were together and had all things in common; and they sold their possessions and goods and distributed them to all, as any had need,

4:32–35 Now the company of those who believed were of one heart and soul, and not one said that any of the things which he possessed was his own, but they had everything in common. And with great power the apostles gave their testimony to the resurrection of the Lord Jesus, and great grace was upon them all. There was not a needy person among them, for as many as were possessors of lands or houses sold them, and brought the proceeds of what was sold and laid it at the apostles' feet; and distribution was made to each as any had need. (RSV)

The setting is the early life of the Christian church. Acts 2:44–45 follows immediately upon the heels of Pentecost. The economic community of distribution is formed by the spirits's being "distributed" among them.

Acts 4:32–35 follows upon the initial proclamation of the Word, the arrest and subsequent release of Peter and John, and the "second Pentecost." The community remains as it was prior to expansion (by 5,000 men according to Acts 4:4) and persecution.

Now the question for us is, "What authority does or might the behavior of this foundational community have for us today? Or, "How does one translate this 'religious communism of love' into practical economics?" Or, "Does one discuss this passage of scriptures as purely time-bound and irrelevant, a 'white elephant' to be shelved, but of no particular value?"[3]

It is Ernst Troeltsch from whom I take the economic description of the early church depicted in Acts as a religious communism of love. Troeltsch contends that these verses point to a religious community whose life involved "a communism which regarded the pooling of possessions as a proof of love and of the religious spirit of sacrifice."[4] It was a communism of consumers, in which all had a moral claim on what others possessed. But it presumed that the "means of production" and productive activity were embedded in a system of private enterprise, allowing Christians to earn income to enable them to practice generosity and sacrifice. Troeltsch further argued that this communism of love (voluntarily entered into) was self-consciously understood to be confined to the Christian community; it must not be understood as having a directionality toward a program of social reform in general.

What is present in this community and in the narrative about it is the positive moment of love to fill the need of the neighbor, even to the point of selling possessions, and the realization that wealth must be feared because of its danger for the health of the soul.

Troeltsch's conclusion is that this religious communism is a by-product of Christianity and not a fundamental idea. He therefore relativizes the particular form of this community while affirming the impulses of love and fear of wealth. Yet, he admits, one of the permanent results of the accounts in Acts is the ideal of a communism of love.[5]

One of the streams of influence of this idea of a religious communism of love is present in the Roman Catholic tradition of orders. A cursory examination of this movement, diverse as it is, points to the remarkable continuance of an appeal to "all things being held in common." In order after order it is a communion of love which holds together community ownership of means of production with the communal sharing of goods and profits. The "surplus" may be used by the community for its capital needs or may be shared with the "secular" community in the form of services or alms. But this way of communal living is classically a "religious way," a way of perfection, not one commended for the society.

Luke T. Johnson, Roman Catholic New Testament scholar, writes in *Sharing Possessions* that the monastic community's appeal to the Lukan depiction of the early community is all founded on a misrepresentation of the biblical message. He writes:

> the idealized picture stands as utopian in the best sense—it presents an image from the past of a kind of spiritual sharing and unity against which later communities could measure themselves. Luke is not proposing this picture as a concrete example to be imitated, by structuring a life on the basis of community possessions. To read these passages in Acts as providing the idiological legitimation for such a structuring of the Christian community is to misread them.
>
> But this is precisely the way in which the monastic tradition of the West has read these passages. The monks sought the origins of their cenobitic life in the primitive Jerusalem community and saw themselves as successors to the apostolic life. The Acts passages appears everywhere in the monastic legislation as the legitimation for having common goods.[6]

Johnson's appeal is not unlike Troeltsch's. He affirms the critical significance of the biblical impulses but demythologizes the Acts verses as gounds for constructing concrete human communities. His proposal for economics is rather alms-giving, or doing justice, the content of which is to be determined by human reason and imagination in the emergent historical situation. The basic problem with the monastic appeals to the foundational literalness of the Acts passages is that they are inaccurate in interpreting the scriptures. They do no recognize that in Acts, Luke is providing:

> the familiar picture of the restoration of the perfect 'primal state' which has analogies with the sharing of goods among the Scythians, Plato's doctrine of the state . . . and the 'primal community' of the Pythogorians in Southern Italy.[7]

They further do not take into account the expectation of the Lord's imminent return.

It is Johnson's conclusion that,

> There is no Christian economic structure to be found in the Bible, any more than there is a Christian political structure or educational system. The Bible does not tell us how to organize our lives together, and still less which things we should call private and which public. Nor does it propose a clear program of social change. It does not even present one way of sharing possessions as uniquely appropriate. A Christian social ethic must be forged (repeatedly, as in theology) within the tension established by two realities: the demands of faith in the one God who creates, sustains and saves us and the concrete, changing structures of the world we encounter in every age.[8]

Yet while Johnson maintains that the use of the Acts passage to justify a particular type of religious economic order is unjustified by the canons of biblical scholarship, another contemporary Roman Catholic New Testament Scholar extends the Acts model from a religious model to a secular one. José Miranda in *Communism in the Bible* appeals to our Acts passages as justification for his view that, "the notion of communism is in the New Testament, right down to the letter."[9] In fact, Miranda writes, "the definition Marx borrowed from Louis Blanc, 'From each according to his capacities, to each one according to his needs' is inspired by, if not directly copied from, Luke's formulation eighteen centuries earlier."[10]

Miranda rejects the monastic use of Acts 2 and 4 as legitimation for a perfectionist or better way. But he does so not to relativize the Lukan model to one time and place but to make it applicable to all Christians. Luke's normative intention was that all Christians should live in this fashion. And Luke's position is consistent with that of Jesus. "Jesus was himself a communist."[11] The early experience of the church failed not because of the expansion of the church's membership, leading to life in diverse situations and with differing claims. It failed because there were too few real Christians. Indeed, "according to Luke, what is optional is not communism but christianity." The death of Ananias and Sapphira is due to their betrayal of communism.

Miranda's passionate defense of the Lukan model of communistic community is not to be equated with a defense of what he calls Russian state capitalism. What he does mean is what he finds in the scriptures, for which our Acts 2 and 4 passages are foci. The characteristics of a biblical economics so displayed is the absence of private property, the presence of a classless society in which there is no differentiating wealth,[12] no private profit,[13] and a community entered freely.

For Miranda the communist project is *the historical* project that will lead to freedom for each and for all. It is a special kind of communism, but its authority base is secure in a literal use of the scriptures.

For both Johnson and Miranda the concern for the poor is a driving and primary norm for economic life. For the former, that concern may be met through economic systems and practices that vary with the times and places. For Miranda, only a communist system can treat the poor's needs and condition.

I have tried to illustrate how two Roman Catholic scholars use the Acts scriptures. Both are compelled to take them seriously as narrative not only because "they are there" but because of the tradition of practice in their church tradition. Johnson fights against the literal authority of the life depicted in the passage because of the behavior's being applied too restrictively, that is, only in monastic settings. Miranda joins that struggle but extends the literal application to a global historical exterprise. His norms are themselves general, and issues of power and governance are not treated. But the ideological vision is preserved. In the one, what has continuing biblical authority is the call to do justice (alms-giving), the impulse of love, and concern for the poor. For Miranda it is a form of life together with specific content that has biblical authority.

We turn to Reformed thinkers next. I have selected three study papers recently published by the Presbyterian Church (U.S.A.) in one or more of its recent incarnations. They are *Christian Faith and Economic Justice, Toward a Just, Caring and Dynamic Political Economy,* and *A Theology of Compensation.* Then I will look at Calvin's treatment of our passages. I am acutely aware of the difference between a study paper and a study done by a single author. But I take all of them as representative of traditions.

It is striking that in all three study documents the Acts 2 and 4 passages are seldom cited. They clearly are not at the center of thinking. In *Christian Faith and Economic Justice*, Acts 2:44–45 is used along with other passages to illustrate the presence in the biblical story of sharing with the poor. Holding all things in common is not treated. *Towards a Just, Caring and Dynamic Political Economy* does not mention the Acts verses. *A Theology of Compensation* proposes an alternative economics for the church. Its sole appeal to the context of the Acts verses is to Acts 5, the Ananias and Sapphira story. This story is used to illustrate the temptation and threat of "a private surplus" withheld from the community. Despite this last paper's explicit concern for egalitarianism as opposed to meritocracy in the church, the appeal of the early church's model is not used.

What conclusions do I draw from the meagerness of references in these papers to Acts 2 and 4? One is that all three papers use a thematic approach to biblical materials. Scripture citations are used to illustrate scriptural motifs such as God's sovereignty, God's doing and demanding of justice, and justice as requiring special concern for the poor and oppressed. There is no attempt at exegesis of particular passages, though exegesis of all passages is assumed. There is clearly no felt need to draw from the one institutional expression of early church economics. I do not mean those conclusions to be pejorative. But what may be clear is that since economics is a more pervasive issue in the Biblical story than a more circumscribed topic such as homosexuality, those of us in the Reformed tradition believe it is appropriate in dealing with economics not to exegete specific passages. Or, there may be biblical images or themes that become biblical bases for our perspective. For example, in *Towards a Just, Caring and Dynamic Political Economy*, the images of jubilee (Luke 4:18–19) and last judgment (Matthew 25:31ff) are cited and may be the underground streams that water the theological and ethical materials. But if that is the case, they are implied, not explicit. Whatever the situation, we tend to speak and to write more in terms of biblical understandings, biblical themes, and biblical perspectives, more than being engaged with specific passages.

How does John Calvin treat the Acts passages? In his *Commentary Upon the Acts of the Apostles* Calvin writes that Acts 2:43–45 teaches that "we must relieve the poverty of our brethren with our plenty." Calvin goes on to reassure the reader against the excess of the Anabaptists who "thought there was no church unless all men's goods were put and gathered together, as it were, in one heap, that they might all one with another take thereof."[14] He affirms that the early Christians's goods were made common only to relieve the "present necessity" of the poor. And in his comment on Acts 4:43–45, he wrote that the faithful did not sell all that they had but only so much as need required.

> For neither doth Luke in this place prescribe a law to all men which they must of necessity follow, while that he reckoneth up what they did in whom a certain singular efficacy and power of the Holy Spirit of God did show itself; neither doth he speak generally of all men, that it can be gathered that they were not counted Christians which did not sell all that they had.[15]

Also, Calvin suggests that the principle of division was not equality but need. "Therefore the goods were not equally divided, but there was a discreet distribution made." [16] He concludes that Luke was not proposing a law for all to follow when he refers to all things being held in common. Luke was showing that those in need must always be cared for and that those who had much were given the heart to share what they had. Calvin in dealing with Acts 2 and 4 retains the voluntary character of sharing in the church and the assumption of private ownership of goods.

To conclude let me draw out some propositions for our reflections.

1. For Protestant Christians of the Presbyterian Church (U.S.A.) family, who have written the papers cited above, scripture is formally authoritative, but in none is there a clear sense of "how" it is authoritative. In these papers, the authors select biblical themes or images without either giving explicit attention to the principle of selection or arguing for their validity. There is apparently an assumption that mere reference to biblical perspectives is sufficient to satisfy issues of biblical authority. Is the question of biblical authority not begged by this type of practice? or, is biblical authority a background question that only emerges if the issue addressed becomes controversial?

2. In Calvin and in the study papers, it is clear that scriptural authority for Christian faithfulness is located in biblical themes or perspectives, not in specific biblical passages. These themes are not un-biblical. They are related, of course, to specific scriptural refer-

ences, finding in the latter both origin and example. But it is by the full range of scriptural themes that any one biblical passage is to be interpreted. Thus, passages such as Acts 2 and 4 become authoritative as they shape, fit into and reflect convictions that reappear consistently throughout the Bible. This type of interpretation invites rather than forecloses questions of which themes are both valid and pertinent, as well as of priority ranking. Authority is dislodged from any single portion of scripture and located in the dynamic interaction internal to the bible and between and among scripture, interpreters, and the Spirit. Questions of authority usher us into the house of hermeneutics.

3. A seldom addressed issue of biblical authority is the way such interpretation is shaped by the particular tradition's institutional history. Often attention is given in hermeneutics to the thought worlds of then and now and to the social environment out of which the scriptures come. But the interpretative consequences of a particular community's social organization are seldom considered. James Luther Adams has instructed us as to the need to explore how different forms of piety affect different kinds of social organization.[17] But we also can be instructed by inquiring as to how different forms of social organization shape differing forms of biblical interpretation. Thus, the presence of monastic communities in the Roman Catholic tradition appealing to Acts 2 and 4 as authorities requires Roman Catholic scholars who treat economic matters to attend to their claims. Roman Catholic scholars are forced by Roman Catholic institutions to attend to Acts 2 and 4 which have legitimated those communities. An institutional hermeneutic is required. The Reformed Tradition, with a different organizational history and agenda had no such obligation or has felt no such need.

4. The Reformed perspectives cited above suggest that when it comes to economic matters there is a kind of "passionate pragmatism" with reference to contemporary policies to be proposed and sought. The passion derives from the grace and mercy of God which joins neighbors to neighbors in affection and caring, and which become specified in such themes as "bias for the poor." The pragmatism refers to the necessity of dealing with changing environments of production, distribution and consumption, which together and individually create new conditions to be addressed. "Passionate pragmatism" rejects any ideology as inadequate finally to the contingencies of history and to a religion of radical monotheism.

5. Finally, one should not be surprised that the issue of "by what

authority" eludes unequivocal answers and invites the interviewer and the interviewee into an exploration of multiple levels of meaning and relationships. The issue of authority will recur in the church whenever controversial matters appear. More to the point of this paper, the issue of biblical authority will be provoked and therefore require attention over and over again as the church grapples with social, political and economic policies. If it does not appear, then the Reformed church's authority—as it has historically understood its own authority base—is in more serious difficulty than has been previously imagined. To put it succinctly, in controversial matters the attention given to biblical authority is a barometer *both* of the significance of the issue addressed *and of* the viability of the church's unique base—scripture—for discerning God's purposes and intentions for the contemporary world.

Endnotes

1. Hannah Arendt in an essay entitled, "What is Authority," *Between Past and Future* (New York: World Publishing Company, 1963) writes, ". . . authority has vanished from the modern world. Since we can no longer fall back upon authentic and undisputable experiences common to all, the term has become clouded by controversy and confusion." (p. 91)

2. *Ibid.*, pp. 119, 120

3. Victor Furnish uses the phrase White Elephant in his book *The Moral Teaching of Paul* (Nashville: Abingdon, 1979) to refer to the view held by numerous Christians that the scriptures are interesting historical documents but have no bearing on contemporary issues.

4. Ernst Troeltsch, *The Social Teachings of the Christian Church*, Vol. I, p. 62.

5. *Ibid.*, p. 63.

6. Luke T. Johnson, *Sharing Possessions* (Philadelphia: Fortress Press, 1981), p. 129.

7. Martin Hengel, *Property and Riches in the Early Church* (Philadelphia: Fortress Press, 1974), p. 9.

8. Johnson, *Sharing Possessions*, p. 115.

9. José Miranda, *Communism in the Bible* (New York: Orbis Books, 1982), p. 1.

10. *Ibid.*, p. 2.

11. *Ibid.*, p. 8.

12. *Ibid.*, p. 19. Miranda cites Mark 10:21–25 as presenting the idea of a classless society.

13. *Ibid.*, pp. 49–50.

"The etymology of *besa* ("profit, gain") is incision, extraction by cutting with a knife. But the conspiracy of the ideologues of the establishment has reached the degree that it manages to keep the truth even from readers who have taken the trouble to study Hebrew. The dictionaries of biblical Hebrew translate *besa* as "unjust profit"—and then forget to add that the Bible has no word for "just profit"! That is because for the Bible there is no such thing as profit. It is as if when we came to the word na'af ("adultery") we were told it means "illicit adultery." Establishment botching knows no bounds.

14. John Calvin. *Commentary Upon the Acts of the Apostles* (Grand Rapids: Erdmans, 1948), p. 130.

15. *Ibid.*, p. 193.

16. *Ibid.*, p. 192.

17. James Luther Adams, *On Being Human Religiously* (Boston: Beacon Press, 1976), p. 131.

Chapter Two

Bitter Bounty: The Dynamics of Political Economy Critiqued by the Eighth-Century Prophets

Marvin L. Chaney

No segment of Christendom has emphasized the Old Testament as Christian Scripture more than the Reformed tradition. When one asks what so significant a portion of the Reformed heritage has to say about economics—particularly about economic justice—the Hebrew prophets come readily to mind. For many Reformed Christians, passages from the eighth-century prophets, Amos, Hosea, Isaiah, and Micah, give classical articulation to this prophetic view of economic realities.

The appropriation of these texts by the modern community of faith has often lacked clarity and effect, however, because of a lack of hermeneutical precision. A penchant for abstraction can sometimes be the culprit. The injunction of Amos 5:24 to "let justice roll down like waters," for example, is frequently quoted in tones which presuppose that everyone agrees about what economics justice is, but that certain people must be persuaded to be for it rather than against it. Such are not the terms of reality. People of faith in the vast majority favor economic justice as an abstraction, even as they can almost never agree about what it is or how to achieve it. The Almighty may create well enough *ex nihilo*, but mere mortals require data, especially when it comes to economics!

If abstraction is the Scylla of an adequate hermeneutic of prophetic economics, particularism is the Charybdis. Under the impress of the extreme individualism of American culture, many modern readers of the prophetic books assume that these texts excoriate a few venal individuals who deviated from norms otherwise observed in what was a healthy and just economic system.

Once again, little could be farther from the realities of ancient Israel and Judah. As a careful reading of the oracles concerning economic dynamics makes clear, the prophets critique certain changes in the political economy as an integrated whole. While these changes benefited the powerful and privileged few who initiated them *as a generic class,* the prophets insist that they did so at the expense of even meager subsistence for the impoverished majority, who are also understood *as a generic class.*

Dozens of oracles in the eighth-century prophets declare the judgment of Yahweh's court against the former because of their oppression of the latter. Although these texts allude to various aspects of the economic dynamics involved, they nowhere describe them in full. All parties to the ancient conflict were familiar with the operations of their economy—even though they valued them quite differently— and thus did not require that they be rehearsed. Modern readers of the prophets share no such preunderstanding, a fact which occasions this preliminary attempt to reconstruct those systemic dynamics for those not participant in them.

Detailed exegesis of the pertinent prophetic texts would require a book far exceeding the bounds of this paper. Attention here will be focused instead on integrating data from disparate sources outside the prophetic books. Against the background thus sketched, it is hoped, many of the more obvious oracles will become self-explanatory.

My address to this task marks a return to matters previously treated far too briefly. In a paper first presented in December of 1981, I wrote as follows regarding the eighth century B.C.E.:

> For historical reasons . . . most freeholding peasants in Israel and Judah were located in the highlands. As many small, subsistence plots in this hill country were foreclosed upon and joined together to form large estates, a change in the method of tillage also took place. Upland fields previously intercropped to provide a mixed subsistence for peasant families were combined into large and "efficient" vineyards and olive orchards producing a single crop for market. The increased production of wine and oil resulting from the formation of these plantations or latifundia played at least two roles in the new scheme of things. On the

one hand, wine and oil were central to the increasingly consumptive lifestyle of the local elite, epitomized in a sodality called the *marzeah*. On the other, since wine and oil were more valuable than most agricultural commodities per unit of weight or volume, they made ideal exports to exchange for the luxury and strategic imports coveted by members of the ruling classes.

But the "efficiency" of these cash crops came at a brutal cost to the sufficiency of the livelihood which they afforded the peasants who actually produced them. The old system of freehold had provided this peasant majority secure access to a modest but adequate and integrated living. The new system saw them labor in the same fields, but only according to the cyclical demands of viticulture and orcharding and at wages for day-labor depressed by a sustained buyer's market. During lulls in the agricultural calendar, they were as unemployed as landless. Jobless or not, they were forced into the marketplace of which they had little or no experience to buy wheat and barley, the staples of their diet. They had previously produced these cereals sufficiently for themselves in their hillside plots, but now the same grains were grown "efficiently" on the large estates of the alluvial plains and piedmont region and shipped to market. In the marketplace, the meager and irregular wages of fieldhands bought even less sustenance than they should have because the vulnerable peasants were cheated with adulterated grain and dishonest weights and measures. Finally, the processes of foreclosure and expropriation which initiated these dynamics were accelerated by a wholesale suborning of the courts. Instead of stopping foreclosures based upon illegal forms of interest, these corrupted courts sanctioned the proceedings.[1]

Although few today would accept without considerable nuance so bald a sketch of these dynamics as this offered in 1981 under the pressures of space and time, a remarkable diversity of scholars has since documented in greater detail many of the factors whose integration I sought then under a concept of latifundialization. The following attempt to delineate those factors necessarily moves seriatim, but its intent is to explore their systemic integration.

The political and military power and territorial expansion of Israel and Judah in the eighth century B.C.E.—particularly during the long and mostly concurrent reigns of Jeroboam II and Uzziah—are beyond doubt. "By the mid-eighth century the dimensions of Israel and Judah together lacked but little of being as great as those of the empire of Solomon."[2] The particulars are well documented elsewhere,[3] and need not detain us here.

I would only highlight briefly two elements in this geopolitical situation. 1) Not since the "United Monarchy" of David and Solomon had Israel and Judah been so secure from immediate, external, military threat. This relative security, coupled with the lengthy tenure in office of both the allied kings, granted a greater than usual opportunity for royal administrations to rearrange their domestic furniture, including that of their economies. The accession of Tiglath-pileser III to the Assyrian throne in 745 B.C.E. may serve conveniently to symbolize the closing of that window of opportunity. 2) That Jeroboam II and Uzziah had incentive, as well as opportunity, to effect change in the economies of their nations is suggested by the evidence for their active participation in international trade.

As David C. Hopkins recognizes, "the expansion of borders not only meant an increase in sources of income and produce for import/export trade, but also could lead, given propitious geopolitical conditions, to an expansion of transit trade."[4] Morris Silver offers a concise, if maximalist, summary of the evidence for such propitious conditions in eighth-century Israel and Judah.[5] Contra Silver, however, M. Elat is surely correct when he writes of this transit trade that "while it produced profits for the royal court and raised the standard of living of those close to it, it had only a limtied influence on the local economy or on the occupational distribution of the country's inhabitants."[6]

It was the import/export trade which heavily impacted the peasant majorities in Israel and Judah and tempted their rulers to become involved in changing the priorities, methods, and distribution of agricultural production. After a penetrating synopsis of the relevant data, Hopkins reaches the widely shared conclusion that "this literary, epigraphic, and artifactual evidence converges on oil, wine, and wheat as the commodities of choice in the monarchic economic network."[7]

These commodities were exported mainly to and through the kingdom of Tyre,[8] a maritime society whose seaborne transportation was cheaper than the overland modes utilized of necessity by the transit trade in Israel and Judah.[9] This differential in transportation costs goes far to explain why a large proportion of Phoenicians could earn their living from transit trade, while most Israelites and Judahites could not. In return for their export of oil, wheat, and wine, Israel and Judah received luxury goods and military materiel. That such was the nature of the trade between Israel and Tyre can now be documented archaeologically as well as from written records, it would appear.[10]

The interface between this configuration of international trade and the pattern of social stratification in Israel and Judah is significant. Foodstuffs produced by the peasant majority were exported. Luxury goods and arms utilized by the elite minority were imported. While agricultural intensification probably raised the absolute amount of edible commodities produced, there were very finite limits to that increase, and exports competed directly with peasant sustenance. For all its erudition, Silver's "supply-side" analysis of the situation never comes to grips with these simple facts.[11]

Faced with a finite supply of exportable commodities but possessed of an almost infinite appetite for imported luxuries, the elites in Israel and Judah had a powerful incentive to increase production of the three major export crops. One method used to gain this increase was a regional specialization of agriculture. At the Annual Meeting of the Society of Biblical Literature in 1981, Anson Rainey and I independently noted that 2 Chron. 26:10—translated according to the known facts of Hebrew syntax and economic geography—records that Uzziah undertook just this process.[12]

> He built guard towers in the Steppe and hewed out many cisterns, for he had large herds; and in the Shephelah and in the Plain (he had) plowmen; and vineyard and orchard workers in the Hills and in the Carmel. . . .

Here we learn that under royal tutelage, herding was increased in the steppe by means of guard towers and cisterns, plowing—the cultivation of cereal crops, the predominant of which was wheat—was intensified in the plain and piedmont region, and viticulture and orcharding were pressed in the uplands. In each case, the economic exploitation of a given region was specialized to the one or two products by whose production that region could contribute maximally to the export trade and/or to the conspicuous consumption of the local elite. Rainey has analyzed in some detail the exact nature and location of these districts in Judah.[13]

Nor need this one verse in the Chronicler bear the whole burden of historical reconstruction. In light of the clarification of the stratigraphy at Lachish and taking this verse as a key, Rainey has been able to demonstrate that the much-discussed *lmlk* seal impressions from Judah witness a system of royal vineyards towards the end of the eighth century B.C.E.[14] Farther north, The Samaria ostraca—despite all the controversies surrounding their exact dating and interpretation—". . . evidence the flow of oil and wine probably to officials of the royal court . . ."[15] sometime during the eighth century B.C.E. Perhaps the easiest reading of these documents is occasioned by the assumption that the existence of both private and royal vineyards and olive orchards is reflected therein.[16] An ostracon from Tell Qasileh probably witnesses the export of oil in about this period.[17] And epigraphic finds continue. Excavations in the City of David in 1978 produced a large stone plaque fragment from the latter part of the eighth century which may well refer to royal stores, either of grain or of treasure articles.[18]

Anepigraphic archaeology, too, provides further evidence, particularly on the processing of olive oil. While rock-cut olive and grape processing installations are probably almost as old as agriculture itself in Palestine, recent surveys suggest a proliferation of and innovations in such installations in the eighth century B.C.E.[19] Of special interest is the evidence for use of the beam press to extract more oil from the olives. The earliest such press found is apparently from the ninth century B.C.E.,[20] but the device appears to have come into widespread use in the eighth century.[21] As already indicated, the export trade was thirsty for every drop of olive oil it could get. Such intensification of the extraction process, in turn, probably led to different grades of oil. The finest resulted from crushing the olives and using water to extract the oil without presses. Subsequent processing of the pulp and the use of presses often introduced impurities into the oil and reduced its quality.[22] One may reasonably assume that certain of the demands of the export trade tended toward quantity—hence, the beam presses. The tastes of both local and foreign elites, on the other hand, preferred quality, an interpretation which appears to be borne out by the appearance of a term for the finer "washed oil" some dozen times in the Samaria ostraca.[23]

If the processing installations for oil and wine give little hint of who initiate their proliferation, 2 Chron. 26:10, when corroborated by the inscriptional evidence for royal vineyards and olive orchards, strongly suggests elements of a "command economy."[24] Hopkins writes appositely, "the centralizing structure of the monarchy and its characteristic institutions bring about an attenuation of the decisionmaking functions of the primary productive units, perhaps a complete usurpation, in the creation of what has been called a 'command economy'."[25] More than one distinguished social scientist has maintained that such "command economies" are characteristic of advanced agrarian societies as a generic class.[26] Both the comparative data upon which these scholars base their general theories and the specific data adduced for ancient Judah and Israel should give pause to anyone inclined to follow Silver in his positing of largely private, free market economies in eighth-century Israel and Judah.[27]

Even Silver agrees that many of the dynamics already discussed combined to consolidate more and more of the arable land into fewer and fewer hands.[28] Once again, Hopkins has stated the matter with precision: "Besides demands to pay for its costs and the possibility of the loss of labor to the royal projects, the monarchical program of agricultural intensification cut into village-based agricultural systems most directly by its pursuit of land."[29]

The land consolidation reflected in the eighth-century prophets had historical roots. Prior to the founding of the Davidic state, Israel's secure holdings were concentrated in the hill country. "Landholdings in the hills were small in comparison with those in the plains,"[30] a pattern similar to that found by Leon Marfoe in southern Syria.[31] In premonarchic Israel, these small, hill country holdings typically supported a mixed, subsistence agriculture.

This configuration changed with David.

> . . . David not only defeated the Philistines, restricting them to their pentapolis and laying solid Israelite claim to the alluvial plains of Canaan for the first time, but succeeded in subjugating his neighbors on all sides. In that process of empire building, he incurred debts. His military retainers, many loyal to his person since his days as a social bandit, expected to be rewarded when he came into his glory. He had conquered an empire, and its administration necessitated the creation and importation of bureaucrats. In an agrarian context, these categories of obligation were payable in grants of land, that is, in patrimonial and prebendal estates.
>
> But what did David have to grant? Certainly not most of the hill country, which supported his core constituency as peasant freehold. (The forces which led to the formation of the monarchy had produced some larger estates in the hill country [cf., e.g., I Sam. 22:6–8], but these were as modest in number and importance as the military professionals whom they supported [Halpern 1981: 86–87 *et passim;* Ben-Barak 1981: 73–91]). But the richer plains had never been a secure part of premonarchic Israel, and were David's to grant by right of conquest. Accustomed to the typical agrarian combination of patrimonial and prebendal domain, the estates of the lowlands simply received new overlords, in this case, newly created Israelite aristocrats and bureaucrats.[33]

If this analysis is correct, the ruling elites of Israel had enjoyed primary control of the "breadbasket" areas of the plains long before the agricultural intensification of the eighth century B.C.E. For them to have implemented on their large, lowland estates measures designed to maximize the production of wheat would have been a relatively simple matter. But what of the hill country? If much of it remained in small plots, tilled by their holders according to the priorities of the village community, such a system would have constituted a major impediment to the goals of the city-based elite.

As already indicated, urban elites in Israel and Judah sought the maximally efficient production of wheat, oil, and wine for export and for their own consumption. Hill country peasants, left to their own devices in a village, would have sought to guarantee the sufficiency of their livelihood by spreading the risks inherent in it as much as possible. "The crucial objective of village-based agriculture dictates the spreading of risk. The concentration of risk in a costly investment runs directly counter to this security-conscious objective."[34]

While direct evidence is sparse, a combination of indirect evidence and broad-based comparisons allows the following sketch of risk spreading in Israelite upland agriculture to be offered with considerable confidence. Fields which produced cereals were not so used every year. To maintain fertility, they were periodically fallowed and probably also sown to legumes in at least some rotations. (Obed Borowski has collected the evidence from the Hebrew Bible and from archaeological remains for the cultivation of leguminous crops in ancient Israel.)[35] As well as returning nitrogen to the soil, these pulses would have been a significant source of protein in the diet. Fallow fields would have supplemented uncultivable grazing land in providing pasture for the herding of sheep, goats, and cattle—in varying numbers and proportions. For subsistence farmers, such herding provided "a hedge against the risk of purely agricultural pursuits."[36] Animals so raised constituted a "disaster bank on the hoof," which stored surpluses from good years to be drawn on in lean years. Their manure helped to fertilize the fallow fields where they grazed, though not so efficiently as if it had been composted. Herding also made use of labor in the village—the very young and the very old—which would not otherwise have been productive. Tree and vine crops would have rounded out the repertoire of village agriculture in the hills. Their labor demands were complementary to those of cereals, and their processed fruit could be stored stably for extended periods, making them valuable contributors to the goal of spreading risk.

The demand or encouragement by the urban elite that only oil, wheat, and wine be produced and in ever increasing quantities

. . . ran counter to the village's objective of spreading risk and optimizing labor through a diversity of subsistence means. Assuming a limitation on labor and land, a relative increase or production of these commodities meant a relative decrease in the production of others. The absolute increase in production if the agricultural village were to contribute a share of its produce to the state and also maintain its level of subsistence necessitated, at least along one likely pathway, an expansion of the percentage of village land given over to cultivation of the preferred commodities at the expense of grazing lands. Sheep and goats which were integral to the risk- and labor-spreading agriculture of the village were not integral to the taxation apparatus, and were pushed out of the village system."[37]

When linked with the evidence in 2 Chron, 26:10 for royal herding in the steppe, such considerations weigh heavily against Silver's statement that ". . . it is not unreasonable to assume that land consolidation facilitated a transition from grain to stock farming to take advantage of the emergence of an affluent, meat-consuming Israelite public."[38] For reasons which are becoming increasingly apparent, we can hardly assume that the Israelite public at large was affluent. Lands in Judah which could support at least seasonal grazing but were too arid to be cultivable were scarcely sufficient to supply meat on a regular basis to the general public. All land which was cultivable was increasingly being pressed into producing one of the three preferred export crops.

A far more probable scenario would see animals headed for the tables of a few privileged urbanites pastured in the steppe during the wet season and then stall-fed in preparation for slaughter. Such stall-feeding would also have facilitated the collection and composting of manure, which in turn would have been in demand for fertility maintenance in the more intensively cropped fields. Lucian Turkowski, at least, reports just such a use of manure in the Judean hills when agriculture was intensified there in the last century:

> From the nineteenth century new systems of increased agriculture spread to the Judaean hills. This demanded that no part of the land should be left unproductive. The part formerly left fallow was now fertilized with manure. . . ."[39]

With the fallow went a significant part of village grazing land and its ability to sustain a "disaster bank on the hoof." In its place came hand weeding of cereal fields to provide fodder for stall-fed animals.[40]

When this fodder proved insufficient to fatten the delicacies of the rich, precious cereals may well have been used. As Marvin Harris concedes, "it is true that the cost-benefits of intensification are not the same for peasants or workers as for members of the ruling class."[41]

As part of this eighth-century intensification of agriculture in the hill country of Israel and Judah, multi-purpose land which had helped to spread risk was gradually converted into terraces growing vineyards and olive trees.[42] While elite demands on their production tended to be steady or to increase, that production itself was subject to the vicissitudes of the environment and, in the case of the olive, to a pattern of alternating yields.[43] Gone was the "inefficient" diversification which had spread the risk of such fluctuations in the past. Hopkins characterizes the changes and their implications as follows:

> A system-wide increase in crop specialization brings an increase in short-term production and efficiency, but also lowers resistance to catastrophe. The former relative self-sufficiency of the agricultural village gives way increasingly to a dependence upon the centralizing forces and the exchange network that they administer. Constant coordination and direction must emanate from this center, lest the whole structure collapse.
> . . . The period [the eighth century] triggered a sharp jump of the needle that monitors movements on the continuum between autonomous village-based agriculture and an economy dominated by the central state.[44]

Although quantitative data are difficult to secure, there is probably a high correlation generally in agrarian societies between such dynamics, on the one hand, and political stability, territorial expansion, growing import/export trade, and royal construction, on the other.[45]

These latter same factors are also correlated with an increase in what is sometimes called "rent capitalism."[46] In such a system, not only are ownership of the land and labor separated,[47] but each of the factors of agricultural production is segmented from the others and subjected to separate rent.[48] While rural residence of the wealthy favors a multi-stranded patron-client relationship with poor cultivators, a single-stranded relationship of economic exploitation is most often the result when the elite are urban-based.[49]

> This estrangement is favoured by the landlord's urban residence ('absentee landlordism') as well as by the situation of the upper classes which

provides both for social prestige and political influence independent of any clientele support.[50]

Inducements for rich landlords to live in the city include import trade in luxury items. "As soon as the market is able to provide luxury goods and gives rise to a corresponding urban life-style . . . [,] then exploitation may be a consequence."[51]

Under such circumstances, the contrast between the splendor of the cities and the misery of the countryside is stark and "can hardly be exaggerated."[52] Recent studies indicate that this configuration characterized Neo-Assyrian society:

> . . . Even under Essarhaddon more revenue was produced from internal provinces than was collected through conquest. Regardless of the wealth of the empire, the economic conditions of the peasant in the countryside never improved, but if anything became worse as the empire expanded. The question was not one of the supply of goods and services but of the demand of a central administration which claimed the right to acquire and redistribute them.[53]

While Israel and Judah were not empires in the sense that Assyria was, every other indication points to similar dynamics there in the eighth century B.C.E.

Such a system pressed the typical peasant cultivator hard even in good years, because there was incentive for the elite to extract every possible surplus, leaving only the barest subsistence necessary to continue production. In less than optimal years cultivators stripped of the insurance of diversification were forced to take out survival-loans. The social systems supported by diversified, subsistence agriculture had most probably included mutual obligations of interest-free survival loans within certain village and/or kinship groupings.[54] But the intensified system saw the only funds available increasingly in the hands of wealthy moneylenders bent on becoming wealthier. "Taking a loan almost automatically leads to long-term or even permanent dependence because of the high interest rates. . . ."[55] In many cases, a cycle of encumbered harvests was created, each pledged to repay debts incurred in the prior procurement of the factors of its production. Usurious interest rates—coupled with the nadir of the annual cycle of agricultural commodity values at harvestime, when the debt contracts came due—insured the need for further, even larger loans. Foreclosure on collateral at the discretion of the lender often become a sword of Damocles hanging over the indebted peasant.

For historical reasons detailed above, the lowlands of Israel and Judah had, for the most part, probably been organized into large estates long before the eighth century B.C.E. Many cultivators there would have been landless tenants, most vulnerable to the dynamics of "rent capitalism." With intensified demand for wheat in the eighth century, these tenants would have been pressed even harder, leading to an increase in all forms of debt incurred for survival reasons, and producing growing numbers of debt-slaves.

The situation in the hill country had been different. Royal vineyards and olive orchards no doubt existed there from the emergence of the monarchy, but in much of the upland a tradition of small freeholders, working their own land in mixed subsistence, had struck deep root. But as seen above, each of the particulars of that system was under pressure to change in the eighth century. Urban elites could structure state taxation to induce, perhaps even force, increased production of oil and wine, with all the attendant losses in the spreading of risk. Bad years began to bring the necessity of loans from the rent capitalists of the cities, with upland plots offered as collateral.

Although the evidence is spotty and difficult and the secondary literature far too voluminous and controverted to be reviewed here, it seems likely that not all hill country plots were equally alienable. Those planted to vines and orchards were probably most often held in perpetuity by a given family, since such intensive cultivation of perennials takes many years to come full fruition, and few cultivators will make such improvements on land which is periodically redistributed.[56] Evidence from later periods in Palestine,[57] as well as various comparisons and allusions,[58] combines to suggest that fields used to grow cereals were often held in common by the village as a whole and periodically reapportioned by lot to individual families.

It appears probable that the vineyards and olive orchards may have been the first lands to slip into the hands of the urban elites. They already controlled most of the best grain fields in the lowlands, and would at first have been primarily interested in oil and wine from the hills. Since vineyards and orchards "belonged" to individual families, they would have been less complicated to offer as collateral, even if they could not be sold outright. (I Kings 21 remains easiest to interpret, I believe, on the assumption that Israelite customary law forbade outright sale or trade of such property.) If the grain lands of the village were taxed in common, as evidence from later periods suggests,[59] heavy state taxes in kind would both have yielded wheat for the export trade and have supplied villagers a powerful incentive to terrace former grainfields and convert them to vines and trees. As Hopkins writes,

> the alienation of land, usually the most productive, decreases the farming household's ability to control a variety of ecological niches and pushes the family, which must somehow provide for its subsistence, onto poorer and poorer lands at greater distances from its village.[60]

Unable to grow all their own grain, and in many cases forced off their lands altogether and relegated to agricultural wage labor, former freeholders went, of necessity, to grain traders to procure the staples of their diet.

The mortgaging of and foreclosure upon family lands, members, and property involved court action. While there was a long tradition of consensus justice in the village courts, state officials had long since enjoyed considerable success in limiting and subordinating local judicial functions in the name of the king.[61] Given the priorities of royal policy in the eighth century B.C.E., there can be little astonishment that such courts did not and could not effectively block land consolidation and its concomitants. The bitterness of those whose dispossession was sanctioned by these courts should occasion even less surprise.

Such a sketch of the dynamics of political economy in eighth-century Israel and Judah can be rendered even more probable by close exegesis of the prophetic texts which both reflect and reflect upon these dynamics. That detailed study must await another occasion, as must any attempt to expicate the extended parallels between the world of these prophets and much of the so-called third world today. My only hope is that a slightly firmer foundation has been laid for both enterprises, for they are both intrinsic to any full dialogue between the Reformed faith and economics.

Endnotes

1. Marvin L. Chaney, "Systemic Study of the Israelite Monarchy," *Semeia*, XXXVII (1986), 72–73. On the sodality called the *Marzeah* in paragraph one of this quotation, see: Robert B. Coote, *Amos Among the Prophets: Composition and Theology* (Philadelphia: Fortress Press, 1981), pp. 36–39.

2. John Bright, *A History of Israel* 3rd ed. (Philadelphia: The Westminster Press, 1981), p. 258.

3. *Ibid.*, 255–59; S. Yeivin, "The Divided Kingdom: Rehoboam-Ahaz/Jeroboam-Pekah," in *The Age of the Monarchies: Political History*, ed. by A. Malamat, Vol. IV:1 of *The World History of the Jewish People*, ed. by B. Mazar (Jerusalem: Massada Press, 1979), pp. 161–72; and Yohanan Aharoni, *The Archaeology of the Land of Israel*, ed. by Miriam Aharoni, trans. by Anson F. Rainey (Philadelphia: The Westminster Press, 1982), pp. 251–54.

4. David C. Hopkins, "The Dynamics of Agriculture in Monarchical Israel," in *Society of Biblical Literature 1983 Seminar Papers*, ed. Kent Harold Richards (Chico, CA: Scholars Press, 1983), p. 195.

5. Morris Silver, *Prophets and Markets: The Political Economy of Ancient Israel* (Boston: Kluwer-Nijhoff, 1983), pp. 49–52.

6. M. Elat, "Trade and Commerce," in *The Age of the Monarchies: Culture and Society*, ed. by A. Malamat, Vol. IV:2 of *The World History of the Jewish People*, ed. by B. Mazar (Jerusalem: Massada Press, 1979), p. 186; cf. Gerhard Lenski and Jean Lenski, *Human Societies: An Introduction to Macrosociology* (5th ed.; New York: McGraw-Hill, 1987), pp. 183–85; and Hopkins, "Dynamics," p. 195.

7. Hopkins, "Dynamics," p. 196; cf. Silver, *Prophets and Markets*, p. 24; and Bernhard Lang, *Monotheism and the Prophetic Minority: An Essay in Biblical History and Sociology*, The Social World of Biblical Antiquity Series, Vol. I (Sheffield: The Almond Press, 1983), P. 123.

8. Elat, "Trade and Commerce," pp. 225–28.

9. Lenski and Lenski, *Human Societies*, pp. 216–19.

10. Shulamit Geva, "Archaeological Evidence for the Trade Between Israel and Tyre," *Bulletin of the American Schools of Oriental Research*, CCXLVIII (1982), 69–72.

11. Silver, *Prophets and Markets, passim.*

12. Anson F. Rainey, "Wine from the Royal Vineyards," *Bulletin of the American Schools of Oriental Research*, CCXLV (1982), 58; Chaney, "Systemic Study," pp. 73–74; cf. Hopkins, "Dynamics," p. 200.

13. Rainey, "Wine," pp. 58–59.

14. *Ibid.*, pp. 57–61.

15. Hopkins, "Dynamics," p. 199.

16. Devadasan N. Premnath, "The Process of Latifundialization Mirrored in the Oracles Pertaining to Eighth Century B.C.E. in the Books of Amos, Hosea, Isaiah and Micah" (unpublished Ph.D. dissertation, The Graduate Theological Union, 1984), pp. 60–62.

17. Silver, *Prophets and Markets*, p. 17; N. Avigad, "Hebrew Epigraphic Sources," in *The Age of the Monarchies: Political History*, ed. by A. Malamat, Vol. IV:1 of *The World History of the Jewish People*, ed. by B. Mazar (Jerusalem: Massada Press, 1979), pp. 33–34; and Benjamin Maisler (Mazar), "The Excavations at Tell Qasileh: Preliminary Report," *Israel Exploration Journal*, I (1950), pp. 208–210.

18. Silver, *Prophets and Markets,* pp. 36–37; and Yigal Shiloh, "City of David: Excavation 1978," *Biblical Archaeologist,* XLII (Summer, 1979), p. 170.

19. David Eitam, "Olive Presses of the Israelite Period," *Tel Aviv,* IV (1979), pp. 146–54.

20. Lawrence E. Stager and S. R. Wolff, "Production and Commerce in Temple Courtyards: An Olive Press in the Sacred Precinct at Tel Dan," *Bulletin of the American Schools of Oriental Research,* CCXLIII (1981), pp. 95–102; and Lawrence E. Stager, "The Finest Olive Oil in Samaria," *Journal of Semitic Studies,* XXVIII (1983), p. 244.

21. Eitam, "Olive Presses," pp. 146–54.

22. Stager, "Finest Olive Oil," pp. 241–44.

23. *Ibid.,* pp. 241–45.

24. Chaney, "Systemic Study," p. 74; Hopkins, "Dynamics," p. 193 and n. 71, p. 200; Premnath, "Latifundialization," p. 56.

25. Hopkins, "Dynamics," p. 193.

26. Lenski and Lenski, *Human Societies,* pp. 183–85; and Robert L. Heilbroner, *The Making of Economic Society* (5th ed.; Englewood Cliffs, NJ: Prentice-Hall, 1975), pp. 7–46.

27. Silver, *Prophets and Markets, passim.*

28. *Ibid.,* pp. 73–77; 259–63.

29. Hopkins, "Dynamics," p. 200; cf. Chaney, "Systematic Study," pp. 72–73; and J. Andrew Dearman, "Prophecy, Property and Politics," in *Society of Biblical Literature 1984 Seminar Papers,* ed. by Kent Harold Richards (Chico, CA: Scholars Press, 1984), pp. 389–91.

30. Lawrence E. Stager, "The Archaeology of the Family in Ancient Israel," *Bulletin of the American Schools of Oriental Research,* CCLX (1985), 24.

31. Leon Marfoe, "The Integrative Transformation: Patterns of Sociopolitical Organization in Southern Syria." *Bulletin of the American Schools of Oriental Research,* CCXXXIV (1979), 21–23.

32. Marvin L. Chaney, "Ancient Palestinian Peasant Movements and the Formation of Premonarchic Israel," in *Palestine in Transition: The Emergence of Ancient Israel,* ed. by David Noel Freeman and David Frank Graf, The Social World of Biblical Antiquity Series, Vol. II (Sheffield: The Almond Press, 1983), pp. 50, 64–65.

33. Chaney, "Systemic Study," pp. 67–68; cf. Albrecht Alt, "Der Anteil des Konigtums an der sozialen Entwicklung in der Reichen Israel und Juda," in *Kleine Schriften zur Geschichte des Volkes Israel,* ed. by Martin Noth, III (Munich: C. H. Beck, 1959), pp. 348–72. On the larger estates in the hill country supporting military professionals, see: Baruch Halpern, "The Uneasy Compromise: Israel Between League and Monarchy," in *Traditions in Transformation: Turning Points in Biblical Faith,* Baruch Halpern and Jon D. Levenson, eds. (Winona Lake: Eisenbrauns, 1981), pp.86–87 *et passim;* and Zafrira Ben-Barak, "Meribaal and the System of Land Grants in Ancient Israel," *Biblica,* LXII (1981), pp. 73–91.

34. Hopkins, "Dynamics," p. 201.

35. Obed Borowski, *Agriculture in Iron Age Israel* (Winona Lake, IN: Eisenbrauns, 1987), pp. 93–97.

36. Hopkins, "Dynamics," p. 191.

37. *Ibid.*, p. 197.

38. Silver, *Prophets and Markets*, pp. 97–98.

39. Lucian Turkowski, "Peasant Agriculture in the Judaean Hills," *Palestine Exploration Quarterly*, CI (1969), p. 24.

40. *Ibid.*, p. 101.

41. Marvin Harris, *Cultural Materialism: The Struggle for a Science of Culture*, (New York: Random House, 1980), p. 103.

42. Hopkins, "Dynamics," p. 200; and Gershon Edelstein and Mordechai Kislev, "Mevasseret, Yerushalayim: The Ancient Settlement and Its Agricultural Terraces," *Biblical Archaeologist*, XLIV (1981), pp. 53–56.

43. Hopkins, "Dynamics," p. 197.

44. *Ibid.*, p. 201.

45. *Ibid.*

46. Lang, *Monotheism and the Prophetic Minority*, p. 167, n. 218.

47. *Ibid.*, p. 118.

48. Eric R. Wolf, *Peasants*, Foundations of Modern Anthropology Series (Englewood Cliffs, NJ: Prentice-Hall, 1966), pp. 55–56; and Robert B. Coote, *Amos among the Prophets: Composition and Theology* (Philadelphia: Fortress Press, 1981), pp. 29–32.

49. Lang, *Monotheism and the Prophetic Minority*, pp. 118–19.

50. *Ibid.*, p. 119.

51. *Ibid.*

52. *Ibid.*, p. 120.

53. Dearman, "Prophecy, Property and Politics," pp. 393–94; cf. J. N. Postgate, "Some Remarks on Conditions in the Assyrian Countryside," *Journal of Economic and Social History of the Orient*, XVII (1974), pp. 225–43; and G. van Driel, "Land and People in Assyria," *Bibliotheca Orientalis*, XXVII (1970), pp. 168–75.

54. Lang, *Monotheism and the Propetic Minority*, p. 120; and Richard Critchfield, *Villages* (New York: Anchor Press/Doubleday, 1983), p. 345.

55. Lang, *Monotheism and the Prophetic Minority*, p. 117.

56. Chaney, "Ancient Palestinian Peasant Movements," pp. 50, 64–65.

57. Turkowski, "Peasant Agriculture," pp. 23–32.

58. Chaney, "Ancient Palestinian Peasant Movements," pp. 50, 64–65.

59. Turkowski, "Peasant Agriculture," p. 23.

60. Hopkins, "Dynamics," p. 201.

61. Dearman, "Prophecy, Property and Politics," pp. 391–92; and Keith W. Whitelam, *The Just King: Monarchic Judicial Authority in Ancient Israel*, Journal for the Study of the Old Testament Supplement Series, Vol. XII (Sheffield: JSOT Press, 1979), *passim*.

Part Two

The Reform Tradition on Economic Justice

Chapter Three

The Reformed Economic Ethics of John Calvin

Ronald H. Stone

The reference to a Reformed economic ethic implies that we are primarily concerned with the economic ethic that originated in John Calvin. The religious vision sustaining John Calvin, of course, has its earlier origins in the history of Christian thought. It also has its latter day exponents. John Calvin is in important ways Augustinian in his thought. Jonathan Edwards and Reinhold and H. Richard Niebuhr are Calvinistic in their religious vision and their economic ethic. While this paper focuses on the economic thought and action of John Calvin in the 16th century, its view also includes perspectives from the dying Roman empire to the contemporary American empire.

James Gustafson's theological ethics locates three characteristics of the Reformed religious vision which are common to Augustine, Calvin, Edwards, and the Niebuhrs. They are: (1) a recognition of the sovereignty of God; (2) the commitment to piety or religious experience in Christian life; and (3) the regulation of life according to the discernment of the will of God.[1]

Economics here refers to the investigation of the system of political-economic decisions which shape the system of distribution and production of a society's goods and services. In the case of John Calvin, economics refers to teaching about the role of money, interest, distribution and welfare practices and to practical decisions made about these subjects in Geneva 1541–1564.

Ethics is the critical reflection upon the morality of people. Christian ethics is the theory and practice, including advocacy, of what the church in both its assembled and scattered life *ought* to do.

So our discussion is a critical reflection on the decisions of John Calvin about church morality in the economic system of Geneva. This paper will limit itself to Calvin's Geneva and not investigate the further development of Calvinist economic ethics. An assessment of economic ethics in Calvin's thought and practice, of course, cannot provide exact norms for our current practice in the political economy of the American empire. But a look at his ethic may be suggestive of themes that a reformed church would want to consider in developing an ethic for political economy. The overall Reformed tendencies of commitment through personal experience to the shaping of life toward the discernable will of a powerful, loving God could be lost only at the cost of Reformed identity.

The confining of the discussion to Calvin in Geneva disconnects the paper from the thesis developed by Max Weber and supported by Ernst Troeltsch and R. H. Tawney that capitalism and Calvinism had a psychological affinity for reinforcing each other. The thesis is regarded as true and important for later Calvinism and the develop-ment of the capitalist ethos. But it does not illuminate well the economic ethic of John Calvin which Weber did not investigate in detail. Of the many critics of the thesis, Andre Bieler's is among the best, and his first point of critique is accepted as determinative for the direction of this essay.

> Weber analyzes a Calvinism which is quite different from its origins. The thought and ways of the Puritanism of the eighteenth century have been strongly influenced by religious and profane factors which were utterly alien to Calvin. Weber's analysis is accurate but is applied to a society which is later than original Calvinism. In other words, Weber's grave fault is to confuse a later form of Protestantism with the original Calvinism.[2]

Middle Class Virtues

Calvin did not develop a philosophic moral theory. Rather he taught moral obedience to the will of the sovereign God. This will was found particularly in the Ten Commandments. The remainder of scripture's moral teaching could be related to the decalogue. Jesus didn't really add any new moral teaching, but purified the morality and returned it to its true meaning in the decalogue. The reformation ethics are not a new ethic, but a return to the Mosaic ethic in light of the new situation. Of course, scripture had to be interpreted and that gave the interpreter of scripture, particularly Calvin himself, a high role in teaching the meaning of God's law. Natural law corresponds to God's law, but in Geneva or wherever Reformed ethics was taught the exposition of the decalogue was the chief guide to morality. The law properly taught: (1) convicted human beings of their sin, (2) constrained the wicked by the fear of public penalties and the fear of hell, and (3) counseled the faithful in reforming instruction on how they should live. Calvin's faith is in a message of grace, but instruction in the things needful to do is required. However, the instruction could serve as grounds for legalistic requirements as it did in Geneva and elsewhere.

Still a nation that did not know of the law of Moses could be well governed by "the common laws of nations."[3] The law of God called the moral law,

> is no other than a declaration of natural law, and of that conscience which has been engraven by God on the minds of men, . . .[4]

The moral law has two chief precepts to love God, and to embrace people with sincere love.[5] All nations are free to enact their own laws as are expedient for them as long as they correspond to love.[6] Some laws which violate humanity should not be considered as laws. Generally, though, people can govern themselves through observing equity and the practices of natural law engraven in human conscience. The law of God is best served as it is promulgated to meet time, place, and circumstance of different peoples and not by insisting that the law of Moses which was given for the circumstances of the Hebrews be slavishly imitated.[7]

Calvin's teaching of the law was to instruct a people who ordered themselves to God's will in freedom. Jane Dempsey Douglass has caught his spirit well.

> Calvin willingly sets aside the vision of freedom offered by the philosophers in favor of his view of Christian freedom: liberation by Christ's work from the power of sin and evil and the anguished conscience in order to worship God, to devote oneself freely and energetically to making the Kingdom of Christ manifest in the world, freedom to participate in history in the Holy Spirit's creation of the new society envisioned and empowered by God.[8]

In Geneva and generally in Reformed circles, the decalogue was expounded to people participating in the growth of urban and citizen power as the feudal system was giving way. The practitioners of Calvin's ethics were becoming middle class people and eventually the owners of European urban civilization. They were roughly originally middle class in economic position, though many protestant refugees flocking to Geneva were in fact poor. They were also middle class in outlook, preferring citizen control to oligarchic or monarchical political control and a mixture of lay-clerical control of the church to a clerical-hierarchical control of the church.

There is a moral seriousness to this ethic of Calvin. God is a judge, the law is known, it is interpreted by a lawyer-theologian in its clear sense with full, moral rigor. If the world does not correspond to the ethic then oridinarily that is so much the worse for the world which must be changed. The pursuit is of a righteousness which confirms the adoption of Christians as children of God.

The Christian life for Calvin is the self-denial and the seeking of the righteousness pleasing to God.[9] This rule of life is expressed in *Titus* as soberness, righteousness, and godliness, fugality, and patience in poverty.[10] He sums up the Christian life as self-denial in the exposition in Chapter VII of Book III of the *Institutes*. His exposition of the Christian life expresses the vision of the Christian life of the monastery applied to the world.[11] Chastity and the seriousness of marriage, the rejection of sexuality outside of marriage suggests the monastic virtue of chastity, but now to reinforce the family. Obedience is to the worldly powers and ultimately to God for the same end of humility which motivated monastic obedience at its best. Poverty, the third monastic virtue, is to be accepted patiently, when present, as it is of God. For those not poor, frugality in consumption is enjoined and they are to share. Whether one has wealth or poverty one is of God. Patience in the knowledge that God controls the world frees the Christian from anxiety about this world.

> In short, whatever happens, because he will know it ordained of God, he will undergo it with a peaceful and grateful mind so as not obstinately to resist the command of him into whose power he once for all surrendered himself and his every possession.[12]

His virtues of temperance in eating and drinking were strongly stated. Drunkenness and gluttony were both to be restrained. Calvin's own style of life was very frugal and he enjoined frugality upon his followers. His frugality was not asceticism, but moderation. Simplicity in food and dress were enjoined, and the temptations of dancing and theater were to be avoided. Card playing was rejected as a waste of time, but the theater and dancing were suggestive of adultery. Who in our society could say he was mistaken?[13]

There isn't much in Calvin about the duty to labor hard. He rather assumes hard work, but he wants it clearly understood that hard labor doesn't give wealth. Only God provides wealth. No one will be advanced unless God advances him or her. Idleness was criticized, humanity since the fall was intended to labor, but the words of Calvin himself do not incite people to frenzied labor. His attitude toward work is revealed in his commentary on the story of Jesus with Mary and Martha. Martha is rebuked only for her frenzied efforts. Her efforts on Jesus' behalf according to Calvin were appreciated. Mary's willingness to sit with him and be instructed was carefully guarded from encouraging indolence. Calvin went on in his commentary to say:

We know that people were created for the express purpose of being employed in labor of various kinds, and that no sacrifice is more pleasing to God, than when everyone applies diligently to one's own calling, and endeavors to live in such a manner as to contribute to the general advantage.[14]

For Calvin there is a time to hear and a time to act. Calvin even concluded from the passage that Christ

would rather have chosen to be entertained in a frugal manner, and at moderate expense than that this holy woman should have submitted to so much trial.[15]

Calvin's example, of course, was of a great activist in constant practical and academic labor. Few have equalled his literary outpouring, but we do not find in Calvin's teaching the advocacy of driving, anxious labor that a simple reading of Max Weber might lead the student to expect. Nor do we find the popular notion that Calvin related salvation to hard labor.[16]

In Calvin's hands *honesty* became honesty of spirit as well as of the strict work. Business trickery or chicanery were condemned as dishonest and also as stealing. The strictures against false witness were broadly applied. The Ten Commandments were interpreted vigorously to reinforce a strict commercial ethos. The common meaning of "business is business" received no toleration from John Calvin.

Even legal practices which deprived people of their property were regarded as stealing. The rich and powerful exploiting of their material edge to increase the poverty of the poor was equivalent to brigandage.

So sobriety, frugalness, family discipline, and honesty all reinforced middle class lives and often contributed to their business success. But the strict enforcement of the Ten Commandment morality with an eye open to the needful protection of the poor separated those who internalized Calvin's moral preachments from cruel business or legal practices. The least received special protection from the Christians and from the government.

> But there is a special reason why God declares that he takes the foreign born, the widows, and the orphans as his wards. Where evil is more flagrant, there is more need of potent remedy.[17]

The virtues of Calvin lead to practical policies assisting the poor, but neither to special blessed place for the poor, nor to a proletariat as a special class.

In Calvin's view money and goods ought to circulate in human society to the welfare of all. Humanity in solidarity one with another would participate in contributing according to one's vocation to the good of all. However, selfishness has led to the theft and hoarding of society's goods by a few. Mammon has come to dominate and to ruin the common life. The natural, relative economic equality and mutual service has been violated. God is using both the church and the state to restore the original intentions. The church teaches and acts to promote equality and restore human solidarity. Calvin said,

> God wills that there be proportion and equality among us, that is, each one is to provide for the needy according to the extent of one's means, so that no one has too much and no one has too little.[18]

The church helps people to put their property to the use of all. "The crying differences between rich and poor thus disappear."[19] In the church the charity one owes to the neighbor is assisted. The church through the restored service of the diaconate reaffirms human solidarity through concrete service. It also through preaching, teaching and lobbying insists that the public organs of society meet the needs of the people. The restoration of the dignity of people beginning in Christ is alive in the church and moves into state policies.

Jesus himself gave up power and riches to enter into the condition of the poor. Jesus is the example of human communication and his combat with the evil of poverty is the work of the church and the state. Cavlin and his pastors lived in conditions close to poverty raising funds for the needy and lobbying the state to act for the poor. The goal is a society of neither the poor nor the rich, but of a working, contributing class with sufficiency for life at a modest level.

Usury

Under Calvin's influence restrictions against lending of money for economic production were put aside. His exegesis of Deuteronomy 23:20 became the rallying cry for the expanding middle class to overthrow the remnants of the legislation of the middle ages which had hemmed in the loaning of money.

Since Jerome (340–420) and Ambrose (340–397), Western exegetes, church councils, and jurists had wrestled with the Deuteronomic prohibition of interest taking.

> To a foreigner you may lend upon interest, but to your brother you shall not lend upon interest; that the Lord your God may bless you in all that you undertake in the land which you are entering to take possession of it. (Deuteronomy 23:20)

All Christians were included as *brothers*, the loaning to foreigners was seen by Ambrose as lending to *enemies* at interest. The trend of medieval writers was to rule out all loans at interest. Various escape clauses were worked out including sometimes the toleration of Jewish lenders to Christians. Casuistry proliferated to make loans possible and before the reformation many ways around the prohibition were established.

Martin Luther dealt differently with usury at various historical crises in his career and was unable to resolve the issue clearly. In the end he surrendered regulation of interest to the princes and authorities. He would regard as usurious only a too-high rate of interest.

Calvin taught that Deuteronomy 23:19 is specifically in reference to the Hebrews. It does not bind Christians who are bound by rules of charity and justice.

> There is a difference in the political union, for the situation in which God placed the Jews and many other circumstances permitted them to

trade conveniently among themselves without usuries. Our union is entirely different.[20]

Usury is not universally permitted and it needs regulation, but the general prohibition of it was smashed by Calvin. "Usury is permitted if it is not injurious to one's brother." Calvin is not, of course, renouncing the call to Christian community; whereas Hebrew community and medieval community had prohibited the taking of interest within the community, the new community permitted it. Benjamin Nelson has likened this shift to a change in the meaning of the term "brotherhood" to "Universal Otherhood."[21]

Calvin and others fixed the maximum amount of interest for the parishes of Geneva at 5 percent, urged the prohibition of the extraction of interest from the poor, and permitted ministers to invest for interest with some restrictions. The records of the city council show that the 5 percent interest rate held from 1543 until 1557 when it was raised to 6.67 percent. In the intervening period the clergy under Calvin's leadership participated in the debates over interest rates, and in one case Calvin's complaints about Pierre Mercier accused of charging excessive interest led to his trial and his being fined. W. Fred Graham's enthusiasm for Calvin on this issue judges him as understanding both the needs of expanding commerce and the needs of the poor. The records do not allow us, however, to conclude that the poor ever received loans without interest. They received charity, but loans even for the peasants were at interest.

Calvin's exegesis and writings reveal a healthy respect for the special structures of Hebrew society and Genevan society. The Hebrew neighbor needed to be helped, God in charity required that the help be without interest. In general interest was permitted. Genevan development required interest-bearing loans, they were to be regulated by standards of justice by the government for otherwise sinful powerful people would exploit them. Calvin rejected the age-old theory of Aristotle and Thomas that money could not produce money and he recognized the right to receive money for the use of one's money.

In summary he recognized God's ordering sovereignty, the need for capital to produce capital, the need for regulation of capital, the need for new practices to meet new situations, and the special needs of the poor.

Although the great banking houses, the Vatican and others before Calvin had found rationalizations for the loaning of money at interest, it had been discouraged and regarded as immoral. The case had been made on scripture, Aristotle and nature.[22] The traditional scriptural prohibition was overthrown by an historical relativist argument. Scripture was God's will for the historical situation of the Hebrews, 16th century Geneva was something else. Aristotle and the argument from nature were discredited by showing that the function of money was more complicated than the philosopher had thought. Aristotle had taught that the "making of money of money" was unnatural. Money was to be used in production, it could not produce income by itself. Calvin's argument was that the money, like land or machinery, was being used to create wealth and that the one who loaned it to another for production deserved part of the income or interest also. "The profit is not in the money itself, but in the return that comes from its use."[23]

Usury was not to be evaluated in Calvin primarily through scripture, but by standards of justice available in natural reason. However, the limits placed on usury reflected Calvin's theocentric ethic and the guidance of that ethic by scriptural seriousness. He hedged his justification of interest taking with several qualifications:

1. Interest should not be taken from the poor who need loans for necessities.

2. One should not become so intent on gaining interest that one scorns the needs of the poor.

3. The rate of interest was to be set in light of equity interpreted by the Golden Rule.

4. The borrower of the funds at interests must profit from the loan also.

5. The rules of God, not secular insights, were to govern the loaning of money.

6. The good of the public was to be served by the loans.

7. Rules of the region could govern the rate of interest. In Geneva the clergy participated in fixing the rate at 5 percent, but rules of the region ought to be taken advantage of. It was ethically better to take too little interest rather than too much interest.[24]

Applied Theology

Calvin's real world involved shopkeepers, traders, and craftsmen as well as clerics and academics. He was relatively free of the medieval distaste for commerce as he was of Luther's preference for the pastoral life. His world was that of urban commerce and he affirmed it. The exchange of money and goods was affirmed. The institution of money itself was not suspect. God had provided the institution for the good of humanity. Andre Bieler's work particularly stresses the teaching of Calvin that "material goods are instruments of God's providence."[25]

Money is a test for humanity, it tests one's humility and it is to be used charitably. The money one receives is a divine favor, totally undeserved, on the one hand. On the other hand, Calvin actively struggles for just wages for clergy, himself, and for other workers.

Evil is found in the use of money since the fall. Though money is good, its historical use leads to distortion, oppression, and economic chaos. People come to follow the human god of Mammon, and Mammon rules over much of humanity by the corruption of the human heart. This takeover of the human heart is a hidden victory. Mammon then works against God by trying to confine God's rule to the things spiritual while allowing Mammon to rule in the economic realm. Bieler puts this particularly well: "Mammon allows man full liberty to practice his own religion and say his prayers."[26]

The reformation in Geneva threw both the ministry and the social welfare organizations of the church into confusion. Calvin's recruitment into the reformation of Geneva left him with responsibilities to reorganize both. The traditions of social welfare of Geneva impacted his work as he impacted on the traditions of Geneva. The civil government had taken over all of the church revenues and attempted to reorganize the welfare system. During his temporary exile in Strasbourg, Calvin came under the influence of Martin Bucer who used the churches to supplement the municipal welfare system. Calvin later adopted Bucer's ideas of the order of the diaconate for ministry to the poor and through a process of adjustment and change applied them to Geneva upon his return to leadership in that city. For Calvin the deacons were not to be subsumed as apprentice priests or priests' assistants, but to fulfill a more Biblical role of primarily ministering to the poor.[27]

Calvin and the pastors supervised and intervened in the affairs of the hospital-general which was supported by the city government. The hospital-general provided housing and food for orphans, the aged, and the needy as well as medical services. It also provided out-client welfare services and its organization included services in times of plague. The hospital-general was clearly an institution where the religious and secular understandings and institutions met in the administration of social welfare.

Other aspects of applied theology led Farel and Calvin to institute the first free public education for both sexes and to found the university. Beyond the welfare system and education the work of Calvin and the pastors reached out to suggestions for railings to protect children on stairs and balconies. Fires and chimneys were regulated and efforts were made to clean the town and for street repair. Of current interest also was Calvin's demand for the securing of strict legislation prohibiting the recruitment of mercenaries from Geneva.[28]

Regulation of prices for the necessities of life was an accepted principle of the early reformation in Geneva. It followed that business practices artificially raising prices received Calvin's criticism:

> "Today when everything has such a high price," Calvin says, "we see men who keep their granaries closed; this is as if they cut the throat of a poor people, when they thus reduce them to extreme hunger."[29]

The state had the responsibility of regulating business both for its own efficiency and just management as in the cases of the medium of exchanges, weights, measures, coins, and contracts,[30] and for the protection of the population. The major example of regulation of an industry from Calvin's time is that of printing. Printing represented the new technology. The industry had been slipping somewhat in Geneva until the arrival of the reformation. Geneva as an intellectual center of the religious revolution had a great need of printing. The religious needs intersected with issues of wages, hours, collective bargaining, and relationships between masters, journeymen and apprentices. The industry in France was subject to conflicts and strikes. In France the government took the side of the owners. In Geneva, with the intervention of the pastors and the leadership of Calvin, a paternalistic council prohibited collusion by both owners and workers. After the demands of two pastors were presented to the Council, the whole industry was regulated after listening to the presentations by the interested parties.[31] Regulation of the printing industry for quality was undertaken by the Council, and when it concerned church publications, the weight of clerical intervention was felt. The ordinances passed at Calvin's insistence lasted until the time of Napoleon.

Geneva's regulation of industry, of course, was not innovative. This regulation preceded laissez faire economics. It was standard, but it was different from France in favoring the workers as well as the owners. The regulation was, of course, reinforced by the high view of government help by Reformed theology and Calvin in particular. The governing authorities were the agents of God for the welfare of the people. Against the practical power and the theological justification of that power owners and workers had to adjust.

Calvin recognized this high doctrine of government in several of his writings. One interesting formulation of this high calling of the civic official is found in his *Instruction of Faith,* a compendium of the *Institutes* which he prepared.

> The Lord has not only testified that the status of magistrate or civic officer was approved by him and was pleasing to him, but also he has moreover greatly recommended it to us, having honored its dignity with very honorable titles. . . . Hence princes and magistrates must think of him whom they serve in their office, and do nothing unworthy of ministers and lieutenants of God. All their solicitude must be in this: to keep in true purity the public form or religion, to establish and to guide the life of the people by very good laws, and to procure the welfare and the tranquility of their subjects, both in public and in private. But this cannot be obtained except through justice and judgment, which two things are to them particularly recommended by the prophet (Jer. 22:1– 9). Justice is to safeguard the innocent, to maintain, to keep and to fill them; judgment is to resist the audacity of evil men, to repress violence, and to punish misdeeds.[32]

Here is Calvin's enthusiastic *yes* to government. However, even in this text the possibility of a *no* to an unjust government is heard. Justice and judgment are required of these lieutenants of God. The text of Jeremiah in which Calvin grounds the requirement of justice and judgment requires one to:

> Deal justly and fairly, rescue the victim from his oppressor, do not ill-treat or do violence to the alien, the orphan or the widow, do not shed innocent blood in this place (Jeremiah 19:3, *New English Bible*).

Jeremiah thunders on that if the people obey, right government will prevail; and if not, there will be destruction. Disobedience will lead to people passing by Jerusalem and crying, "Why has the Lord done this to such a great city?" (Jeremiah 19:8a, *New English Bible*) Rule then is subject to justice and judgment. Within two paragraphs, Calvin states plainly that any orders by governors contrary to God's will are to be disregarded. Peter is turned to with his witness that we must obey God and not human authorities (Acts 4:19).

The welfare of the people, then, is a clear responsibility of the government as Calvin understood it. The tendency toward governmental control of business is clear in Calvin's writings and actions. Tendencies of many later-day Calvinists towards affirmations of laissez faire economics and social Darwinism do not seem to have a grounding in Calvin. The cruelty of unregulated social Darwinism certainly is not consistently compatible with Calvin's teachings.

At one level an affinity with laissez faire economics seems possible. If it were more efficient, if it produced more goods for people in need, would Calvin have not accepted it? He was able to adjust Christian ethics to changing times, but laissez faire economics are beyond the level to which he could have adjusted. He was a person of the 16th century with a sense that a theonomous society was possible. An autonomous society of all competing according to their own passions and desires was unthinkable. To many, Geneva with Calvin probably seemed heteronomous, but to Calvin it was moving into theonomy in the free acceptance of God's law. The heteronomy of medieval Europe and the autonomy of modern capitalism were both foreign to Calvin, in fact he was closer to the medieval Europe.

All of his economic ethics are secondary to serving the Kingdom of Christ. After affirming the priority of the divine blessing: "We must prize the blessing of God as more valuable than the entire world," he could turn to economic ethics as a secondary matter. In this second rank came the need to "honestly work for a living," the requirement to live moderately, the duty to "employ the power which riches give in aiding neighbors and relieving them from suffering." "Riches are a means to help the needy. That is the way to proceed and to keep a happy medium."[33]

Themes for Present Reflections

Reformed church practice which wants to take John Calvin's work in economic ethics seriously could consider several themes from his work. First, Reformed ethics is characterized by a high degree of human solidarity and mutuality. As Calvin put it in commenting on the creation story: "The commencement, therefore, involves a general principle, that humanity was formed to be a social animal."[34] Secondly, life is lived within the context of a gracious, sovereign God whose will for practical living may be sought in scripture and natural reason. Thirdly, the church and the state must cooperate in regulating the common life and in caring for the poor. The struggle for justice is their common task. In commenting on the difficulty of establishing justice Calvin wrote:

> The term applied by Matthew is very emphatic, and is intended to inform us, that justice is not established in the world without a great struggle and exertion. The devil throws all possible difficulties in the way which cannot be removed without violent opposition.[35]

Finally: while economics is a practical matter, the goals of the process are mutual support among all people and for the common good; no one is to have too much and no one is to be condemned to having too little. Work is for the common good and not for selfishness. He put it in commenting on the parable of the Good Samaritan from Luke:

> For here, as in a mirror, we behold that common relationship of people which the scribes endeavored to blot out by their wicked sophistry, and the compassion which an enemy sowed to a Jew demonstrates that the guidance and teaching of nations are sufficient to show that one was created for another. Hence it is inferred that there is a mutual obligation between all.[36]

Endnotes

1. James C. Gustafson, *Ethics from a Theocentric Perspective* (Chicago: University of Chicago Press, 1981), pp. 163–164. Paraphrased here.

2. Andre Bieler, *The Social Humanism of Calvin* (Richmond: John Knox Press, 1964), p. 60.

3. John Calvin, *The Institutes of the Christian Religion*, The Library of Christian Classics, XX (Philadelphia: The Westminster Press, 1960), IV, xx, 14.

4. *Ibid.*, IV, xx, 16.

5. *Ibid.*, IV, xx, 14.

6. *Ibid.*

7. *Ibid.*, IV, xx, 16.

8. Jane Dempsey Douglas, *Women, Freedom and Calvin* (Philadelphia: The Westminster Press, 1985), p. 121.

9. *Institutes*, III, vii, 2.

10. *Ibid.*, III, vii, 3.

11. Professor David Little reminded me at the Ghost Ranch Colloquium

discussion in the summer of 1986 that this was a point made by Max Weber in his *Protestant Ethic and The Spirit of Capitalism.* He is correct and my own method of Christian ethics owes a lot to Max Weber's insights. My intention in this paper is not to attack the Weber thesis as applied to later Calvinism, but only to distance my interpretation of Calvin from Weber's interpretation of a later type of Calvinism.

12. *Institutes,* III, vii, 10.

13. Georgia Harkness, *John Calvin: The Man and His Etics* (New York: Henry Holt and Company, 1931), p. 168.

14. John Calvin, *Commentary on a Harmony of the Evangelists* (Grand Rapids: Baker Book House, 1979), II, p. 141

15. *Ibid.*

16. Robert E. Weigand is a typical of this popular misconception. The professor of marketing at the University of Illinois wrote: "John Calvin, the 16th century theologian taught that hard work and an abstemious life brought salvation. These values also bring prosperity." *The New York Times* (April 19, 1986), p. 15.

17. John Calvin, *Calvin's Commentaries,* The Library of Christian Classics, XXIII (Philadelphia: The Westminster Press, 1957), p. 330.

18. Quoted in Bierler, *The Social Humanism,* p. 37.

19. *Ibid.*

20. Quoted in Benjamin Nelson, *The Idea of Usury* (Chicago: The University of Chicago Press, 1969), p. 78.

21. *Ibid.*

22. Harkness, *John Calvin: The Man and His Etics* discusses the usury question in detail in perhaps the first major book on Calvin's ethics in English. Her work is made particularly useful by her long quotations from Calvin himself on disputed points.

23. Quoted in Harkness, p. 206.

24. Listed in Harkness, p. 207.

25. Bieler, p. 30.

26. *Ibid.,* p. 34.

27. See: William C. Innes, *Social Concern in Calvin's Geneva* (Allison Park: Pickwick Publications, 1983), pp. 103–116, for an excellent analysis of Calvin's diaconate.

28. *Ibid.,* p. 152.

29. Quoted in Bieler, p. 53.

30. *Ibid.,* p. 52.

31. Fred Graham, *The Constructive Revolutionary: John Calvin and His Socio-Economic Impact* (Atlanta: John Knox Press, 1971), pp. 127–144. Graham's discussion of the regulation of commerce in Geneva is the most complete I have found.

32. John Calvin, "Instruction in Faith," in Harry Emerson Fosdick (ed), *Great Voices of the Reformation* (New York: Random House, 1952), p. 237.

33. *Ibid.*, p. 63.

34. John Calvin, *Commenting on Genesis* (Grand Rapids: Baker Book House, 1979), p. 128.

35. John Calvin, *Commenting on Harmonization of the Evangelists* I, p. 62.

36. *Ibid.*

Chapter Four

Calvinism, Racism, and Economic Institutions

Preston N. Williams

The familiarity of the terms in the title of this article to the readers of this collection of essays makes necessary only the most general definitions. Calvinism or the Reformed tradition embodies all those persons, institutions, and values that have been greatly formed by the Reformations of John Calvin in Geneva, John Knox in Scotland, and the Puritans in England and the United States of America. In this article they are to be understood in their broadest North American usage.

Racism shall be understood as the belief or practice of discrimination against another racial group based upon the conviction that one race is by nature superior to another. By race we shall mean those groups of persons usually classified as Caucasian (white), Negroid (black), and Mongolian (brown or red). Economics, the economy, and economic institutions shall refer to those societal institutions designed to distribute the benefits and rewards produced within a nation and its communities.

The intention of the article is to indicate how Calvinism in the United States of America helped to establish and maintain a pattern of race relations that influenced economic institutions as well as social, political, and religious institutions. The thesis is that Calvinism has contributed not only to the economic political, social, and religious character of America but also to the patterns of racism found in its economic as well as in its social, political, and religious institutions.

Ernst Troeltsch has stated that both Roman Catholicism and Calvinism were systems of religious thought that created universal visions of civilization. In Calvinism this orientation follows from the high conception of the sovereignty of God, a conception that led in the thinking of some to the so-called doctrine of double predestination. Important for our consideration is the fact that such an understanding sees all of the universe as being under the total control of an all powerful, just, and loving God. This embraces nature and society including all the social, political, and economic orders. If one can accept this teaching, and for many years the majority of Calvinists did, then, at the level of the relationship between creator, creation, and creature all things and individuals received justice or we might say were treated equally. These relationships, however, are metaphysical and theological and frequently have little influence upon the natural and human relationships that exist on earth and which one might think were entailed by them.

Calvinists have always taken these relationships seriously and have sought to create human institutions and practices which corresponded to the divine economy, God's manner of managing the world and the creatures therein. The results have often been very surprising, but they do disclose how men and women have understood the divine and natural law of God as well as the Words of the Lord. The pattern that has developed in America is not very different from what has emerged in Switzerland, the Netherlands, Scotland, and England. It is a conception which suggests that God has in some mysterious way divided people into two categories: the saved and the damned, the elect and the non-elect, and that while this is a mystery the division can be presumptively associated with some visible particular entity: church membership and baptism, piety and style of life, nation, ethnicity or race. This way of understanding God's household has had enormous consequences for the manner in which stewardship was established in respect to all things. This way of conceiving things has left its mark upon our ideas of community. Troeltsch captures the historical consequence accurately when he states that Calvinism has no doctrine of abstract equality. It affirms instead an inequality of earthly vocations and an essential inequality of human life.

Much has been said in our day about Puritan notions of community, especially John Winthrop's address on the Arabella, but what is often forgotten is that his conception of community was exclusive. God's grace and wisdom placed some people over and above other people. The conceptions of duty, obligation, and bondedness applied only to the "in group" and had a different significance for the relationship between the members of the Arabella's party and those persons inhabiting the mainland or who for other reasons were outside the covenant community. This notion of exclusive covenant was pervasive throughout the colonies and was used to justify not only religious divisions but those of race, culture, class, and sex. Much of the power in present day appeals to community rest still upon this Calvinist notion of separation and exclusion which is set at the heart of the Puritan conception of community. In the American community this translates into an implicit, often explicit practice of racism.

Such also has been the case historically within the Reformed tradition in America, especially the Presbyterian churches. David E. Swift has written that the classical pattern of Presbyterian concern for slaves was set in the middle of the eighteenth century by Samuel Davies who was one of the most eloquent preachers in the colonies and one who was concerned for the neglect of the soul of the African slaves because they shared immortality and the gospel in common with their masters. His Virginia mission to the blacks indulged therefore in no double standard for blacks and whites in respect to the profession of piety and holiness, yet he was unable to see any contradiction between the slave's status as property and the status of white persons as free. He sought then to make blacks literate and fully Christian while at the same time controlling what they read and heard in order that they might not create or join in any untoward social and political activity. Following the death of Jonathan Edwards, Davies became the president of the College of New Jersey (Princeton). Moreover, it was Davies' views that were affirmed in the official statement in 1787 by the Synod of New York and Philadelphia (forerunner of the General Assembly) in stressing education of blacks as more important than freeing them. In doing so the synod was asserting the superiority of white Americans and the rightfulness of slavery for blacks because they were not yet fit for citizenship in the American nation.

> The Synod of New York and Philadelphia do highly approve of the general principles in favor of universal liberty that prevail in America, and the interest which many of the States have taken in promoting the abolition of Slavery; yet, inasmuch as men, introduced from a servile state, to a participation of all the privileges of civil society without a proper education, and without previous habits of industry, may be in many respects dangerous to the community; therefore they earnestly recommend to all the members belonging to their communion to give those persons who are at present held in servitude, such good education

as to prepare them for the better enjoyment of freedom; and they moreover recommend that masters, whenever they find servants disposed to make a just improvement of the privilege, would give them *a peculium*, or grant them sufficient time and sufficient means of procuring their own liberty, at a moderate rate; that thereby they may be brought into society with those habits of industry that may render them useful citizens and finally, they recommend it to all their people to use the most prudent measures consistent with the interests and the state of civil society, in the countries where they live, to procure eventually the final abolition of slavery in America.

The teachings of the synod and Samuel Davies were institutionalized in the church by the Reverend John Holt Rice, the first white man assigned by the General Assembly, over a period of years, to do mission work with blacks. Two Afro-Americans, John Chavis (1801–1807) and John Gloucester (1807–1813), served in a similar capacity. The inequality between whites and blacks was accepted. Whites saw themselves as engaged in the uplift of blacks through catechism, word, and sacrament. Recognition of the slave's soul and possible immortality was undertaken not only in order to teach them to fear and to love God but also, as the General Assembly suggested, to protect civil society and as many whites stated, with a regard to the self-preservation and safety of their families.

While then affirming a metaphysical and theological equality in this life, the Reformed tradition taught persons to accept white superiority and black inferiority. Moreover, they taught the blacks that slavery was lawful and that the peculiar institution should not be removed by any activity not approved of by whites. The soverign God who ruled nature and persons had brought into existence in America a notion and religious tradition in which natural and God-given rights were bestowed upon persons according to the wishes of white men and women of power and presumably piety.

From a letter of John Holt Rice to a friend one is able to learn in addition about the willingness of religious persons to modify their conception of the sovereignty of God when applying the doctrine to economic institutions. Rice wrote to his friend that the church and clergy should not attack the slave system because slaves were property and Americans were extremely reluctant to accept any interference with their property rights.

> I am most fully convinced that slavery is the greatest evil in our country, except whiskey; and it is my ardent prayer that we may be delivered

from it. . . . The reason why I am so strenuously opposed to any movement by the church or the ministers of religion on this subject, is simply this. I am convinced that anything we can do will injure religion, and retard the march of public feeling in relation to slavery. . . . As slavery exists among us, the only possible chance of deliverance is by *making the people willing* to get rid of it. At any rate, it is this or physical force. The problem to be solved is, to produce that state of *public will,* which will cause the people to move spontaneously to the eradication of the evil. Slaves by law are held as property. If the church or the minister of religion touches the subject, it is touching what are called the rights of property. The jealousy among our countrymen on this subject is such, that we cannot move a step in this way, without wakening up the strongest opposition, and producing the most violent excitement. . . . Under this conviction, I wish the ministers of religion to be convinced that there is nothing in the New Testament which obliged them to take hold of this subject directly. In fact, I believe that it never has fared well with either church or state, when the church meddled with temporal affairs. And I should—knowing how unmanageable religious feeling is, when not under the immediate influence of divine truth—be exceedingly afraid to see it brought to bear *directly* on the subject of slavery. . . . Let the subject of slavery be discussed in the political papers . . . as a subject of political economy . . . ; and treat it as a matter of State concernment [as against the federal government]. Examine its effects on the agriculture, commerce, and manufacture of the State. Compare the expense of free and slave labour. Bring distinctly before the people the evil in its unavoidable operations and its fearful increase. Set them to calculating the weight of their burdens. Consideration of this sort, combined with the benevolent feelings growing out of a gradual, uninterrupted progress or religion, will, I believe, set the people of their own accord to seek deliverance. They will foresee the necessity of a change; soon begin to prepare for it; and it will come about without violence or convulsion. (Letter of February 24, 1827, to William Maxwell. Maxwell, *Memoir of Rice.*)

American intransigence in respect to their property rights made Rice attempt to persuade clergy that the New Testament did not require Christians to oppose slavery and that Christianity was bound to the policies of economic freedom and least government. The fate he sought to avoid by this distortion of religion, the usage of physical force to end slavery, was not forestalled. Instead the Reformed tradition which had been long associated with the teaching of the virtues of literacy, industry, fidelity, submissiveness, temperance, and honesty as forms of moral and religious discipline became associated also with these virtues as instruments for determining political and economic institutions supportive of slavery. In the period following the Civil War, these same virtues would be harnessed to the Calvinism which the Weberian hypothesis asserted helped to create the "spirit of capitalism." In both pre- and post-Civil War America Calvinism supported racism and helped to link it to the economic order.

In outlining the interrelation between Calvinism, racism, and economic institutions several matters need to be observed. One needs to note that the pattern established by Davies and Holt continued to dominate the life of the Reformed tradition in the South and to a considerable extent in the nation at large in spite of the split of Presbyterian bodies over the issue of slavery. The entire tradition remained deeply divided over matters of race and this led to its acquiescence in and legitimation of a system of social, political, and economic exploitation of Afro-Americans. The self-respect and dignity of black people were denied; their political franchise stolen; and their means of economic livelihood severely restricted. This practice continued without any significant protest by the white members of the tradition until the end of World War II. The Southern branch was most concerned to continue as much of the pattern of slavery as was possible in a legally segregated and pervasively discriminatory society while the Northern branch held to a pattern of aristocratic paternalism in relation to its nonwhite members, adhering as much as possible to Rice's admonition not to mix religion with protest against prevailing property arrangements.

Thus, insofar as the Reformed tradition influenced the political and economic order in respect to race relations, it was content to advocate the equality of rights and duties among all persons but within a framework which affirmed white superiority and black inferiority as God-given and natural. Calvinism can be seen therefore as being in deep complicity with the national practices of racial discrimination. Most importantly one must see, as Aldon Morris has so convincingly shown, that this was a pattern of economic exploitation defined in terms of race as well as social and political exploitation defined in terms of race.

With the victory of the Union armies in the Civil War there emerged in America not only a strong federal government but also a triumphal industrial capitalism. The new industrial order which developed was greatly influenced by the Reformed cultural and religious tradition because its industrial captains and political leaders were members of that tradition or from societies in which that tradition was very strong.

Cities like New York, Philadelphia, Newark, Pittsburgh, and Chicago symbolize its economic strength and form whereas Presidents Theodore Roosevelt, Woodrow Wilson, William G. Harding, and Calvin Coolidge point to its political influence. The *Report of the National Advisory Commission on Civil Disorders,* the Kerner Commission Report of 1967, documents how under a society largely shaped by this tradition two Americas continued to grow. Black Americans were excluded from the ladders of economic mobility by the huge importation of European people, and the new white immigrants used the power of their numbers not only to deny blacks access to economic institutions but also to exclude them from political power in the large cities.

These practices continued until the rise of the union movement prompted some employers to utilize a more aggressive dual race employment policy in which blacks were employed to stifle union growth but were still shut off from equal opportunity for participation in the work force. It would be foolish to contend that the dual race employment and professional system that developed in America was due to the influence of the Reformed tradition alone but it would be equally foolish to assert that the tradition which produced Adam Smith, the original industrial revolution, the normative definitions of poverty and charity, and the dominant American cultural values had no part to play in the creation of two Americas, one rich and one poor, one white and one black. In respect to equality of opportunity and treatment for black Americans, the new industrial America was only slightly more hospitable than the legally segregated South. The black members of the Reformed tradition and the black citizens of America did not have equal access to or equal place in the economic institutions built with the wisdom and guidance of Reformed people in America.

The period from Franklin D. Roosevelt's New Deal reforms until the conservative administration of Ronald Reagan embodied some important changes in the American economy and its pattern of race relations. Monsignor John A. Ryan, director of the Social Action Department of the National Catholic Welfare Conference suggested that the New Deal was the enactment of the economic program suggested by the Roman Catholic Bishops in their 1919 letter, "Social Reconstruction: A General Review of the Problems and Survey of Remedies." The monsignor's claim may have been too large but it pointed to the fact that the influence of Calvinism upon the economy had lessened.

The new political coalition also meant a change in race relations. European ethnic groups who had not participated in slavery and who had felt themselves to have been victims of Anglo-Americans and Northern Europeans assumed power in the new Democratic party. Although this four decade period could be divided into several eras, I shall treat it as a whole because its direction of change was not forcefully challenged until the Reagan presidency (1980–88). Reagan questions as no other president the notion of the welfare state and New Deal economic policies and sought to reverse the understandings of racial justice that grew from its seeds.

America underwent many economic and social changes during the period from Roosevelt to Reagan but most of these changes rested upon the acceptance of the belief that the federal government had a responsibility to be the employer of last resort and the protector of the most weak and needy in society. The performance of this task justified the intervention of the federal government in the economy and in local affairs. The depression of the thirties was worldwide in scope and caused many white persons to see that poverty could be the result of unavoidable misfortune as well as moral inadequacy or the will of God. They supported therefore the establishment of a partial welfare state which sought to make the federal government their protector against the extremes of poverty and unemployment.

While these programs were not intended to aid black Americans overcome their oppression and on occasion increased the discrimination against blacks, the programs of the New Deal on the whole aided blacks to enlarge their opportunities in the society and to maintain their sense of hope. The nation's participation in the war against Hitler's Germany similarly led inadvertently to advances for black Americans in the social, political, and economic structures of the American society. The programs of decolonization in Africa and Asia following World War II likewise contributed to the inauguration of a civil rights and black power revolution in America that further increased black access to and participation in the social, political, and economic institutions in society. This even slight improvement in race relations made possible a higher status for black Americans. Coupled with the continuing economic affluence resulting from the mobilization for war and victory in war, this social progress permitted a narrowing of the gap between white and black income. Not until the Vietnam War and the economic recovery of Germany and Japan did America experience a major challenge to and decrease in its economic growth. Limited economic growth led to a resistance by a sizable portion of the middle class to the welfare state and to more equal justice for black Americans.

The superpower status of the nation and its economic dominance in most world markets made progress in race relations possible but value shifts in America contributed also to this change. During the age of the New Deal the immigrant groups that had entered the nation in such large numbers at the turn of the century were able to convert their numbers into political power and their political power into economic power. In the fifties and sixties the combination of numbers and political and economic power was used to define America as a pluralistic nation, and since most black Americans were Protestants, the redefinition often carried racial overtones. The nation's Calvinistic cultural influence was reduced thus making possible the justification of many elements of a welfare state and power sharing with European ethnic groups in social, political, and cultural institutions. Since the cultural traditions of the new immigrant groups and the Reformed tradition were overwhelmingly white, the racial customs of the land were not greatly modified even though some change took place.

The Reformed tradition was not unaffected by these changes. It sought therefore to respond to these social and cultural changes by finding within itself a more adequate understanding of the relationship between the metaphysical and theological affirmation of God's sovereignty and its historical manifestation. Andrew Murray in his volume, *Presbyterians and the Negro: A History* (Philadelphia, 1966) indicates that one can understand the history of blacks and whites within the church in terms of the prepositions: by, for, and with. Only in the recent past has there been a structure of governance and an attitude conducive to cooperative work based upon the assumption of equality. The participation of Eugene Carson Blake, the Stated Clerk of the United Presbyterian Church in the United States of America, in the Civil Rights movement and his submittal to arrest and imprisonment dramatized the new understanding. The National Committee on the Self-Development of People perhaps best symbolizes the changes, for its name and program points to the concern for advocacy, self-determination, and the ennoblement of all people. Most of this committee's work and program is, however, at the edge of the church's life.

Much more change needs to take place. The historical understanding of God's sovereignty must have consequences for economic institutions and it must entail the understanding of covenant as inclusive.

The tradition's understanding of an inclusive church in an inclusive society must be oriented to understanding the family of God as one family in which equality and justice prevail.

The Reformed tradition's revised understanding of its teaching concerning the sovereignty of God indicates its recognition that a metaphysical and theological affirmation of equality requires historical embodiment in social, political, and economic institutions. Thus, it is no longer adequate to omit race relations and economic activity from these considerations or to assert that existing practices and institutions are basically natural and God-given. The tradition's new conception of itself can support, if properly developed, a model of society that insists that rights and duties should not only be equally applied to all persons but that the social order in which they exist should also be one exhibiting racial and economic equality and justice. The spirit of capitalism and economic freedom need not be abandoned but they must be constrained by a concern for equality and justice. A moral and religious discipline must be accepted by social, political, and economic institutions as well as the self.

Troeltsch asserted that Calvinism possessed a universal vision. I have argued that Calvinism's vision was flawed because in America it did not develop properly the implications of God's sovereignty especially in relation to its teaching concerning the covenantal community. It spoke about an exclusive covenant and this had the effect of cultivating attitudes of superiority on the part of one class of persons over against another or it permitted a too easy justification of inequality. The former orientation aided and abetted discrimination not only among persons within the Reformed tradition but also between its members and the people of African descent who were brought to this shore and the immigrants from eastern, southern, and central Europe who were not Reformed.

This attitude of superiority helped to create racism against black Americans and ill treatment against European ethnic groups because it could only enlarge community by conquest. Religious and social transformation required the replacement of one religion or culture by another. Racism was one sin that emerged from this process. It has and it continues to affirm that some people are by nature unable to undertake the task of moral and social improvement that will make them the equal of the white Calvinist.

The pluralism endemic to America and made actual by the changes which took place in the nation between the presidencies of Roosevelt and Reagan together with the revision of covenantal thinking by

Calvinists has persuaded the Reformed tradition to alter its conception of community and to affirm that God's covenant is inclusive. It is a covenant with all the people of the universe and it is actualized within a variety of cultural and religious traditions. Having taught America much of its conception of white superiority, the Reformed tradition is now seeking to take a leading role in the removal of the discrimination based upon race, sex, ethnicity, and religion. The conception of God's sovereignty and covenant is now understood in a manner which helps to form a more inclusive community in America and in a Reformed tradition which is largely white and middle class.

While it is possible to see positive revisions in the Reformed tradition in respect to its teaching about and practice of race relations, it is more difficult to see the development of sensitive concerns for economic justice. This is due in part perhaps to the long period of prosperity which followed the Great Depression and which allowed the nation to reduce the perception of economic injustice among all its people and at the same time be relatively generous to people abroad. Such a period of national affluence could permit a people to perceive not only themselves as an economically just society but also a society that did not need to employ regulations to procure economic justice. Lack of change within the Reformed tradition on economic matters has been due also to the middle class status of most of its members and their blindness to matters of economic injustice. Whatever the reasons for the failure to become more perceptive concerning the economy, the consequence was the survival of the older ideas of economic freedom and little government even within the framework of government policies that pointed in a different direction.

The recent reduction in economic prosperity and the better understanding of God's sovereignty point, however, to the need for the tradition to rethink its teaching concerning the economy. This is needed in order to remove racism and to be fair to all members of the covenant community. An inclusive covenantal community requires the enlargement of one's sense of special obligations and duties beyond the bonds of race, class, and family. It requires the recognition of special obligations to racial minorities, the poor, and the disadvantaged, at home and abroad. The more comprehensive understanding of neighborly love should cause the tradition to see the need for more adequate private and governmental economic institutions. Calvin's conception of the state as a positive order of creation and of economic institutions as compatible with the will of God should stimulate the tradition to devise institutions appropriate for maintaining the general welfare of an inclusive community. Economic freedom would be required then to exist within the context of consideration of justice, and market systems would be encouraged to become fair. Such occurrences would enable the tradition to approximate more closely its vision of a universal civilization responsive ultimately to the rule and authority of God.

Such an approach would not be unaware of the need for productivity and efficiency. The world societies' failure to handle these issues was in part the cause of the Great Depression. On these matters of productivity and efficiency the Reformed tradition is as Weber noted quite capable. Concern for an inclusive covenantal community and attention to the needs of all others cannot be a reason therefore to set these issues aside. Productivity and efficiency must be made to better serve all people and not simply those with natural abilities and talents of an exceptional nature. Consideration of the welfare of all from the perspective of the economy requires then a concern for limits. The important point is that all persons and not just an unfortunate few will be encouraged to govern wisely their usage of the earth's resources and to share in its largess.

Since much of this task for the Reformed tradition lies in the future, only a thin outline can be given here. Acknowledgement of the sovereignty of God is to be related to the functioning of economic institutions and all persons are to be supplied, within the framework of existing resources, with the basic requirements for living. Government will not be unlimited but its limits will be related to the needs for social and economic justice.

In this paper I have outlined the pattern of interaction that has existed in the United States of America between Calvinism, racism, and economic institutions. The interaction has been substantial but not always in accord with the best insights of democratic government or the basic understanding of the Christian faith, even if persons and communities are themselves implementing the teachings of those two systems of action. Over time there has been improvement, and, if I am correct, the Reformed tradition's concern with a universal civilization under the sovereignty of God can yet be the basis for a guideline toward the realization of racial and economic justice in a world community in which all persons are equally respected and share equally in the rights and duties and rewards and benefits of that society.

Chapter Five

Economic Justice and the Grounds for a Theory of Progressive Taxation in Calvin's Thought

David Little

Sometime before the passage of the Tax Reform Act of 1986, the *Washington Post* admitted editorially that the act was insufficiently progressive. To apply "genuinely progressive rates," the editorial recognized, would involve "a substantial increase in the tax burden of the rich." But true as that might be, the editorial went on, 1986 was not the right time to campaign for increased progressivity. People worried about the issue should wait: "That's next year's argument," announced the *Post*.[1]

Just why is was next year's argument was never made clear. In any case "next year" has come and gone, and neither the Post nor anyone else seems to be taking up with much vigor this piece of unfinished business. Whatever the Posts's excuse for its lack of perseverance, Reformed Christians have no excuse for ignoring the question of progressive taxation. The Reformed tradition raises the question in unmistakable terms, even if it does not entirely resolve the question of its own accord.

The Background: Calvin's Theory of Community and Economic Justice

The necessary starting point for a Reformed approach to taxation is the thought of John Calvin, and, more specifically, his general understanding of economic life and responsibility. This aspect of Calvin's thought is probably best described as "communitarian," to invoke a currently fashionable term. For Calvin, human solidarity lies at the heart of God's providential design. Commenting on Genesis 2:18—"It is not good that man should be alone," Calvin writes:

> Moses now explains the design of God in creating the woman: namely, that there should be human beings on the earth who might cultivate mutual society among themselves. Yet a doubt may arise whether this design ought to be extended to progeny, for the words simply mean that since it was not expedient for man to be alone, a wife must be created, who might be his helper. I, however, take the meaning to be this, that God begins, indeed, at the first step of human society, yet designs to include others, each in its proper place. The commencement, therefore, involves a general principle, that man was formed to be a social animal.[2]

Or, as Andre Bieler puts it, citing Calvin's comment on Luke 10:30:

> The primary character of the social order created by God is the *solidarity* that unites all beings one with another. 'The human race is conjoined together by a sacred bond of community. All are neighbors one of another. . . . We must never wipe out our common nature.'[3]

Moreover, while Calvin's vision of an ideal human community is of course cast, to an important degree, in spiritual or religious terms, it is simultaneously and pervasively portrayed in material or "economic" terms, as well.

> [H]ence we infer what was the end for which all things were created; namely, that none of the conveniences and necessaries of life might be wanting to men. In the very order of the creation the paternal solicitude of God for man is conspicuous, because he furnished the world with all things needful, and even with an immense profusion of wealth before he formed man. *Thus man was rich before he was born.*[4]
> The Prophet makes it known that God not only provides for the needs of men and gives to them as much as is sufficient for the ordinary needs of this life, but by His mercy He treats them still more generously when He gladdens their hearts with wine and oil.[5]

In fact, while the family is important for Calvin as a vehicle for the development of cooperative life, in some ways it is economic relationships that provide an even more significant expression of his understanding of social interdependence. In Bieler's apt summary,

'God has created man,' Calvin says, 'so that man may be a creature of fellowship'. . . . Companionship is completed in work and in the interplay of economic exchanges. Human fellowship is realized in relationships which flow from the division of labor wherein each person has been called by God to a particular and partial work which complements the work of others. The mutual exchange of goods and services is the concrete sign of the profound solidarity which unites humanity.[6]

It is in the connection that Calvin's proverbial emphasis upon hard work in a worldly vocation must be seen. The vulgar impression, partly encouraged by Max Weber, that individual labor, especially if it is crowned by personal prosperity, is somehow an end in itself for being a sign of individual election, radically distorts Calvin's idea by ignoring the social context of labor, and thus misconstruing the proper objectives, in Calvin's mind, of individual initiative and effort. Calvin clearly does emphasize the importance of self-initiated hard work in worldly vocations.

It is not the will of the Lord that we should be like blocks of wood, or that we should keep our arms folded without doing anything; but that we should apply to use all the talents and advantages which he has conferred upon us. It is indeed true that the greatest part of our labors proceeds from the curse of God; yet although men had still retained the integrity of their primitive state, God would have had us to be employed, even as we see how Adam was placed in the garden of Eden to dress it. Solomon, therefore, does not condemn watchfulness, a thing which God approves; nor yet man's labor, by which when they undertake it willingly, according to the commandment of God, they offer to him the acceptable sacrifice. . . .[7]

Still, the point of such action is decidedly for the sake of the common good.

[Paul] applies the appellation of disorderly persons, not to those that are of a dissolute life, or to those whose characters are stained by flagrant crimes, but to indolent and worthless persons, who employ themselves in no honorable and useful occupation. For this truly is *ataxia* (disorder)—*not considering for what purpose we are made, and regulating our life with a view to that end,* while it is only when we live according to the rule prescribed to us by God that this life is duly regulated. Let this order be set aside, and there is nothing but confusion in human life. . . . *For God has distinguished in such a manner the life of men, in order that every one may lay himself out for the advantage of others.* He, therefore, who lies to himself alone, so as to be profitable in no way to the human race, nay more, is a burden to others, giving help to no one, is on good grounds reckoned to be *ataxia* (disorderly).[8]

Because "it is certain that a calling would never be approved by God that is not socially useful, and that does not redound to the profit of all,"[9] Calvin proposes the notion of "general usefulness: as the standard for evaluating economic performance. Accordingly, he envisions a system of material benefits that are efficiently produced by the dedication and hard work of all employable human beings, and that are universally and justly exchanged and distributed so as to satisfy the basic needs of all, and, in addition, so as to stimulate continued production. Thus, in the primitive community, that community originally designed by God, material benefits are, so to speak, the tokens of a shared life. As the fruit of divided labor, they function to remind human beings of their fundamental interdependence and mutual responsibility. And as rewards or "payment" for contributing to the common good, they symbolize the ultimate purpose of economic endeavor.

Calvin's idea of property fits in against this general background. Again, contrary to the popular conception, property for Calvin is nowhere understood as something exclusively subject to individual interests. As usual, Bieler summarizes Calvin's view accurately:

> If a person is a property-holder, he alone is responsible before God for the management of his goods; his property is conditioned by the needs of others. Whatever a person possesses, is held with reference to the service of the community. . . . [According to Calvin,] the Bible never gives property a purely individualistic meaning. It does not recognize any other conception of property than for the purpose of service.[10]

Or, as Calvin himself puts it,

> Let those, then, that have riches, whether they have been left by inheritance, or procured by industry and efforts, consider that their abundance was not intended to be laid out in intemperence or excess, but in relieving the necessities of the brethren.[11]

Indeed, Calvin elaborates this point in an interesting way.

> For in order to be purged of all anger, hate, and enmity, you have to begin at this point: that it isn't enough for you to have abstained from

insult and injury and violence, for you not to have attempted anything against your neighbors, or harbored in your hearts any hate or malice against them. It isn't enough for you not to have been poisoned with ill will, but it is crucial for you to live in charity. . . . For God does not want us to be lazy in this world. He did not simply create us to abstain from evil. Rocks and trees and other unconscious things achieve that quite well. Rather it is crucial for men to give and apply themselves to accomplishing good. Therefore let us understand that when our Lord wills for the life of our fellowmen to be precious and dear in our sight, he shows that, as far as he is concerned, each time we fail to help our neighbor in need, we kill him. For we are not only murderers when we harbor ill will and secretly hate our neighbors, but even when we do not help them in their need and do not attempt to engage ourselves in their behalf when they need our help, we are guilty before God.[12] Therefore, let none of us think that it is only lawful for us to guard what we have, rather, as the principle of charity exhorts us, let us see that *we preserve and procure our neighbor's property as much as our own.*[13]

In short, Calvin appears to expand the duties of justice to include certain duties of love or charity. On this reading, one is not being fully just simply by refraining from doing injury, by forbearing abuses of various kinds, but also by failing to assist those in need. Such acts are of a piece with "insult, injury and violence": "each time we fail to help our neighbor in need, we kill him." This intriguing interconnecting of justice and love is related, as we shall see more fully in our discussion of taxation, to Calvin's notion of *equity.*

It is clear, then, that Calvin's conception of economic justice is emphatically not individualistic, if individualism is understood to mean that the common good is finally determined by the aggregated subjective preferences of the members of a community. The idea of economic justice for Calvin is unmistakably wedded to a trans-subjective or "objective" vision of right relations among human beings. That vision is not something human beings may invent for themselves.

There is, to be sure, an important role for individual initiative and responsibility in economic life, as we have seen. Each person ought ideally to be motivated from the heart to perform vigorous productive activity. In fact, as the passage about using riches quoted above suggests, material reward is, among other things, justly allocated according to a person's "industry and efforts," according, that is, to *individual desert.* Calvin even concedes that differences in individual calling and achievement provide support for certain kinds of legitimate status differences within society.

> I acknowledge indeed that we are not bound to such an equality as
> would make it wrong for the rich to live more elegantly than the poor;
> but *there must be such an equality that nobody starves and nobody hordes his
> abundance at another's expense.*[14]

But as this passage makes clear, individual economic initiative must
be controlled, in Calvin's mind, by "the necessities of the brethren,"
and by the basic needs of all members of the human community.
That economic system alone is truly just that optimally serves those
basic needs, that supplies the *fair shares* of the means of survival that
are the birthright of every human being. There is no doubt that in
Calvin's mind the "fair survival shares"—enough to eat, sufficient
shelter, affordable medical care, access to education, employment
opportunity, protection against arbitrary injury[15]—constitute a relatively objective standard of justice, above and beyond the subjective
interests of individual human beings, and according to which economic performance can and must be judged.

If Calvin enunciates *individual desert* (based on "industry and efforts") and a fundamental right to *fair survival shares* as two criteria
for the just distribution of material benefits, he appears to affirm at
least one more criterion, at least by inference—*merit*, based on social
contribution, especially contribution to "necessities of the brethren."
In other words, special benefits are justly due those, like political and
economic leaders, who make singularly important contributions to
the peace and welfare of all citizens, to promoting, that is, the "fair
survival shares" that are the rightful possession of everyone.[16]

What we have outlined so far is, so to speak, Calvin's ideal or
normative model of economic life, a model that to his mind is part of
God's ultimate design for human community. It is associated, therefore, with social life in the "edenic" or "pre-fall" condition.[17]

By contrast, the fall, according to Calvin, produced a severe disrup-
tion or perversion of the model. In rejecting God's authority, sinful
human beings simultaneously corrupt the desirable pattern of socio-
economic organization intended by God. Where there was harmony
and a vivid sense of interdependence through economic exchange
and mutual effort for the sake of "general usefulness" or the common
good, there is now alienation, conflict, vicious competitiveness motivated exclusively by self-interest and systematic disregard for the
needs of others. In a word, this is all the bitter fruit of the "victory of
Mammon" over God's design, a victory that is no less destructive for
being temporary and provisional, for being ultimately subject to
God's vindication.

The victory of Mammon over man does not produce only the crooked-
ness of the individual; it immediately also brings about the perversion
of society. . . . Immense perturbations follow in economic life, engender-
ing social disorder. Selfish appropriation of wealth, hoarding, cornering,
monopolization, greed, avarice as well as waste, prodigality, luxury, or
absence of sobriety—visible expressions of sin—block the harmonious
circulation of goods foreseen in God's order. These disorders falsify the
just reparation and distribution of money within creation according to
the purpose of God. They clog the equitable redistribution of the
benefits of wealth among all. Misery and luxury together, and between
them the social irresponsibility of the moderate individualist, are the
sign of this fundamental vitiation of society.[18]

For Calvin, God's response to the fall makes up the remainder of
the Christian drama. Christ's encounter with the forces of evil, and
his triumph over them, which is even now in the process of being
fulfilled, has, in Calvin's hands, a markedly socio-economic and
communitarian cast to it. This is true in three respects. Interestingly
enough, in characterizing Christ's redemptive accomplishment, Calvin finds it natural to adopt none other than economic language and
imagery:

Those who employ usefully whatever God has committed to them are
said to be engaged in trading. The life of the godly is justly compared
to trading, for they ought naturally to exchange and barter with each
other, in order to maintain intercourse; and the industry with which
every man discharges the office assigned him, the calling itself, the
power of acting properly, and other gifts, are reckoned to be so many
kinds of merchandise; because the use or object which they have in view
is, to promote mutual intercourse among men.

Now the gain which Christ mentions is general usefulness, which
illustrates the glory of God. For, though God is not enriched, and makes
no gain, by our labors, yet when every one is highly profitable to his
brethren, and applies advantageously, for their salvation, the gifts which
he has received from God, he is said to yield profit, or gain, to God
Himself. So highly does our heavenly Father value the salvation of men,
that whatever contributes to it He chooses to place to his own account.
That we may not become weary in doing well, Christ declares that the
labor of those who are faithfully employed in their calling will not be
useless.[19]

Second, Calvin regularly uses economic metaphors to portray life
in the Body of Christ, the church:

'The Communion of Saints' . . . very well expresses what the church is. It is as if one said that the saints are gathered into the society of Christ on the principle that whatever benefits God confers upon them, they should in turn share with another. This does not, however, rule out diversity of graces, inasmuch as we know the gifts of the Spirit are variously distributed. . . . If truly convinced that God is the common Father of all and Christ the common Head, being united in brotherly love, they cannot but share their benefits with one another.[20]

This "diversity of graces" is nothing other than a spiritual division of labor. Accordingly, God's benefits ("gifts") are variously distributed so that in the process of exchanging them for the common benefit of all, the members of Christ's body will come to realize how profoundly interdependent and mutually responsible they all are.

Third, while Calvin emphasizes that this pattern of sharing gifts involves more than material benefits, it nevertheless does include as a signal feature of Christian life the redistribution of goods within the church for the sake of the needy brethren. In fact, such acts are of the deepest theological significance. They exemplify in a special way one of the central lessons of Christ's redemptive activity.

Having mentioned love [Paul] now refers to Christ as the perfect and unique pattern of it. 'When He was rich,' he says, 'He gave up possession of all His blessings that He might enrich us by His poverty.' [Paul] does not explain why he has mentioned Christ but leaves that for [the Corinthians] to consider for themselves, for it must be clear to everyone that by Christ's example we are incited to beneficence so that we should not spare ourselves when our brethren require our help. Christ was rich because He was God, under whose power and authority are all things, and even in our humanity, which He put on, He was, as the apostle says, 'the heir of all things,' since He was placed by His Father over all creatures and all things were put in subjection under His feet.[21]

[Paul] mentions the twofold result of God's blessing upon us—first, that we have sufficient for the support of life and then that we have something to give to relieve other people's necessities. For as we are not born for ourselves alone, so a Christian man ought not to live for himself or use what he has only for private purposes.[22]

[I]n the Church sharing of resources must be counted a necessary duty. By helping the brethren in Jerusalem, the Corinthians and the rest were offering God a sacrifice and discharging a rightful service that was binding upon them.[23]

As Weber saw, then, Calvin did indeed give special prominence to economic life, though Weber did not sufficiently highlight or examine the unmistakable communitarian cast to Calvin's thought. Nevertheless, if it is important to demonstrate the concern with community in Calvin's thinking, we must not overreact, and lose sight completely of the crucial place that individual, voluntary action—properly understood—does in fact occupy in the Calvinist perspective.

The key here was suggested by our comment above that in Calvin's scheme each person ought ideally to be motivated *from the heart* to play a productive economic role: active, voluntary, "self-imposed" endeavor is essential in the normative economic order. Indeed, it should now be clear that such endeavor is a crucial expression of Christian redemption. Of course, individual initiative is proper only if it is inspired by the vision of common usefulness, interdependence, and just distribution we have outlined. Sin, as we know, is misdirected individual initiative; it is inspired by private, subjective interest to the exclusion or to the subordination of the objective common good. So understood, a major objective of the Christian cause is to reform and redirect individual motivation so as to bring it into line with the general welfare of all.

This central objective creates a deep dilemma for the Calvinist, as to just how far it is permissible to try by political-legal means to coerce the desired reform of individual motivation. On the one side, the communitarian economic order ought properly to constitute a model for governmental action. If the criterion of fair survival shares for all—including sufficient food, shelter, employment opportunities, etc.—is as much a part of justice as Calvin argues, then it clearly follows that such a criterion must serve as a fundamental guide for the enforcement of justice by the state against disruptive and perverse economic action. Calvin's own interventionist economic policies in Geneva exhibit this impulse.[24]

On the other side, if correct motivation is something "we impose . . . upon ourselves of our own free will," rather than being "compelled from the outside to do" by "forced consent,"[25] then the external enforcement of economic justice by the civil authority contradicts that objective. In keeping with the concern for free consent, so central to the Calvinist scheme, it would appear that individuals ought to be left free of external restraint so as to have the opportunity of acting voluntarily.

It is, incidentally, this concern for the importance of free consent, for voluntary agreements, in Calvin's outlook that provides the foundation for the "convenantal" or "contractual" emphasis that was to become so central to the Puritan and (Lockean) liberal traditions.

At the same time, the emphasis upon free consent in economic and other social relationships does, as we say, run into conflict with the countervailing emphasis upon a mandatory economic order. Neither Calvin nor his Puritan descendents ever clearly resolved this dilemma. For our purposes, it is enough to understand the sources of the dilemma, the better to grasp accurately the basic characteristics of Calvin's theory of community and economic justice.

Calvin and Progressive Taxation

If "taxes" may conveniently be defined as "compulsory payments to government to support public expenses,"[26] it is obvious that the question of taxation is closely tied to a consideration of the "common good." Public expenses paid by a government must finally be justified in reference to the public or shared benefit that they produce. If those expenditures go for defense or transportation or a judicial system, such things are normally regarded as "common goods." Even if a government, for one reason or another, provides financial support for particular groups or "special interests" within the society, those expenditures, too, must be accounted something the society as a whole has a common interest in, such as providing welfare relief for the poor, or special assistance to the farmers, or emergency aid for disaster victims.

The two underlying questions, therefore, that lurk behind any discussion of taxation are: (1) What is (or are) the common good(s) for which taxes may legitimately be paid? and (2) What constitutes a legitimate system of tax collection?

So far as an explicit theory of taxation goes, the comment by S. I. Benn and R. S. Peters would appear to apply to Reformed thinking in the sixteenth century:

> Until the nineteenth century, taxation was simply a matter of raising money to cover government expenses, and ease of collection counted for a good deal more in the choice of a tax than concern for fair distribution of the tax burden. Indirect taxes which bear most heavily on lower incomes, provided the bulk of government revenue. [However,] there were plenty of protests. . . .[27]

Accordingly, Calvin did not devote much extended attention to the subject of taxation as such, and certainly he did not worry expressly about utilizing the tax system as a scheme for the fair distribution of wealth. In fact, as we might guess from the sketch laid out above, there would be some ambivalence in his thinking about equality and fairness in the distribution of wealth. Any conclusions we may draw from his writings will have to be mainly inferential, and no doubt selective.

Still, much that he did have to say has direct implications for taxation, and even, as we shall see, for a theory of progressive taxation. Some of Calvin's ideas provide the grounds for a belief in progressive taxation. At the same time, the ambivalence and incompleteness of his thought on this subject may help to explain the obscurity and instability of the notion in the Reformed tradition.

As we say, Calvin did not devote much explicit and sustained attention to the subject of taxation. The two primary places where he provides some comment do not help much. In the *Institutes*, Calvin writes:

Lastly, I also wish to add this, that tributes and taxes are the lawful revenues of princes, which they may chiefly use to meet the public expenses of their office; yet they may similarly use them for the magnificence of their household, which is joined, so to speak, with the dignity of the authority they exercise. . . . [However, princes ought] in turn remember that their revenues are not so much their private chests as the treasuries of the entire people . . . which cannot be squandered or despoiled without manifest injustice. Or rather, [they ought to remember] that these are almost the very blood of the people, which it would be the harshest inhumanity not to spare. Moreover, let them consider that their imposts and levies, and other kinds of tributes are nothing but supports of public necessity; but that to impose them upon the common folk without cause is tyrannical extortion.

These considerations do not encourage princes to waste on expensive luxury, as there is surely no need to add fuel to their cupidity. . . . And this doctrine is not superfluous for private individuals in order that they should not let themselves rashly and shamelessly decry any expenses of princes, even if these exceed the common expenditures of the citizens.[28]

And in his *Commentary on Romans*, Calvin says much the same things:

Paul takes the opportunity of mentioning tributes, and he bases his reason for paying tribute on the office of magistrates. If it is their responsibility to defend and preserve uninjured the peace of the upright and to resist the impious attempts of the wicked, they cannot do this

unless they are assisted by force and strong protection. Tributes, therefore, are paid by law to support such necessary expenses. This is not the
proper place to enter into a fuller discussion concerning the manner of
paying taxes or tributes, nor is it our concern either to prescribe to
rulers how much they ought to spend for individual purposes, or to call
them to account. It is right, however, that they should remember that all
that they receive from the people is public property, and not a means of
satisfying lust and luxury. We see the uses for which Paul appoints the
tributes which are paid, viz. that heads of state may be furnished with
assistance for the defense of their subjects.[29]

While it is true, as Donald Shriver and Richard Knox write, that
particularly the comment on Romans suggests public security as the
primary common good for which tax revenues should go, it is a
peculiar reading of even these passages to conclude, as Shriver and
Knox do, that "Money is useful for government, in the first instance,
not for the service of public good but for the acquisition of the 'force'
basic to proper government."[30] In support of this conclusion, Shriver
and Knox go on to quote Michael Walzer's puzzling remark: "Calvin's
recognition of political authority was also the end of political mystery.
The state was a fact, a matter of force and organization."[31]

These observations are off the mark because it is unwarranted to
ascribe to Calvin such a sharp contrast between "public good" and the
use of force for public safety, as Shriver and Knox do, or to attribute
to him the idea that the state is exclusively "a matter of force and
organization," an "order of repression" in face of human sin, as
Walzer does.

Clearly, Calvin believed that the use of force in protecting public
safety (both internally and externally) is itself a function of achieving
the public or common good on behalf of all the citizens. In his
comments on Romans 13:4, two verses before the remark on taxes,
Calvin leaves no doubt that the whole point of political rule is "for the
public good." He continues, significantly: "Nor do [magistrates] have
unbridled power, but *power that is restricted to the welfare of their
subjects.*"[32] (Incidentally, these remarks obviously illumine the statements in *Institutes* IV.xx.13 and in the *Commentary on Romans* 13:6
(quoted above) concerning the need for a ruler's restraint in spending
public money as "a means of satisfying personal lust and luxury.")
Insofar, then, as a magistrate's primary responsibility is to serve the
public good, and as the public good is in Calvin's mind unquestionably served by using force, where necessary, to protect public safety,
the proper use of police and military force *is* for the public good.

If the use of force, properly applied, serves the public good, rather than being contrasted with it, there is also strong reason to believe that, for Calvin, coercive protection of public safety is not the *only* common good that government is in business to promote, contrary to what I regard as Walzer's thoroughly unreliable account of Calvin's thought.[33]

It is true that in Calvin's famous summary description of the function of magistrates, he singles out as their "sole endeavor" providing "for the common safety and peace of all," by means, as he says, of protecting and vindicating "public innocence, modesty, decency, and tranquility. . . ."[34] Still, as in the case of the comments on Romans, it is important to consider the context in which these remarks occur. This summary is immediately preceded by a crucially important discussion of the magistrate's obligation to uphold the Second Table of the Decalogue.

> As far as the Second Table is concerned, Jeremiah admonishes kings to "do justice and righteousness," to deliver him who has been oppressed by force from the hand of the oppressor," not to "grieve or wrong the alien, the widow, and the fatherless" or "shed innocent blood." The exhortation which we read in Ps. 82 has the same purpose: *that they should "give justice to the poor and needy, rescue the destitute and needy, and deliver the poor and needy from the hand of the oppressor.*[35]

And, in this connection, Calvin's futher remarks in his *Commentary on the Psalms* are most revealing.

> We are here briefly taught that a just and well-regulated government will be distinguished for maintaining the rights of the poor and the afflicted. . . . [F]or it cannot be doubted that rulers are bound to observe justice towards all men without distinction. But the prophet, with much propriety, represents them as appointed to be the defenders of the miserable and oppressed, both because such persons stand in need of the assistance of others, and because they can only obtain this where rulers are free from avarice, ambition, and other vices. *The end, therefore, for which judges bear the sword is to restrain the wicked, and thus to prevent violence from prevailing among men, who are so much disposed to become disorderly and outrageous. According as men increase in strength, they become proportionally audacious in oppressing the weak.* . . . From these remarks, it is very obvious why the cause of the poor and needy is hear chiefly commended to rulers: for those who are exposed as easy prey to the cruelty and wrongs of the rich have no less need of the assistance and protection of

magistrates than the sick have of the aid of the physician. Were the truth deeply fixed in the minds of kings and other judges, *that they are appointed to be the guardians of the poor, and that a special part of this duty lies in resisting the wrongs which are done to them, and in repressing all unrighteous violence,* perfect righteousness would become triumphant through the whole world.[36]

These passages begin to suggest that, in addition to providing for public safety ("repressing all unrighteous violence"), a related and equally important public benefit or common good that any just government must attempt to promote is assistance to and protection of "the poor and afflicted."

In short, there already emerges a foundation in Calvin's thought for *twin commitments* to safety *and* sustenance as the basic obligations of government. In fact, in a most interesting way, Calvin knits these dual concerns together as but two parts of the same central purpose. If the prevention by the government of "unrighteous violence" is unquestionably of overriding public benefit, abuse and neglect of the poor would, according to the above words, appear to be simply one manifestation of unrighteous violence. Properly speaking, therefore, provision for both safety and sustenance are interrelated, indefeasible features of the essential responsibility of magistrates to promote the "public good."

It follows that to the extent governmental responsibility for safety *and* sustenance is as indispensable as the above passages suggest, then there is every reason to think that Calvin would favor the levying and collection of taxes for "public expenses" involving assistance to the poor, every bit as much as he favored taxes for purposes of defense.

While, to my knowledge, there is no evidence he ever explicitly said as much, his practice in Geneva appears to reinforce the logical inference we have just constructed. Calvin and the city fathers handled the high incidence of poverty in mid-sixteenth-century Geneva by intervening in various ways to provide shelter, medical care, and work for the indigent and refugee.[37]

Calvin and the magistrates also had an "industrial policy," supported no doubt by public funds. They were particularly active in providing job training and in creating new trades and industries to provide work and means of livelihood for the indigent and refugee. "As early as December 29, 1544," writes Williston Walker in his biography of the reformer, "[Calvin] urged the Little Council to develop the weaving industry as an aid to the prosperity of the city.

His efforts in this direction had very considerable success. . . . Geneva prospered in a material way under his influence."[38]

In addition, as is well-known, Calvin helped to institute a public education system in Geneva, and supported a range of regulatory activities by the government of a religious, moral, and civil, as well as of an economic, character. All of these activities, like the others mentioned, undoubtedly required some public support.

It therefore seems reasonable to infer that though Calvin does not apparently ruminate specifically on the subject, he had no trouble supporting, both on theoretical and practical grounds, the use of taxes for promoting public benefits beyond defense.

So far, however, we have simply been sketching out the beginnings of an answer to our first question concerning a theory of taxation—What are the common goods for which taxes may legitimately be paid? We shall still need to say more about that, but, in the process, we must not lose sight of our second question—What is a legitimate system of tax collection?

It is in respect to this second question that some of the ambivalence about taxes emerges that is so much a part of the liberal tradition. To my knowledge, Calvin says nothing at all about what, to his mind, makes up a 'legitimate tax collection system.' Nor, so far as I can determine, does he ever say anything about using taxes to redistribute wealth, as would be done, for instance, in a progressive system.

And though, as I shall argue, it is possible, again, to infer from his writings something along these lines, it must also be admitted that Calvin holds some ideas that decidedly do not support a redistributive tax system, and, in fact, run in the opposite direction. In this connection, three passages come to mind: In his *Harmony of the Fur Last Books of the Pentateuch,* Calvin states:

> God, therefore, permits every one to reap his corn, to gather his vintage, and to enjoy his abundance; provided the rich, content with their own vintage and harvest, do not grudge the poor the gleaning of the grapes and corn. *Not that He absolutely assigns to the poor whatever remains, so that they may seize it as their own; but that some small portion may flow gratuitously to them from the munificence of the rich.* He mentions indeed by name the orphans, and widows, and strangers, yet undoubtedly He designates all the poor and needy, who have no fields of their own to sow or reap. . . .[39]

In the same volume, Calvin contends that although the poor be oppressed by the wealthy, they possess no legal claim against their oppressors—"they may not sue . . . at law." "[I]t is sufficient for [the poor] to appeal to the faithfulness of God." "The more patiently he who is despoiled shall bear his wrong, the more ready will God be to undertake his cause; nor is there any louder cry to Him than patient endurance."[40] Thirdly, Calvin takes a related line, again, in his *Commentary on the Psalms:*

> We may farther learn from this passage, that *although magistrates may not be solicited for succor,* they are accounted guilty before God of negligence, if they do not, *of their own accord,* succor those who stand in need of their interference.[41]

These passages conclude only that both the magistrates and the wealthy owe God a stringent obligation to lend assistance to the poor, an obligation that God has every right to enforce against them. However, the poor do not possess a legally enforceable claim for assistance against either the wealthy or the state, such that they might legally "solicit" the magistrates "for succor," nor might they with justice "seize for their own" some small portion of the bounty of the rich for basic sustenance.

Rather, in these remarks, Calvin construes the duties of charity that magistrates and wealthy alike owe the poor as voluntary and discretionary, as performed of the magistrates' "own accord," or "gratuitously from the munificence of the rich." Where benefits are not extended, Calvin advises the needy to appeal to God and no one else for righteous treatment.

There are, I believe, two reasons for Calvin's resistance here to the idea that assistance to the poor is a matter of legally enforceable right, which would justify compulsory taxation in the interests of redistributing wealth. First, against the radical Anabaptists of his age, some of whom favored abolishing private property, Calvin stands firmly behind that institution.

> For it is necessary for the preservation of human society that each should possess what is his own; that some should acquire property by purchase, that to others it should come by hereditary right, to others by the title of presentation, *that each should increase his portion in proportion to his diligence, or bodily strength, or other qualifications.* In fine, political government requires, that each should enjoy what belongs to him; . . .[42]

And Calvin goes on in the same passage to reinforce his belief in the voluntariness of assistance to the poor:

And Paul also, wisely makes the distinction, in enjoining that there should be an equality, not arising from a promiscuous and confused use of property, but by the rich spontaneously and liberally relieving the wants of their brethren, and not grudgingly or of necessity.[43]

The idea here is clearly that wealth and income is appropriately distributed in society by means of "honest industry," as well, of course, as by means of inheritance, gifts, purchase, and so on. Calvin gives special attention to the importance of honest industry as a distributive criterion, as, for example in his *Commentary on II Thessalonians,* 3:6–13.[44]

Interestingly enough, Calvin also frequently makes room for the same merit criterion of distribution that is to be found later in the Puritans and in Locke, namely the fitting return due those who actively contribute to the common good. This consideration clearly governs his remarkable and quite revolutionary opinion that, within limits, usury is permissible. Contrary to the scholastic tradition, Calvin reasoned that those forms of usury that did not gouge the poor could actually perform an economic service by creating working capital and production loans.[45] Indeed, in passing judgment on the whole subject of usury, "it is necessary," writes Calvin, "to concede to the common good."[46] The implication is that a fair return to the money-lender on a loan that enriches the economy and thereby serves the general advantage is legitimate.

The second reason Calvin frequently resists construing assistance to the poor and needy as a matter of legal right is his fear of rebellion and anarchy, a fear that pervades his writings. To put into the hands of the dispossessed a title to sustenance is to provide them with a rallying cause for legitimate revolution against those who deny them their rights. Such talk deeply worried Calvin. Better to leave these things up to the discretion of the magistrates and the rich, and to counsel the neglected poor and needy to wait for the Lord's vengeance.

These considerations—the emphasis upon the legitimacy of private property, the voluntariness of beneficence and the fear of rebellion, should the poor get it into their heads they have a right to assistance—explain Calvin's reservations toward the idea of redistributive taxation.

Is it proper, then, to conclude that while, on the one hand, Calvin leans strongly toward redistributing wealth in the interest of assisting the poor and needy as a thoroughly desirable governmental objective, he nevertheless, on the other hand, leaves the question entirely up to the individual discretion of the magistrates, the wealthy, and to God's providential reckoning to make good this desideratum? Does he, after all, give his full, if somewhat uneasy, support to the "individualism" associated in the liberal tradition with the sovereignty of private property and the right to personal discretion in disposing of that property, including all charitable contributions?

As we have shown, there can be no doubt that the grounds for this interpretation do exist in Calvin's writings, and, without question, that interpretation has, in one way or another, been influential in the Protestant Ethic and liberal traditions. My overall view, however, is that this interpretation coordinates in too tidy a fashion a set of convictions about law, government and the distribution of wealth that, in fact, Calvin himself never entirely reconciled, just as the Protestant Ethic and liberal traditions have never entirely reconciled them. The best conclusion is that the Reformed legacy in regard to this subject is, as in other areas, a deeply unstable one. It presents to us a set of convictions and considerations that are, as we have said, ambivalently related, that pull in different directions, and that, therefore, require continuing efforts at coordination.

In conclusion, therefore, we need to try to reinforce the "other side" of Calvin's outlook, the side that countervails against the "individualistic," absolute-right-of-private-property view we have just outlined. It is the side that emphasizes, instead, the centrality of governmental responsibility for promoting, by means of legal enforcement, if necessary, the basic common goods including assistance to the poor and needy that constitutes the fundamental purposes of government.

The heart of this "other side," which we have already glimpsed, is located in a concept that is essential to all Calvin's moral, political, legal and economic thinking, the concept of *equity*. In a decisive passage from the *Institutes*, Calvin begins to clarify this notion and to underscore its centrality.

> What I have said will become plain if in all laws we examine, as we should, these two things: the constitution of the law, and the equity on which its constitution is itself founded and rests. Equity, because it is natural, cannot but be the same for all, and therefore, this same purpose ought to apply to all laws, whatever their object. Constitutions have certain circumstances upon which they in part depend. It therefore does not matter that they are different, *provided all equally press toward the same goal of equity.*

It is a fact that the law of God which we call the moral law is nothing else than a testimony of natural law and of that conscience which God has engraved upon the minds of men. Consequently, the entire scheme of this equity of which we are now speaking has been prescribed in it. Hence, this equity alone must be the goal and rule and limit of all laws.[47]

Although Calvin repeatedly employs the idea of equity as the ground of moral reflection, he nowhere systematically elucidates the idea. The reader is therefore left to piece together and infer what specifically Calvin means by the term. For one thing, the idea is close to and appears to encompass "the rule of charity" or the Golden Rule. For example, in his sermon on Job, Calvin defines *equite'* as doing to others as you would have them do to you.[48] And his *Commentary on Exodus* 20:20, he elaborates as follows:

This, then, is the rule of charity, *that everyone's rights should be safely preserved, and that none should do to another what he would not have done to himself.* It follows, therefore, that not only are those thieves who secretly steal the property of others, but those also who seek for gain from the loss of others, accumulate wealth by unlawful practices, and are more devoted to their private advantage *than to equity.*[49]

In his *Commentary on Second Thessalonians,* he goes on:

This is the first law of equity, that no one makes use of what belongs to another, but only use what he can properly call his own. The second is, *that no one swallow up, like some abyss, what belongs to him, but that he be beneficent to neighbors, and that he may relieve their indigence by his abundance.* In the same manner, the Apostle exhorts those who had been formerly idle to labor, *not merely that they may gain for themselves a livelihood, but that they may also be helpful to the necessities of their brethren. . . .*[50]

Finally, in his *Commentary on Second Corinthians,* Calvin further clarifies the idea of equity as follows

Equality can be taken in two ways, either as meaning mutual compensation, when each side gives an equal amount, or as a *fair apportioning.* I take *isotayta* to mean that each should give a fair proportion of what he has. . . . Thus the Lord commends to us this fair apportioning of our resources that we may, in so far as funds allow, help those in difficulties *that there may not be some in affluence and others in want. . . .* We are thus told that in exercising beneficence *we should look to present need if we wish to observe the rule of equity.*[51]

We may now attempt to organize Calvin's ideas on equity in a systematic fashion. Four crucial points need to be made. (1) Equity is the organizing principle and ultimate objective of *all* law, including, Calvin says explicitly, *civil or positive law.* It is, therefore, the final *standard of legitimacy* for all who are charged with making, adjudicating and applying the law (all legislators, judges, and political executives). (2) The rule of equity, which includes the rule of charity, dictates, as the comments on Exodus 20:20 make clear, that "everyone's rights should be safely preserved." According to Calvin, these rights include protection of life, limb, and property against arbitrary interference or injury. Protecting these, which is a basic responsibility of government, is of course what it means to "repress all unrighteous violence" (*Commentary on the Psalms,* 82:3–4), or, what is the same thing, to maintain public safety.

(3) In addition to rights to basic security, the rule of equity also includes a set of *economic rights,* or rights to sustenance or material "fair shares." The idea obviously is that, according to God's original intention, all human beings by virtue of being human are entitled to *both* safety *and* sustenance, and that all civil constitutions and political arrangements ought to be designed and evaluated according to how successful they are in complying with these basic conditions. It follows that the task of developing and administering laws is constrained by this dual principle of legitimacy.

(4) But even more than that, the "second law of equity" seems, according to Calvin's comments on II Thessalonians 3:12, to control the "first law of equity." While the first prescribes the right of personal sovereignty over lawfully acquired property, the second prescribes "beneficence to neighbors," that one "may relieve their indigence by his abundance." In other words, it appears that the *final point* of acquiring property in the first place is at one and the same time self-supprt and mutual assistance. Those who are "more devoted to their private advantage than to equity" (according to Calvin's comments on Exodus 20:20), who, that is, give priority to the first law over the second, are simply "thieves." They are those who engage in "unrighteous violence" every bit as much as do those who forcibly rob another of one's rightful possessions.

The major inference from all this is clear. In the last analysis, Calvin's central notion of equity underwrites an idea of common good that guarantees "initial fair shares" to all citizens as a matter of basic right, and concomitantly entails that the well-off bear a primary and direct duty to support that common good. Insofar as the state is governed by "the law of equity" as described, then it follows that the state has a responsibility within certain limits to enforce the requisite duty by imposing, if need by, "a substantial increase in the tax burden of the rich."

There is, though, one important loose end to be tied up. How does the conclusion we have just reached about the dual standards of legitimacy (basic rights to safety and sustenance) undergirding civil or positive law and government square with our earlier conclusions? Did we not show that in part of his writing, at least, Calvin himself appeared to favor—so far as evaluating the performance of governments—the first law of equity over the second: the rights of private property before and above the rights of assistance?

As might be expected, our final verdict is that this discrepancy in Calvin's thought is exactly the point of tension or ambivalence that we have previously called attention to. But we may also add that there is a further, though related, point of ambivalence in Calvin's thought. If, as we pointed out, one reason for Calvin's reluctance to call duties of assistance out-and-out, legally enforceable rights was his fear that such a doctrine would inspire rebellion and anarchy, it is well to remember that for much of his adult life he held the same view in respect to what we have labeled the "rights of security" (life, bodily integrity, property). Though he clearly believed the protection of these rights to be a primary responsibility of any magistrate, again and again Calvin counseled private citizens *not* to believe they were entitled to demand, or to attempt themselves to enforce, their rights of security against a tyrannical ruler. As in the case of abuses against the duties of charity, Calvin frequently urges patience and prayerful appeals to God for vindication of the natural rights and liberties of a citizen.

However, as is well-known, Calvin does not urge complete passivity on the part of citizens in respect to enforcing their rights. He makes room, and in fact frequently supports, the righteous efforts of "lower magistrates" to discipline, and, if need be, displace, arbitrary rulers. Particularly in his more mature years, Calvin begins to talk in quite revolutionary ways about active defiance of illegitimate regimes.[52] "Indeed," he writes in the *Institutes* that "the magistrates ought to apply themselves with the highest diligence to prevent freedom, whose guardians they have been appointed, from being in any respect diminished, far less violated. If they are not sufficiently alert and careful, they are faithless in office, *and traitors to their country*."[53]

My suggestion is, that just as Calvin begins, toward the end of his life, "to take the gloves off" in regard to holding earthly rulers accountable according to one of his standards of legitimacy, the "safe" preservation of the rights of security, so nothing stands in the way of eventually extending the same revision to rights of assistance, if, that is, rights of security and assistance ("safety and sustenance") are as deeply interconnected in Calvin's understanding as I have tried to show. Were that the result, then the way would be cleared for beginning to speak of the "basic-need" or "initial-fair-shares" distributive criterion as legally enforceable by means, if need be, of compulsory redistribution through taxes. We would thereby have inferred a foundation in Calvin's thought for a theory of progressive taxation.

Endnotes

I wish to express special thanks to John Feldman, who, as a graduate student in Religious Ethics at the Univesity of Virginia, stimulated my interest in the subject of taxation. By means of his edifying dissertation, he helped me to organize my thinking and understand better some of the ethical dimensions of the problem.

1. "A Progressive Income Tax," *Washington Post* (June 2, 1986), p. A14. As with the Post, there was a shocking degree of indifference in regard to the appropriate tax burden of the wealthy among members of Congress. Virtually the only senator who lifted his finger was Sen. George Mitchell. He offered an amendment to the Tax Reform Act on June 18, 1986 that would have added a rate of 35% for wealthy taxpayers on top of the two rates stipulated in the Act. ("Progressivity in Taxes: Back to the Campaign?" *Washington Post* (June 17, 1986)). The amendment was defeated.

In the light of one-and-a-half years' experience the issue of progressivity won't go away. In a recent letter to the *Washington Post*, Joseph A. Pechman, one of the country's leading tax experts, responds as follows to Bruce Babbitt's proposal of a consumption tax as an appropriate way to raise revenues: ". . . Babbitt says that he will stick to his proposal for a flat consumption tax until 'anyone else has a real alternative.' The alternative he is looking for is the progressive income tax. As a result of the 1986 tax reform, the base of the income tax will amount to about $2.5 trillion at the end of this decade. Thus, an increase of one percentage point in the two rates we now have—i.e., the 15 percent rate to 16 percent and the 28 percent rate to 29 percent—would raise $25 billion a year. An increase of three percentage points in each rate would raise $75 billion" (*Washington Post*, February 3, 1988). Pechman does not go on to calculate what the return would be if the top rate were, in addition, raised still more steeply than the designated 28 percent rate, but that clearly ought to be considered.

2. Calvin, *Commentary on Genesis* (Carlisle, Pa.: Banner of Truth Trust, 1979), p. 128.

3. Andre Bieler, *La Pensee Economique et Social de Calvin* (Geneva: Librairie de L'Universite, 1959), p. 234 (my translation . . . Here as elsewhere in quotations, emphasis is added)

4. Calvin, *Genesis*, 1:26, p. 96.

5. Calvin, *Commentaires Sur Les Psaumes* (Geneva, 1909), Ps. 104:15, cited in Bieler, *La Pensee*, 233 (my translation).

6. Andre Bieler, *Social Humanism of Calvin* (Richmond, Va.: John Knox Press, 1964) pp. 17–18.

7. Calvin, *Commentary on the Book of Psalms* (Grand Rapids; Baker Book House, 1981), 127:1; v. IV, p. 104.

8. *Commentary on II Thessalonians* in *Commentaries on Galatians, Ephesians, Philippians, Colossians, I & II Thessalonians, I & II Timothy, Titus, Philemon* (Grand Rapids: Baker Book House, 1981), 3:5, p. 104.

9. *Sermon XXXI Sur L'Epitre Aux Ephesians,* 4:26–28, cited in Bieler, *La Pensee,* p. 405 (my translation).

10. *Ibid.,* p. 353 (my translation).

11. Calvin, *Second Epistle of Paul the Apostle to the Corinthians* (Grand Rapids: Eerdmans Pub. Co., 1964) 8:15, p. 114.

12. Calvin, *John Calvin's Sermons on the Ten Commandments,* trans. and ed. by Benjamin W. Farley (Grand Rapids: Baker Book House, 1980) pp. 162–3.

13. *Ibid.,* p. 200.

14. Calvin, *II Corinthians* 2:8, p. 114.

15. See esp. Bieler, *Social Humanism,* 39–47; W. Fred Graham, *Constructive Revolutionary, John Calvin and His Socio-Economic Impact* (Richmond, Va.: John Knox Press, 1971), chs 6 and 7.

16. Calvin, *II Corinthians,* 2:8, p. 114.

17. See Bieler, *La Pensee,* pp. 233–236; cf. David Little, *Religion, Order and Law* (Chicago: University of Chicago Press, 1984), pp. 57–60.

18. Bieler, *Social Humanism,* p. 35.

19. Calvin, *Commentary on a Harmony of the Evangelists* (Grand Rapids: Baker Book House, 1981), Matthew 25:20, p. 443.

20. Calvin, *Institutes of the Christian Religion* (Philadelphia: Westminster Press, 1960), IV, 1, 3.

21. Calvin, *II Corinthians* 8:9, p. 110.

22. *Ibid.,* 9:10, p. 124.

23. *Ibid.,* 9:11, p. 125.

24. See Graham, *Constructive Revolutionary,* ch. 7.

25. Calvin, *II Corinthians,* 9:7, p. 122.

26. "Taxation," *Encyclopedia Americana* (1956), v. 26, p. 287.

27. S. I. Benn & R. S. Peters, *Principles of Political Thought* (New York: Collier Books, 1959), pp. 174–5.

28. Calvin, *Institutes* IV, 20, 13.

29. Calvin, *Calvin's Commentaries: Romans and Thessalonians* (Grand Rapids: Eerdmans, 1976), Romans 13:6, pp. 283–4.

30. Donald Shriver and Richard Knox, "Taxation in the History of Protestant Ethics," *Journal of Religious Ethics* 13, 1 (Spring, 1985), p. 138.

31. *Ibid.*, cited at p. 138.

32. Calvin, *Commentary on Romans*, p. 282.

33. I have criticized Walzer's views on Calvin in "Max Weber Revisited: The 'Protestant Ethic' and the Puritan Experience of Order," in *Harvard Theological Review 59* (1966), 415–428.

34. Calvin, *Institutes* IV, 20, 9.

35. *Ibid.*

36. Calvin, *Commentary on the Psalms*, 82:3, pp. 331–2.

37. See Graham, *Constructive Revolutionary*, esp. ch. 8.

38. Williston Walker, *John Calvin: Organiser of Reformed Protestantism,* 1509–1564, New York: Putnam's Sons, 1906), p. 359.

39. Calvin, *Four Last Books of the Pentateuch*, Leviticus 19:9, p. 152.

40. *Ibid.*, Exodus 24:14, pp. 114–5.

41. Calvin, Commentary on the Psalms, 82:3–4, p. 332.

42. Calvin, *Four Last Books of the Pentateuch*, Exodus 16:17, p. 279.

43. *Ibid.*

44. *Commentary on II Thessalonians*

45. See Benjamin Nelson, *The Idea of Usury* (Princeton: Princeton University Press, 1949).

46. From Calvin's letter to Sachinus (November 7, 1545), cited in Georgia Harkness, *John Calvin: The Man and His Times* (Nashville: Abingdon, 1958), p. 205.

47. Calvin, *Institutes*, IV, 20, 16.

48. Calvin, *Sermons . . . Upon the Book of Job* (London: Impensis T. Woodcocke, 1584) (film, University of Virginia Library), 1:6–8.

49. Calvin, *Four Last Books of the Pentateuch*, Exodus 20:20, pp. 110–11.

50. Calvin, *Commentary on II Thessalonians*, 3:12, p. 358.

51. Calvin, *Commentary on II Corinthians* 8:14, p. 113.

52. See Little, *Religion, Order and Law*, fn. 66 at p. 46.

53. Calvin, *Institutes*, IV, 20, 8.

Part Three
Contemporary Policy Issues

Chapter Six

Tax Ethics: An Oxymoron?

Robert L. Stivers

From the vantage point of the community, taxes are a means of withholding a portion of the social product to pay for public goods and services. From the vantage point of the taxpayer they are a compulsory extraction from the product of individual labor. So long as taxes are viewed almost exclusively from the latter vantage point, as they are today, the tax system will be a battleground for selfish individuals trying to garner as much of the social product for themselves and to pass as much of the social burden on to others as they can. And, as a corollary, tax ethics will continue to be an oxymoron, for the common good will take back seat to attitudes of tax avoidance and self-aggrandizement.

It is time, therefore, to bring ethics back into taxes, if not to reverse individualistic attitudes, which may be too ingrained, then at least to counter them and to put the ethical dimension back into tax discussions where it belongs. Christianity has something to offer discussions of taxation. It has a rich legacy on economic matters, a legacy which in recent years has been enhanced by the increasing attention of the churches.

The occasion for a discussion of tax ethics is the ongoing debate over taxes which has resulted in two major changes in the federal tax law in recent years. The perspective which informs the discussion is that of reform, in particular a Reformed theological perspective augmented by recent ecumenical developments and coupled to re-forming zeal in the public sector. On the one hand, a reforming perspective assumes the adequacy of the current economic system to provide most North Americans with economic necessities, and on the other the need to move toward greater equity.

The purpose of the discussion is to develop a Reformed ethical perspective for assessing tax proposals and for advocating a more progressive overall tax system on grounds of equity as one way to finance essential programs to reduce domestic poverty.

In the preceding essay David Little develops a Reformed perspective on tax equity. According to Little, "Calvin's central notion of equity underwrites an idea of common good that guarantees initial fair shares to all citizens as a matter of basic right, and concomitantly entails that the well-off bear a primary and direct duty to support the common good." Little concludes, ". . . that the state has a responsibility within certain limits to enforce the requisite duty by imposing, if need be, a substantial increase in the tax burden of the rich."

The problem with Cavlin's point of view, Little goes on to elaborate, is that he couples this community oriented perspective with individualistic views on private property, voluntarism in charity, and the fear of rebellion. These views left him no means but the discretion of government officials, the charity of the rich, the patience of the poor, and God's inscrutable providence to realize fair shares for all citizens.

The result has been a tradition which gives ethical support to tax equity and redistribution but provides few means of countering the economic and ideological power which wealth conveys to its possessors. Little advocates "taking the gloves off," giving primacy to Calvin's "fair shares" concept, and seeking redistribution through the power to tax.

Little's discussion is a good starting point, for it grounds the Reformed tradition in the biblical concern for the poor, insists on the importance of an ethical dimension in tax policy, and holds governments responsible for tax equity or fairness. Recent ecumenical developments add a contemporary dimension to Little's historical analysis, a dimension which complements and reinforces his conclusions.[1]

Before turning to the ethical dimension and these ecumenical developments, it is important to consider the empirical world of economic reality and understandings of it offered by social scientists. The case for a more progressive tax system stands on both empirical and ethical legs. An empirical investigation is needed to establish the degree of poverty, the distribution of income and private physical wealth, and the progressiveness of the tax system in the United States. Numbers alone, however, are insufficient. They need to be interpreted to discover the economic and ideological forces at work producing them. Only then should they be evaluated in light of ethical norms.

Poverty, Distribution and Taxes

The empirical description begins with views of poverty, distribution, and taxes through the eyes of selected economists and sociologists. The purpose is to establish the extent of poverty, the degree of departure from equality, and the progressiveness of the tax system.

Poverty in its most general sense is a lack of adequate resources to provide basic needs.[2] Economic poverty is insufficient income to meet the dollar cost of the minimal goods and services essential to a family's provision of basic physical needs. This dollar cost varies from location to location and is related to differeing tastes and lifestyles.

To cut through the complexity of the definition, relativity, and tastes, government officials have developed a set of income thresholds adjusted for inflation, size of family, head of and number of children in a household, but not for transfer payments or taxes paid.[3] In 1988 the official poverty line was $11,750 for a family of four. This measure is imprecise, but does allow comparisons and calculations of who and how many are at the bottom of the income and wealth pyramid.

By the official measure, which includes some but not all transfers, 19 percent of the population was poor in 1964 before the inception of the new social programs of the 1960's.[4] By 1973 this percentage had dropped to 11.1 percent. It subsequently steadied and then after 1979 rose to a level of 15.2 percent in 1983. When adjusted for transfer payments this percentage is considerably lower, 10.2 percent in 1983. The percentages for minorities and single head of household women are much higher. In 1983, 35.7 percent of Blacks, 28.4 percent of Hispanics, and 40.2 percent of women heads of households had income below the line, figures only slightly lower than in earlier years. In contrast, for the elderly there has been a sharp drop in poverty from 28.5 to 14.1 percent.

A study of poverty statistics reveals that the percentage of poor in advance of transfer payments has remained about the same for the past twenty-five years. Approximately 20 percent were poor in 1964 before transfers and the same held in 1983.[5] These percentages fluctuate around the 20 percent mark depending on the state of the economy, reached a high for the period of 24.2 percent in the recession year of 1983, and have declined slightly since. This suggests that little or no progress has been made in the past twenty-five years in eliminating dependence on transfer programs. It also makes clear that one-fifth of the population, especially minorities, women, and children, does not participate in the economy to the point of earning poverty level wages.

Perhaps most significantly, the figures on poverty reveal a definite correlation between changes in real GNP per household and the percentages of those beneath the poverty line. During boom periods the percentages go down, during bust they go up.[6] This is powerful evidence that having a job is critical to avoiding poverty, although this partially hides the steady unemployment and hence poverty of minorities and single head of household women.

Turning to the distribution of income, one finds consistently wide differentials.[7] The year 1929 was the year of greatest inequality in recent times. This was followed by a narrowing during World War II when greater equality was seen as a sharing of the burdens and made a matter of public policy. This narrowing remained after the war until the past decade when some widening has occurred.[8] The bottom fifth of families takes home 4 percent of total income, the top fifth 49 percent, and the top 5 percent gets 24 percent of income.[9] These differentials are considerable but are fairly typical of industrialized countries and less skewed than most third world countries.[10]

As one might expect, the distribution of private physical wealth is much more skewed. The poor and those in the middle must spend a higher proportion of their incomes for basics. The rich have the luxury of savings. In addition a few individuals win large fortunes which are subsequently passed on through inheritances.[11] Although the figures on the distribution of private physical wealth are not very adequate, enough data are available to indicate a continuing heavy concentration. The top 1 percent of wealthholders owns about 25 percent, the top 2.5 percent owns 44 percent, and the top 20 percent owns 76 percent.[12] Four percent of consumer units owns approximately 90 percent of publicly traded stock and other marketable securities. The top .5 percent owns 44 percent of corporate stock.[13] Inheritance taxes are negligible, especially since the 1981–82 tax reduction package, or can be avoided by a number of devices such as trusts.

The combination of federal, state, and local tax systems is a potentially important tool for changing the distribution of income and private physical wealth. At present the combination of systems is not serving as such a tool, although the concept of progressivity has been enshrined in federal income tax laws since their inception. (A progressive tax is one in which the percentage of income taxed rises with income, as in the graduated income tax. A regressive tax is the opposite, for example, the sales tax, which takes a higher percentage of a poor person's income.)

The distribution of income and private physical wealth are substantially the same before and after taxes.[14] The average overall tax rate for all income groups is within a percent or two of 25 percent. Between 1966 and 1985 the progressivity of the combined system declined largely due to a decline in effective rates on capital gains and corporate income taxes, and an increase in payroll taxes.[15] Federal taxes are slightly progressive, state and local slightly regressive, with the combination producing an effect of overall neutrality.[16]

Tax systems have multiple objectives only one of which has been tax equity. Other objectives include the stimulation of economic growth, the attraction of new industries, and the promotion of social goods, for example, home ownership through the mortgage deduction. Many of these objectives can be realized in the short run only by increasing regressivity, so that tax politics is a constant battleground between conflicting interests and ideologies.

Changes in distribution are at present most influenced by the ups and downs of the unemployment rate and the increasing proportion of the population in traditionally poor groupings.[17] Jobs and transfer payments, including social security, welfare, Medicare and Medicaid, and food stamps are the main tools to relieve poverty. The tax system plays only a minor role.

While the tax system is a potentially important tool to redistribute income and wealth, it is less potent for the direct relief of poverty since the poor have little income to pay taxes on to start with. The elimination of regressive taxes, such as the sales tax, would help the poor some but, in the absence of more jobs or transfers payments, would make little impact.

The two recent federal tax revisions are noteworthy. First came the tax cuts of 1981–82 which reduced revenue significantly and was one factor in the high budget deficits of the 1980's. The deficit has in turn been used to argue for cut backs in transfer programs. Increasing pressure has been brought to bear on all social welfare projects. The tax cuts of 1981–82 also brought substantially lower rates for the wealthy and overall decreased the progressivity of the federal tax system. These factors, when combined with the high unemployment of the 1982–83 recession, also led to a shift in the distribution of income in favor of the rich and increasing numbers below the poverty line. Whether the swing to better times and increased investment reverses this remains to be seen.

Another feature of the 1981–82 package was the virtual elimination of inheritance taxes. In terms of poverty and distribution this had little effect. Income from a job is by far the most important factor in distribution. Inheritances are tiny by comparison and the poor seldom receive them anyway. Finally, the action only ratified what had been the accepted practice of finding ways to avoid substantial inheritance taxes anyway.

Second came the Tax Reform Act of 1986. It is supposed to be revenue neutral and should not by itself bring further pressure on transfer programs. Its distributive effects are unclear. The reduction in ways to avoid high nominal rates, the increase in taxes on business, the increase in the personal exemption, and the limit on deduction of interest payments are progressive steps. The reduction of top income rates to 33 percent and then to 28 percent, the retention of the deduction for intangible drilling costs, and new taxes on unemployment and workmen's compensation are regressive.

Forces at Work

What factors in the American economy and culture account for the high rate of poverty, substantial differentials in the distribution of income and private physical wealth, and an overall tax system which is distributionally neutral?

Some causes of *poverty* are obvious. Racial and sexual discrimination, lack of skills and abilities, inadequate wages in seasonal and low paying jobs, insufficient education, inadequate retirement benefits, personal crisis, and, of course, cyclical and structural unemployment lead the list. Less obvious is privation attributable to the so-called "culture of poverty," to the disincentive effects of the welfare system, and to the lack of power to influence legislation.

A few choose poverty. Others do not take the initiative to upgrade their skills. Still others resign themselves prematurely to their condition. Even so, most individuals do not set their wage rates. Nor do they determine their sex or racial group, the level of employment in the economy, or the relative capitalization of various industries. These are social factors and their presence cannot be dismissed with platitudes about individual initiative.

Several factors determine *income differentials* and hence the degree of inequality. The first and by far the most important is the relative wages and salaries from one's job. Differences in wages and salaries account for 40 percent of total inequality according to economist Alan Blinder, who cites four reasons for these differences: (1) the innate ability of individuals; (2) unequal educational attainment resulting from differing abilities, unequal opportunity, and differences in taste; (3) discrimination in wage rates; and (4) unions and other departures from competitive labor market conditions. Another 30 percent of inequality Blinder attributes to life cycle influences which disappear when a person's entire lifetime is taken into account. Twenty-eight percent comes from "differences in tastes," and only two percent from unequal inheritances.[18]

Lester C. Thurow plays down the role of innate ability and education in the determination of wages and salaries.[19] Discrimination is a major part of it for Thurow. Minorities and women are paid significantly less that white males for a number of reasons, the most important of which is the increased training costs employers expect to incur.[20] In particular, members of minority groups are thought by employers to have higher training costs because of a higher rate of "unsatisfactory" performance for their group as a whole; while women are thought to drop in and out of the labor force at higher rates than men. Whether or not these expectations are accurate, to minimize costs the employer hires white males first ignoring individual characteristics.

More significant than discrimination in the determination of wages and salaries, according to Thurow, is the sociology of wage determination. Wages are determined in some industries by supply and demand, but increasingly non-market factors are playing a significant role.[21] For example, the historical relation between different job categories has become an important determiner of relative wage rates. Persons in one category compare themselves to several reference categories and judge the fairness of their own wage rate accordingly. "Wage contours" develop among categories and are enforced by group pressure. Efforts to "leap frog" occur if traditional differentials get out of line. What has developed is a cultural pattern of relative wages for different jobs, including top executive jobs, which is extremely difficult to alter because of the many interrelationships.

While wages and salaries account for two-thirds of income, another one-fifth comes from dividends, interest, rent, and other property income.[22] They accrue, as one might expect from the data on wealth distribution, overwhelmingly to top wealthholders. This income is a result of patient saving, gifts, bequests, inheritances, and, in the cases of instant fortunes, entrepreneurial skill and good fortune.

One-tenth of total income comes from government transfer programs, including unemployment benefits, welfare for the poor, and Social Security. These payments, according to economist Arthur Okun, are the "equalizer" and accrue mostly to those with low incomes.[23]

Okun is correct about the beneficiaries of direct transfer payments, but has revealed only part of the picture. Counting only direct disbursements as transfer payments overlooks the so-called "welfare program for the rich." This alternate welfare program does not consist of disbursements to individuals. Rather, transfers are made indirectly or taxes are never collected on certain forms of income. In the view of sociologists Jonathan Turner and Charles Starnes, this alternate program includes: (1) government purchases in the market, (2) government price supports, (3) government market regulation, and (4) government tax expenditures.[24]

The fourth is especially interesting and a matter of great debate. Turner and Starnes estimate that in 1975 $65–77 billion was bestowed on individuals and large corporations by way of federal tax codes alone through tax exclusions, tax deductions, tax credits, special tax rates, and tax shelters. The figures are much higher today due to inflation, but should be lower after the Tax Reform Act of 1986 takes full effect. The inclusion of these in the tax code means reduced taxes for those able to take advantage of them. The effect on the budgetary balance and on the income of privileged recipients is exactly the same as that which occurs when welfare payments are made. A dollar not paid in taxes contributes both to government deficits and to personal income just as much as a dollar paid to a poor person. The overall effect of these so-called tax expenditures is a reduction in the progressiveness of the tax system.

Private physical wealth needs to be considered in its own right irrespective of its contribution to income distribution. Lester Thurow estimates that one half of great fortunes are inherited and the other half are gained within the lifetime of an individual over a relatively short period of time.[25] The former are maintained through low inheritance taxes and the various methods available to escape taxes.

The generation of new fortunes is more complex. With Okun,

many attribute wealth accumulation to a lifetime of patient savings and investment.[26] This is true for smaller accumulations and for maintaining larger ones, but for the initial generation of really large fortunes some skill and a lot of luck count most. Thurow details the process of rapid accumulation which he calls the "random walk."[27] In brief, talent is involved in positioning an individual to take the walk, that is, to take advantage of market forces. Talent is a necessary but not a sufficient condition of acquiring instant riches, however. Many have these skills, but few hit the jackpot. Almost none hit it twice.

> Large instantaneous fortunes are created when the financial markets capitalize new above-average rate of return investments to yield average rate of return financial investments. It is this process of capitalizing disequilibrium returns that generates rapid fortunes. Patient savings and reinvestment has little or nothing to do with them. To become very rich one must generate or select a situation in which an above-average rate of return is about to be capitalized.[28]

The usual pattern following this lucky strike is to diversify one's portfolio to eliminate risk, to earn the market rate of interest, and to settle down to further patient accumulation.

> The net result is a process that generates a highly skewed distribution of wealth from a normal distribution of abilities. Fortunes are created instantaneously or in very short periods of time. Personal savings behavior has little or nothing to do with the process. Once created, large fortunes maintain themselves through being able to diversify and through inheritance.[29]

Finally, there is the task of interpreting the jungle of federal, state, and local taxes. While the value of progressivity is widely shared, the combined tax systems, as discussed above, are neither progressive or regressive. The gap between value and reality is partly accounted for by the multiplicity of goals. Progressivity is but one of several important economic and social goals served by the tax system.

Particularly important here is the debate over the trade-off between the goals of equity and efficiency. Highly progressive taxes, claim proponents of efficiency, would reduce incentives to work and invest. The economy would be worse off as a result, and the rate of unemployment would rise negating the gains from progressivity and making everyone a loser. This is the so-called "leaky bucket." It is not just a matter of pouring a dollar from the rich to the poor. In the process of transfer part of the dollar leaks away.[30]

While not denying that trade-offs exist, proponents of progressivity tend to minimize the problem of reduced efficiency.[31] They point out there is no strong evidence that the disincentive effect is substantial, and there are ways around what effects there are. Indeed, many capitalist countries have more progressive tax systems and more equal distributions without the incentive effects claimed for the wealthy in the United States.

Beyond the multiple goals of the combined tax systems several other factors contribute to the lack of progressivity. Ease of collection and the need for a balanced tax system to prevent fluctuations in revenue make some regressive taxes attractive. The phenomenon of "bracket creep," the tendency of inflation to push taxpayers into higher brackets, has given the graduated income tax a bad name. The concept of progressivity is poorly understood reducing the number of potential supporters. Finally, income and wealth convey power which can be used in the political arena to produce favorable outcomes.

To conclude, what social scientific interpretations reveal is that poverty, the distribution of income and private physical wealth, and taxes are not a result of some predetermined order of nature. Poverty and distribution are in part a matter of individual initiative. Much more they result from social factors including discrimination, unequal access to education and jobs, the highly unequal distribution of wealth, ideological bias, and old fashion luck, as in Thurow's "random walk." The tax system is a thoroughly political animal for whose favors ethics must compete with a host of other powers.

Values, Beliefs, and Power

Interpreting the data is a revealing exercise but still does not give a sufficient understanding of poverty, distribution, and the tax structure. As Lester Thurow hinted in his analysis of this historical interrelation of job categories, persistent attitudes and perceptions are also involved. How individuals in groups perceive their wages in relation to other individuals in other groups, for example, has an important influence on their perception of fairness and their acquiescence to a given distribution.

Important to the holding of attitudes and perceptions are basic values and beliefs. Values are the general criteria used for judging ethical behavior. Beliefs are more specific, give content to abstract values, and guide feelings about what should be going on in specific situations.

Values and beliefs are handy instruments of power and most often are wielded unconsciously by powerful groups in pursuit of their interests. They allow for a decreased reliance on force by making the victors appear legitimate and existing arrangements natural. By the same token they can be employed to challenge power and to delegitimize existing arrangements.

In the United States the dominant ideology of market capitalism is well supported by an array of values and beliefs which make differences in income and wealth appear equitable, give the impression the rich are deserving and the poor undeserving, and make economic activity appear highly praiseworthy. Sociologist Robin Williams has isolated thirteen elements of the American value system.[31] For the purposes of the present discussion, ten of them are relevant: (1) efficiency, (2) practicality, (3) achievement, (4) materialism, (5) progress, (6) freedom, (7) individualism, (8) equality, (9) morality, and (10) humanitarianism.

Why do these values and not others appear on this list? A materialist would answer that they are dominant values because they reflect and support existing productive arrangements. Six of the ten directly enhance market capitalism: efficiency, practicality, achievement, progress, materialism, and individualism. The other four contribute through special interpretations.

A few examples will illustrate how these values work to buttress the existing distribution and affect the lives of the poor. The value of freedom has been interpreted primarily to mean freedom from government restraint. As a result, political freedom as opposed to freedom from the miseries of poverty has been stressed and *laissez-faire* attitudes have predominated. Freedom as absence of restraint has also been allied with individualism. This combination translates into a belief in the free play of individual competition and the assumption that the outcomes of the competition are equitable, even if unequal.

Conveniently for the victors at last, inequality of opportunity and the increasing dominance of large organizations over individuals are overlooked. These realities notwithstanding, the American interpretation of freedom and individualism has led to a general acceptance of the end product, reluctance to interfere, and a glossing over of the many advantages the rich have in the struggle.

The values of efficiency, practicality, achievement, and individualism are part and parcel of the work ethic. The work ethic is alive and well at least in the realm of ideology in spite of premature death notices and concessions to consumerism. It rewards the victors and stigmatizes the poor. That many rewards come not as a result of hard work and achievement, and that poverty is often not a consequence of laziness are also overlooked. The end result is that the rich are thought to be hard workers justly rewarded with income and wealth, while the poor are regarded as lazy and shiftless justly condemned to poverty.

The value of efficiency is particularly important. Efficiency, both in terms of productivity and in terms of growth, is critical to industrial society. The promotion of efficiency is perhaps the single most often heard justification for departures from equality.[32] But efficiency as a value also has ideological currency. It becomes a potent tool to pry loose extra rewards above and beyond those actually required to increase productivity and growth.

On the other side are the values of equality, humanitarianism, and morality. Actually, the value of equality serves both sides. It serves to increase inequality if interpreted merely to mean equality of opportunity or equality before the law. For many Americans, however, it also means some measure of equal outcomes and some proportionality of reward and contribution.

Humanitarianism and an emphasis on morality serve to create compassion for the less fortunate and acceptance of social justice. Without these values and the derived belief that society is responsible for meeting basic needs, the plight of the poor and the distribution would be much worse.

Buried in this are the shortcomings of capitalism. Longer on productivity, shorter on equity, capitalism still needs legitimation. Karl Marx's aphorism that the ruling ideas are the ideas of the ruling class still has validity.

Ethical Foundations

It is now appropriate to continue the ethical discussion begun with a review of David Little's development of Calvin's thought. The two purposes of this discussion are the development of ethical guidelines to assess tax proposals and to advocate a more progressive tax system. The following ethical foundations are derived from ongoing discussions in ecumenical circles and are meant to build on David Little's analysis.

Three norms dominate this foundation: justice, sustainable sufficiency, and participation.[33] Of these, justice and the sufficiency aspect of the second norm are most important for discussions of tax equity. The third norm, participation, and the sustainability aspect of the second add some interesting insights, however.

Justice is rooted in the very being of God. It is an essential part of God's community of love and bids Christians to make fairness or equity the touchstone of their social relationships. Justice is not the love of Christ (agape). Justice involves the calculation of rewards and deserts and is less personal than love. Love is the foundation of justice and lends passion to its deliberations.

In simplest terms justice means fairness, treating equals equally and unequals unequally. For biblical writers, and later for the Christian tradition, the poor are the special concern of justice. The Bible is biased in favor of the poor but without making any claim that poverty leads to salvation or moral superiority.

Concern for the poor is found throughout the Bible. In Exodus it is expressed as the liberation of the oppressed slaves in Egypt. For the prophets it is simple justice for the poor, widows, and orphans. In Luke it is a special identity with the poor and the promise of good news. For Paul it is sharing.

This concern and identity leads to what liberation theologians and the National Conference of Catholic Bishops have called "the preferential option for the poor."[34] On the one hand for Pope John Paul II this means "a special sensitivity toward those who are extremely poor, those suffering from all the physical, mental, and moral ills that afflict humanity including hunger, neglect, unemployment and despair."[35] On the other hand justice implies more than sensitivity. It is substantive. It involves the impoverishment of real people, a change in their condition, as well as the procedural safeguard of equality of opportunity. It also conveys a sense of solidarity with the poor through concrete acts of justice. It means seeing things through the eyes of the poor. Finally, and most radically in the words of the Catholic Bishops, it points to "an emptying of self, both individually and corporately. . . . Indeed, the option for the poor is the social and ecclesiological counterpart of the emptying (*kenosis*) of Jesus in the incarnation."[36]

Western philosophical traditions have developed this biblical understanding further. Justice is understood to have two regulative principles, liberty and equality, the latter the more important for discussions of taxation and distribution. Equality is, of course, a biblical norm in its own right. All persons are made in the image of God and in Christ all are one.

Equality as a religious norm does not necessarily mandate equality of income and wealth. Still, equality as a religious norm cannot be approximated where great differentials exist. An empty stomach has its way of intruding on one's relation to God and other people and one's sense of equality. Communities are torn asunder when inequality becomes too great.

As with the biblical understanding of justice, the understanding of equality is substantive. Equal starting points or equality in theory are not enough to satisfy the biblical mandate. Equal outcomes, or at least some reasonable approximation thereof, are also warranted.

To see how equality as a norm works conceptually both the ethical ideal of perfect equality and the human reality of accepting less that full equality in order to achieve fairness or equity must be considered. Equality in terms of income and private physical wealth is an ethical ideal. It would be the condition which would hold in a moral and abundant world or the kingdom of God when it comes. This ideal is important, if not fully realizable. It serves as plumbline to measure and limit concessions to inequality in order to achieve other goods. It pushes and pulls unequal institutions to higher levels of justice.

In the everyday world inequality and scarcity abound and must be addressed with real programs, not just concepts. Measured against the plumbline of perfect equality, all human attempts to establish real equality fall short, although in varying and morally important degrees. In some cases it is legitimate to depart from equality. For example, the sufficient supply of basics, such as food, clothing, shelter, transportation, and health care will mean some departures from equality so long as individuals must be given incentives to produce these necessities. This is the issue of efficiency mentioned above. The common good is frequently enough served by extending extra monetary incentives in hopes of providing a needed social service to allow some trade-off of equality for a little more or less of the social good. Thus equity or fairness, that is, equality reduced by the need to achieve other ends, becomes an appropriate consideration.

The problem in a materialistic society is that the good of efficiency, extended to mean ever increasing affluence, has tended to displace equality as the primary ethical plumbline. From a Christian perspective this is not acceptable. While sufficiency in terms of basic needs must be given the same priority as equality, the provision of ever increasing affluence does not, although this does not mean affluence is an irrelevant good. Material abundance beyond basic needs, however good, is just not a priority norm for Christians.

This leaves the following: equality is the primary ethical norm for judging the equity or fairness of tax proposals. The moral presumption is in favor of equality. In the slightly different words of Lester Thurow, ". . . deviations from economic equality must be shown to be beneficial, placing the burden of proof on those who advocate inequality." And to this, echoing the concern of the prophets, Thurow appends that "some minimum economic prize is an essential ingredient in economic equity."[37] Similarly the Catholic Bishops establish "a strong presumption against inequality of income and wealth as long as there are poor, hungry and homeless people in our midst. . . . This presumption can be overridden only if an absolute scarcity of resources makes the fulfillment of the basic needs of all strictly impossible or if unequal distribution stimulates productivity in a way that truly benefits the poor."[38]

But what are the grounds for determining what is beneficial and therefore a permissible departure from equality? Two additional subprinciples inform this determination. The first is the principle of relevancy which establishes a procedure to specify on Christian ethical grounds the acceptance of proposals calling for departures from equality. Sufficiency, for instance, has been offered as an acceptable reason for departing from equality, so far on self-evident grounds. Its justification comes from the obvious insight that basic necessities are the prerequisite of all else in human life. Thus proposed departures from equality to ensure sufficiency are acceptable.

What other departures are acceptable? If sufficiency does qualify and the provisions of great riches does not, where is one to draw the line? Short of a list of "dos" and "don'ts," the following will have to suffice as tentative general guidelines. Once basic necessities are met, departures are acceptable if they: (1) help the poor; (2) are a matter of deserved reward, as in receiving extra pay for working longer hours at the same job, all other things being equal; and, even more tentative, (3) provide some clear social good.

The second subprinciple is proportionality, a principle which limits the above departures. If a person or group warrants a reward, the reward should be roughly proportional to the good to be supplied. Thus, if one worker puts in twice as much time as another, it is fair to pay him or her roughly twice as much. Pay should be proportional to the time worked. Applied to the discussion of taxes, any tax concession allowed should be roughly proportional to the social good provided.

In summary, equality is a regulative principle of justice. With sufficiency, it is the primary norm by which to judge claims for tax equity. In a moral and abundant world it might be the only principle to consider. In a sinful and scarce world other things demand attention, not the least of which are incentives to assist in the problem of providing basic needs. Proportional departures from equality are permissible provided they promise beyond a reasonable doubt to produce a demonstrable social benefit which would otherwise go unrealized.

Finally, the goal of justice in any tax system should not be perfect equality but rough equity or fairness. It should lead to a distribution where the poor at least have access to basic necessities, and inequalities are accepted only on the grounds that some relevant social good will be provided. Tax proposals should be assessed on the basis of equality and the overall economic benefit they will provide with special consideration for the poor.

Sustainable sufficiency is the second norm. The preceding discussion assumed sufficiency without developing it as a norm. Sufficiency is the timely supply to all persons of basic material necessities defined as the resources needed for food, clothing, shelter, transportation, health care, and some margin above subsistence. The emphasis is on basic needs, not the supply of each and every human want. Its Christian basis is the Gospel's preferential option for the poor, justice, and understandings of the idolatry of materialism.

Sustainability is closely related to sufficiency. It is the long-range supply of sufficient resources for basic needs. It takes its cue from the Christian understanding of stewardship which means care of the earth and of persons.

Sustainable sufficiency reinforces the norm of justice through its emphasis on the provision of basic needs. It also adds new dimensions to tax policy including environmental concern, resource conservation, the promotion of recycling and durability, and the restraint of resource-intensive forms of consumption. These social goods are now candidates for inclusion in the tax code, although Americans would do well to recognize that other vehicles are better suited than the tax systems to the achievement of these objectives.

The norm of sustainability both increases and decreases the importance of efficiency as a consideration. Efficiency as an increase in productivity becomes much more significant. In the future societies will be forced to expend far fewer resources than at present for a given output in order to reduce scarcity. A trade-off of equality for productivity may be inevitable. Efficiency as increasing Gross National Product regardless of its content is another matter. Economic growth must be limited by considerations of sustainability.

Participation is the third and final norm. Participation finds its grounding in the Christian stress on community. The essence of community is *koinonia,* which is the spirit of fellowship and unity in Jesus Christ and the glue of the church. The ideal is established in the opening chapters of the Book of Acts and includes sharing through work and gifts. Paul confirms this in Romans 12 and in his call to the churches to share with those in Jerusalem. For some Christians, in particular the early community in Jerusalem, the ideal also included the holding of possessions in common.

The Reformed perspective on community has been ably developed in the preceding essay by David Little. To translate the ideals of the early church and Reformed notions on community into a statement about the wider society is problematical. The *koinonia* and human communities are not coincidental. At best they overlap. In the Reformed tradition, the two are never separated with the ideal of the community in the church serving as a beacon for both the social institution of the church and for the state. It is the basis for reform and from the Reformed perspective sets the tasks of sharing, fellowship, and unity for church and state. It also establishes the community as prior to the individual.

For the present discussion participation at minimum means having a voice in critical tax decision. Democracy, however imperfect, provides adequate mechanisms in the United States for political participation. But it would be naive to assume these mechanisms serve all groups equally well. The voices of the poor are barely heard, the voices of well-financed special interest groups are loud and clear. The facade of democratic participation conceals a house with several levels of participation with the poor on the least involved level.

Participation also extends to production and consumption. A meaningful job and an income sufficient for basic necessities are prerequisites for economic participation. When combined with the preferential option for the poor, the implications here are clear, at least to the Catholic Bishops.

> Increased economic participation for the marginalized takes priority over the preservation of privileged concentrations of power, wealth and income. This principle follows from the fact that economic rights and responsibilities must find expression in the institutional order of society. It grants priority to policies and programs that enhance participation through work. It also points out the need for policies to improve the situation of groups unjustly discriminated against in the past. And it has very important implications for the institutions that shape the international economic order.[39]

Finally, a consideration of participation leads to a very sticky question in tax matters: who owns property? Social convention in the United States has given wide scope to individual appropriation of property. As a consequence, taxation is seen as "taking away" something which rightfully belongs to the individual. This is a useful fiction for some purposes, but contributes to the problems of tax avoidance, distrust of government, and the neglect of the public sector.

The norm of participation, with its priority on community, offers a different way of looking at this problem. At the most fundamental level the answer to the property ownership question is that neither individuals or governments own property. Property belongs to God and human beings are stewards. Property is a trust from God to be organized in ways which enhance all created life. As for more specific guidance on how this trust is to be organized in terms of ownership, the Bible and the tradition are not of one voice. Both individual and social ownership are possibilities, and the decision between them is a pragmatic one.

Without getting into the complicated and often emotional debate over social versus private ownership, what can be maintained is a limited priority for the community. The community is the holder of property in trust from God, even though in its wisdom it may delegate this responsibility to individuals. Taxes are not a "taking away" but a "withholding," that is, a holding on by the community to the socially generated product for purposes of extending the common good.

The priority of the community and participation in community also point in the direction of a tax system which produces sufficient revenue for community needs and promotes participation in community as a value. It also suggests that extremes of wealth and poverty, since they so easily fracture community, are to be avoided.

Policy Questions

In light of these three norms, the following questions are relevant to any new tax proposal and should be answered in the affirmative.

1. Does the proposal increase progressivity?
2. If the proposal is regressive, is the departure from equality clearly supportable on other ethical grounds, such as the significant increase of some social good?
3. If the proposal is regressive, is the departure from equality roughly proportional to the good to be realized?
4. Does the proposal satisfy the preferential option for the poor? In slightly different terms, does the proposal add to or relieve poverty?
5. Does the proposal increase incentives, for example, to work, to take responsible risks, to increase skills, or to provide needed services?
6. Does the proposal add to, relieve, or help to compensate for the various forms of discrimination?
7. Does the proposal foster community and participation in community?
8. Does the proposal promote environmental soundness, resource conservation, and sustainable forms of consumption?
9. Is the proposal flexible and easily administered?

Measuring Up

Making a case for a more progressive tax system is difficult in these times. Legislators and voters seem uninterested. The poor who would benefit usually do not exercise their political power and are a minority of Americans anyway. Economic far outweigh ethical considerations in most people's minds. The owners of private physical wealth have much at stake in preventing progressive taxes.

The case rests on several fundamental arguments derived from applying the three norms from the above to the facts and interpretations of earlier sections.

1. Continuing high levels of poverty in the midst of affluence is a serious violation of the norm of justice and the gospel's preferential option for the poor. A more progressive tax system is one way to raise the revenue to finance workable social programs to reduce poverty.

2. Spurious departures from equality including discrimination, unequal opportunity and political power, wage contours, and even chance, all butressed by materialistic ideological considerations, are significant factors in the wide differentials in the distribution of income and private physical wealth. A more progressive tax system would partially compensate for these unjustifiable departures.

3. An over-emphasis on efficiency gives this consideration more importance in setting taxes than can be justified, producing disproportionate rewards for those who control capital and scarce resources and an overall tax system which is neutral in terms of its distributional effects. A more progressive tax system would restore the norm of equality to its place of priority.

4. The perception of equity in the distribution of social burdens and rewards is an important determiner of the unity and harmony of the community. A more progressive tax system would help to restore this perception.

In conclusion, the case here is not for an egalitarian revolution, but for a more progressive tax system, that is, for reform. Egalitarian societies have almost all been poor. There are valid reasons to depart from equality. The problem is that Americans have been more than generous to the rich in their determination of equitable departures.

Tax ethics is not an oxymoron. The ethical challenge from a Reformed perspective is to provide jobs, to reduce poverty, to narrow income and wealth differentials, and to adopt a more progressive tax system. Changes in the tax structure combined with transfer payments and legislation to eliminate the effects of discrimination would seem to be the best path to meet this challenge.

Endnotes

1. Roger L. Shinn, ed., *Faith and Science in an Unjust World* (World Council of Churches, 1980), vol. 1; Paul Abrecht ed., *Faith and Science in an Unjust World* (World Council of Churches, 1980), vol. 2; and Robert L. Stivers, *Hunger, Technology, and Limits to Growth* (Minneapolis: Augsburg Publishing House, 1984).

2. Report on Section VI, "Energy for the Future," *Faith and Science in an*

Unjust World, vol. 2, Paul Abrecht, ed., p. 93. Also see the Report of Section V, p. 70.

3. Sheldon Danziger, Robert Haveman, and Robert Plotnick, "Antipoverty Policy: Effects on the Poor and the Nonpoor," *An Institute for Research on Poverty Conference Paper* (Institute for Research on Poverty, University of Wisconsin, Madison, 1985), p. 7.

4. Danziger, *et. al.,* pp. 9, 12.

5. Danziger, *et. al.,* p. 14.

6. Rebecca M. Blank and Alan S. Blinder, "Macroeconomics, Income, Distribution, and Poverty," *An Institute for Research on Poverty Conference Paper* (Institute for Research on Poverty, University of Wisconsin, Madison, 1985), pp. 4, 11.

7. Lester C. Thurow, *Generating Inequality* (New York: Basic Books, Inc., Publishers, 1975), pp. 58f.

8. Blank and Blinder, "Macroeconomics," p. 41.

9. Joseph A. Pechman, *Who Paid the Taxes, 1966–85?* (Washington, D.C.: The Brookings Institute, 1985), p. 44.

10. Herman P. Miller, *Rich Man Poor Man* (New York: Thomas Y. Crowell, 1971), pp. 23f.

11. Thurow, *Generating Inequality,* Ch. 6.

12. Thurow, pp. 14f.

13. Jonathan H. Turner and Charles F. Starnes, *Inequality: Privilege and Poverty in America* (Santa Monica: Goodyear Publishing Company, Inc.), Ch. 2.

14. Miller, *Rich Man,* p. 16.

15. Albert Ando, Marshall E. Blume, and Irwin Friend, *The Structure and Reform of the U.S. Tax System* (Cambridge, MA: The MIT Press, 1985), p. 4. Also see Pechman, *Who Paid the Taxes,* p. 8.

16. *Ibid.,* Ch. 1.

17. Blank and Blinder, "Macroeconomics," p. 4.

18. Alan S. Blinder, *Toward an Economic Theory of Income Distribution* (Cambridge, Mass.: The MIT Press, 1974), p. 125.

19. Thurow, *Generating Inequality,* pp. 165ff.

20. *Ibid.,* Ch. 7.

21. *Ibid.,* Ch. 5.

22. Okun, *Equality and Efficiency,* p. 67.

23. *Ibid.,* pp. 73–75.

24. Turner and Starnes, *Inequality,* p. 66.

25. Thurow, *Generating Inequality,* p. 129.

26. Okun, *Equality and Efficiency,* Ch. 3.

27. Thurow, pp. 142–154.

28. *Ibid.,* p. 149.

29. *Ibid.,* p. 152.

30. Edgar K. Brown and William R. Johnson, "Trade-off Between Equality

and Efficiency," *Journal of Political Economy*, Vol. 192, No. 2, April 1984, The University of Chicago Press.

31. Robin M. Williams, Jr., *American Society: A Sociological Interpretation*, second ed., rev. (New York: Alfred A. Knopf, 1967), pp. 437–500.

32. *The Economic Report of the President 1987* (Washington, D.C.: GPO, 1987), pp. 81ff.

33. Stivers, *Hunger, Technology, and Limits to Growth*, Chs. 7, 8.

34. U.S. Catholic Conference, "First Draft of the U.S. Bishops' Pastoral Letter on Catholic Social Teaching and the U.S. Economy, *Origins, National Catholic Documentary Service,* 15 Nov. 1984, Vol. 14, no. 22/23, pp. 52ff.

35. Bishops' Pastoral, article 52, p. 347.

36. Bishops' Pastoral, article 54, p. 347.

37. Thurow, p. 32.

38. Bishops' Pastoral, article 99, p. 352.

39. Bishops' Pastoral, article 104, p. 352.

Chapter Seven

The 1986 Tax Reform in Perspective

William L. Raby

The Reagan Tax Revolution, so-called, can be epitomized by contrasting the top marginal tax rates in the law when Ronald Reagan took office in 1981 with those likely to exist when he leaves in January, 1989:

	1981	1989
Individual income tax	70%	28%
Corporation income tax	46%	34%
Estate and gift taxes	70%	55%

Tax law changes were sold with the slogan, "Simplicity, equity, and economic growth." The reality? Complication; tax reductions for the wealthy and increases for the middle-class and the aged; with encouragement for neither saving nor the expansion of capital intensive industry.

In the meantime, national deficits roll on, and the reality of inflation seems likely to impose the most hidden and hideous tax of all— the continued depreciation of the dollar's purchasing power. At "only" 6% a year inflation, the value of the dollar becomes fifty cents in twelve years, twenty-five cents in twenty-four years, and twelve and one-half cents in thirty-six years. (The use of six percent is merely to illustrate the impact of what this author views as a low estimate of inflation for the next third of a century.) Someone retiring on a fixed pension at age 60, in other words, may find what was barely adequate at 60 only 12½% adequate if he or she is unlucky enough to survive to ninety-six. By insisting that tax "reform" be revenue neutral, the

1986 Act did nothing at all about this deficit and the inflationary pressures to which it contributes. The December 1987 budget reconciliation legislation did nothing more, either.

Presbyterian Policy Statements

The General Assemblies have spoken twice on tax questions in recent years. (Parenthetical comments contrast the effects of the Reagan Tax Revolution with the topic being discussed.)

In 1973, the 185th General Assembly of the United Presbyterian Church adopted a Policy Statement on State and Local Tax Reform. This statement declared that "several criteria should be employed in the evaluation of taxes and tax systems." These include:

1. Fair progressivity. "In evaluating fairness, the primary concern should be for the impact of the total 'tax system' which means the aggregate of all taxes levied by all levels of government." That impact "should be on a broadly progressive curve with a minimum impact on the poverty levels of income and wealth." (If social security taxes are engrafted onto the 1988 tax schedules, the federal income tax system is progressive at the very bottom and then becomes regressive beyond about $44,000 of income. The social security tax imposes a 7.51% tax on the first dollar of wage income; personal exemptions and the standard deduction prevent income tax on roughly the first $7,000 of wages, so that 7.51% is the effective tax rate. The 15% income tax rate on the next $17,850 raises the effective tax rate to 22.51%; the income tax rate on the next $25,300 is 28%, raising the effective tax rate to 35.51%. By contrast, an unmarried taxpayer earning a salary of $100,000 is paying a tax of 28% on his or her last dollar of income.)

2. Uniformity. "All persons in approximately the same situation with the same income level should pay approximately the same total amount of tax." (The federal situation has improved in this regard, but homeowners will still pay less than renters, those who borrow heavily will pay less than those who finance from savings, ordained church employees will pay less than others, people with passive income can more easily shelter that income from tax than those with income from jobs or investments, employed persons who live together without marriage will often pay less than employed marrieds, etc.)

3. Flexibility. Tax Systems should be structured to provide maximum flexibility for governing bodies, both in funding and in expenditure decisions. (If we consider the constraint imposed by the Admin-

istration and accepted by the Congress that the 1986 tax reform was to be revenue neutral, the process could hardly have had less flexibility.)

4. Acceptance, in the context of political acceptability. "This includes:

   a. Ease of Administration

   b. Simplicity of Compliance

   c. Understanding of Impact by the Real Taxpayer"

(Almost all commentators, including the IRS, seem in agreement that the 1986 Act sets a new high for complexity of compliance and difficulty of administration. The implementation of the rule that children under 14 pay tax on investment income at the marginal parental tax rate, especially when parents are divorced; the analyses required to determine how much interest can be deducted on a relatively straightforward 1040; and the level of analysis required to determine whether a loss on rental real estate is deductible are but a few examples, out of dozens, of almost unbearably sophisticated decisions being forced on ordinary taxpayers.

(Nor do taxpayers understand either the new law's direct effects or the indirect effects of the changes in corporate taxation. Most middle-income taxpayers will be shocked to find that their 1987 taxes on a given package of income and deductions will be greater than in 1986, even after requiring greater work and expense to prepare a return. To the extent that corporate capital recovery allowances were major sources of the funds used to reduce individual taxes, it is likely that, for at least many industries, the ultimate effect will be seen in higher consumer prices than would otherwise exist.)

The 189th General Assembly of the UPC adopted the Report of a special Committee on Federal Tax Reform. Among other conclusions, that Report pointed out that:

• "Inflation is a form of taxation and is Regressive in effect."

• "A fiscal system that spends more than it receives is self-destructive."

• "A growing economy tends to offer expanding opportunities for maximum human welfare."

• "Capital formation and private investment are vital to the American Economy."

The Policy Statement that resulted emphasized equity, moral integrity, simplicity and efficiency as the criteria for considering tax reform and tax law.

Evaluation

The Reagan administration seems to have firmly believed that lowering the marginal rate of tax (i.e., the tax on the last dollar of income) was of sufficient importance that almost any compromises were worthwhile to achieve that goal. Reduction in marginal rates, or so goes the argument, will unleash private investment and provide the energizing force for unparalleled economic growth. We are now in the midst of testing the validity of that hypothesis. It is certainly true that the present prosperity is unparalleled in its duration. But it is also true that the drop in energy prices and the size of the national deficits are also unparalleled. What causes what? And who pays for and who benefits from what?

The economic state of the nation, let alone of the world, is evaluated by the numbers that are available and not by qualitative standards. Is low unemployment, compared to a few years ago, the product of how unemployment is measured (e.g., not reflecting as unemployed those who have ceased looking for work) or even of what is measured? Does a manufacturing job paying $12.50 an hour equal $3.35 an hour in a fast food establishment? The numbers say it does.

A major focus? Gross National Product. But in spite of its name, this basically measures inputs rather than outputs. What adjustments should be made in a number like GNP to reflect the decline in the value of the dollar relative to the yen, the mark, or the pound in the past few years? Only as domestic price levels change will we see GNP responding to what is happening to the values of the U.S. dollar.

How will consumers react to the stock market drop of October 19, 1987? Some down-sizing of expectations could have major impacts on consumer spending in 1988, perhaps triggering the recession that business economists see as likely in 1989.

The 1986 Act's approach to "fairness" as a criteria sought to insure that "no one can get away with anything." This has been a major cause of the complexity added by the law. The Statute reflects nitpicking run amok. But the justice concerns of the church are not so much concerned with extracting the last full measure of the law as they are with the effect on those at the bottom of the economic and social ladders. As to them, the 1986 Act achieves little. Some are dropped from the income tax rolls. But social security taxes, excise taxes, and state and local taxes easily aggregate 14–16% of the income of those at the bottom of the heap (e.g., 7.51% social security tax plus a 7% city and state sales tax = 14.51%, only partially offset by the refundable earned income credit (a sort of negative income tax for those with low incomes who are raising children). The maximum earned income credit for 1987 was $851, for someone earning $6,080, with the actual earned credit reducing by 10 cents for each dollar of earnings exceeding $6,920 and disappearing entirely when adjusted gross income exceeds $15,431. In a sense, the disappearing aspect of the credit imposes an extra ten point tax on income between $6,920 and $15,431, thus accentuating the low income rate progressivity discussed previously.

While simplicity was initially a major stated goal for the tax reform movement, it rapidly dropped by the wayside. In fact, the realities of the political process and its financing appear to provide substantial incentives for complexity in the law as well as constant change in the law, such change and threat of change being itself a major contributor to complexity. Thus, while the 1986 Act was passed in October 1986, one year later both Senate Finance Committee and House Ways and Means Committee were considering major tax legislation, including a substantial Technical Corrections Act to fine-tune the 1986 Act provisions.

The result has been to make the members of the two tax-writing committees, but especially the Senate Finance Committee, popular objects for political contributions and lecture fees and similar honorariums. In fact, they are far more popular than their colleagues on any other Congressional committees. And they will probably stay more popular, as measured in the marketplace, so long as they keep churning the tax law. That is hardly an incentive towards simplicity, which would undoubtedly include limited change from decade to decade let alone massive change from year to year.

Capital intensive industries are relatively less attractive after the 1986 Act than before. Capital recovery allowances have been sharply reduced. In addition, equity investment is relatively less attractive than debt since the investor will pay the same rate of tax after 1987 on interest income as on long term capital gains. Since such changes are hardly contributors to economic growth (in the Gross National Product sense), it can be easily predicted that these provisions will be quickly changed once the next recession sets in. The change will be in response to demands that Congress "do something," just as the December 1987 charade of tax legislation was in response to demands that Congress do something about the deficit in the wake of the October 19 stock market drop. Whether what is done could logically solve the problem is less important than that there be at least the illusion that government is providing leadership in coping with a perceived crisis.

Cost of determining and collecting 1987 taxes under the new law will rise 15% to 25% according to some estimates, as compared to the cost of determining and collecting 1986 taxes. Tax controversies are expected to escalate as the result of Congressional decisions, reflected in recent tax statutes, to opt for more massive penalties and increased enforcement activities (e.g., all children of five or more must have social security numbers on parent and child's returns to better control exemptions).

Conclusion

Involvement with the fiscal affairs of the state is very much in the Calvinist tradition, and involvement in the formation of tax policy has been a part of Presbyterian social witness. The considerations surrounding such tax-related issues as charitable contribution deductions are not, however, narrowly fiscal. Thus, tax reform is really much too serious to be entrusted to tax specialists.

If, as the 189th General Assembly determined, equity, moral integrity, simplicity and efficiency are the criteria by which the church should evaluate the tax system, then that which we have as of the end of 1987 is seriously in need of reform in spite of its alleged reform in 1986.

Tax reform was used as a red herring in preparing for and waging the 1984 Presidential campaign, and as a rallying cry for tax law changes that fell far short of effective reform under the criteria of the General Assembly. The battle is not yet won, and the church should therefore continue its involvement with the issue of a tax system, federal and state, that contributes to rather than frustrates justice.

It is this author's personal belief that a massive public outcry, similar to that which resulted in enactment of Proposition 13 in California, will be necessary before massive change takes place. That outcry should be led by the Presbyterian Church. But before that can happen, the church must itself be willing to abandon its institutional vested interests (e.g., in the exclusion from income of ministerial housing allowances, the deductibility of charitable contributions, and the exclusion from taxation of investment income and unrelated business income). Given the present state of affairs, a progressive tax on adjusted gross income may well be the only approach which will meet the criteria which past General Assemblies have laid down. The political process will inevitably produce some exceptions to that "clean" concept, but absent such a goal, the future of income tax legislation appears to be "more of the same." Yet those who argue for the Church retaining its privileged status can point to the position of the Church in Calvin's Zurich, and Calvin's zealous actions to preserve that favored position, as indicating that such enlightened self-interest is not in the Calvinist tradition. To which one might reply with the thought that "whoever loves his own life will lose it;" and we would speak prophetic words in our day must not first and foremost count the cost to us of radical change or we are likely to prove false prophets, indeed.

Chapter Eight

Creation, Reformed Faith, and Sustainable Food Systems

Gordon and Jane Douglass

In the real world, "agricultural sustainability" means different things to different groups of people. One group thinks of sustainability as supplying enough food to meet everyone's demand. We call this the "food sufficiency" or "productivity" school. Agriculture, in this view, is primarily an instrument for feeding the world—or at least for feeding those who can afford to buy food on world markets—and preserving the resource base or the culture of rural life is usually of secondary importance.

A second group regard agricultural sustainability primarily as an ecological phenomenon. We call it the "stewardship" school. Its proponents measure sustainable production not by total output, or output per unit of scarce input during a limited period of time, but by the average level of output over an indefinitely long period which can be sustained without depleting the renewable resources on which it depends.

Yet another group pays most attention to the effects of different agricultural systems on the vitality, social organization, and culture of rural life. We call it the "community" school. Its members also are ecologically minded, but their primary interest is in promoting vital, coherent rural cultures that encourage the values of stewardship, self-reliance, humility, and holism. They favor "equity" in the distribution of opportunities and rewards.

Few people would take out membership in just one of these schools of agricultural sustainability. Most of us no doubt prefer agricultural systems that are economically viable AND ecologically sound AND socially just. But is it really possible to achieve all these good things at once? Do not further population growth, the tightening of economic constraints, and the rediscovery of ecological limits confront us with important trade-offs among desirable objectives?

Since the answer to this question depends in part on the clarity with which objectives are stated, the first purpose of our paper is to distinguish among the objectives of these three schools of agricultural sustainability and the trade-offs among them.[1] The next three sections are devoted to this task. The paper's second purpose is to confront these objectives and trade-offs with the wisdom of the Bible and the traditions of our Reformed faith, especially in relation to the doctrine of creation. Thus section four evaluates the three approaches to agricultural sustainability for consistency with the perspectives of Reformed faith, as we understand them. Section five extends the analysis by comparing the findings of section four with the recommendations of three recent statements issued by the church: Chapter 5 of the U.S. Catholic Bishops' pastoral on the economy, and statements on the farm crisis by the 190th and the 197th General Assemblies of the Presbyterian Church. Finally section six draws some tentative conclusions about public policies needed to achieve sustainable agricultural economies at home and abroad.

I. Sustainability as Food Sufficiency

Defenders of large-scale, highly specialized, mechanized, chemical-intensive farming methods frequently justify them with references to the expansion of world population. Now growing at the rate of 1.7% per year, today's population of 5 billion people is expected to exceed 6.0 billion by the turn of the century and to climb higher still during the 21st century. As development accelerates in some Third World countries, moreover, growth of incomes will tend to encourage more meat eating, which lengthens the food chain and exaggerates the effect on grain consumption of rising levels of per capita income. The overall result will be a chronic tendency in rapidly developing countries for food demand to outpace its supply from domestic sources, leading to continuing high export demands on breadbasket countries like the United States. "The key to achieving the increased food output needed to feed the greatly enlarged world population in prospect, and to feed it more adequately, is the further application of science and technology to agriculture."[2]

For such people, estimating the future demand for food is the essential first step in achieving agricultural sustainability. The tools of economists are used to estimate the effects of changes in population, income per capita, the relative price of foodstuffs, and other variables on the demand for particular food groups (cereals, oil seeds, meat, etc.) by country or group of countries.[3] The estimates from this approach normally only take account of demands expressed in the marketplace; therefore, the estimates sometimes are adjusted upwards to acknowledge the need to find ways to supplement the diets of the poorest groups whose nutritional levels fall below minimum standards. Finding ways to alleviate the dietary deficiencies of the poorest classes in developing countries is an extremely complicated quest, however, adding considerable uncertainty to the task of estimating future levels of "sufficient" demand.[4]

Once reasonably plausible estimates of demand for foodstuffs are made, the next step is to estimate the supply of economically useful agricultural resources and their productivities per unit of resource. This task often is based on projections of past trends, adapted for what is known about likely changes in the prices of agricultural inputs, the possible effects of resource depletion and environmental stress[5] and the expected consequences of continued research and development.[6] There is a winsome quality to most of these projections, because they usually indicate that supply will match demand for at least the remainder of this century. In most instances, this happy result is made possible by assuming that production and distribution systems will adjust quickly as economic signals change, and that the host environment to these systems is extremely adaptive.[7] These assumptions, embraced explicitly in the neoclassical training of most American economists and implicitly by most representatives of the American agricultural establishment, virtually assure the balancing of supply and demand in conventional market forecasts.

Thinking economically about the supply of agricultural resources leads to the conclusion that the supply of foodstuffs can always be increased, at some cost. Physical limits of resources almost never bar increase in the output of particular goods or services as long as society is willing to incur the economic, environmental and human costs of attracting needed resources from other potential uses. The capacity of agricultural resources begins to be reached only when the costs rise so high that the ability of society to achieve other broadly shared goals is undermined. Since adequate nourishment is an important goal, people who think economically about food supplies tend to believe that the capacity to supply food is unlimited for all practical purposes.

The remarkable record of technological accomplishment in agriculture—of substituting biological, mechanical, and chemical inputs for land—has reinforced this impression.[8] Thus people who subscribe to the food-sufficiency school assume that scientific research and development can be counted on to increase future yields at least as rapidly as they have in the past. Even if farming methods lead to erosion in excess of the rate of soil regeneration, they can be justified as long as the additional output they produce exceeds the costs of producing it. The true legacy that we leave our children is the capacity to produce, rather than the assurance of a sustainable resource base. Resource preservation is regarded as a needlessly high standard of performance as long as technological advances can more than make up for the effects of resource depletion on output.[9]

In fairness, progress has been made recently in reconciling the objectives of producing more, even in the absence of technological advance, and preserving environmental quality. With the help of benefit-cost analysis and other techniques, natural systems managers are beginning to explore how the renewable resource base and the productivity of natural systems can be maintained under varying circumstances. But one must retain modest expectations from these efforts, since economic valuation of benefits and costs relies critically on understanding and measuring the physical, chemical, and biological effects of production activities, and many of these "externalities" escape valuation. Thus policies that otherwise seem economically optimal may deplete resources. Attempts to account for the uncertainties or irreversibilities associated with resource use by applying artificially low discount rates when calculating benefits and cost may lead to over-investments and even greater damage to the natural environment in the future.[10]

II. Sustainability as Stewardship

People who think ecologically about sustainability take environmental costs much more seriously than do conventional agriculturalists of the food-sufficiency school. They believe that nature imposes physical limits on our capacity to grow food—limits based on finite supplies of natural resources and on their limited capacity to absorb waste. When modern energy-intensive agricultural processes yield significant environmental costs, stewards of nature generally regard them as unsustainable, regardless of temporary additions to output which they may make possible.

Indeed, many ecologically-minded people believe that applying nonrenewable resources to natural systems will eventually decrease the productivity of renewable resources—either because using too many nonrenewable resources generates erosion, pollutants, and other outcomes that impair the vitality of biological resources, or because too rapid application of nonrenewable resources may cause a society to raise population and consumption levels unsustainably, leading eventually to a crisis breakdown.

Thus, combining nonrenewable with renewable resources can raise or lower agricultural yields depending on the strength of productivity-raising and productivity-lowering effects of fossil fuels and other nonrenewable inputs. For the last several decades, especially in the United States, yields have been enhanced. Since the beginning of the 1970's, however, momentum has been lost and the rate of advance in cereal yields, for example, has dropped to 1.5% annually, slightly less than the growth rate of world population. The variability of yields has greatly increased also.[11] The Worldwatch Institute estimates that global per capita productivity has now begun to decline for all four primary renewable resources in the world: cropland, grassland, forests, and fisheries.[12] Some of these trends may be reversed with heavier applications of nonrenewable resources, especially for crops and in regions where fertilizer application rates are low. But members of the stewardship school believe this is an unlikely prospect as we continue to deplete the most easily available nonrenewable resources and population growth rates remain high.

Rather than depend on the technologies and policies of the past, therefore, the ecological approach focuses on the need of agricultural managers to adopt new methods that enhance and conserve the renewable resource base and reduce dependence on nonrenewable technological fixes.[13] Its important principles include: (1) the optimization of farm output over a much longer time period than is usual in industrial farming activities; (2) the promotion and maintenance of diversified agroecosystems whose living components perform complementary functions; (3) the building up of soil fertility with organic matter and the protection of nutrients from leaching; (4) the promotion of continuous cover and the extensive use of legume-based rotations, cover crops, and green manures; and (5) the limiting of imported fertilizer applications and pesticide uses.[14] The idea of integrated farming systems is an important new development in the ecological approach to sustainability.[15]

While membership in the stewardship school includes many who subscribe to these principles largely for ideological reasons,[16] an increasing number of recruits have embraced some of them for intensely practical reasons. As the prices of petroleum-based energy inputs have risen during the last dozen years, many farmers have sought ways to limit increases in production costs. Conventional techniques use two to five times as much energy per unit of output as do the methods of ecological agriculture—a margin of difference which their superior productivity no longer is assured of overcoming.[17] Accordingly, many large-scale producers are beginning to show interest in the energy-saving features of ecological agriculture, for example, the rapid spread of low-till agriculture.

In the ecological approach, agricultural sustainability depends on the availability of a renewable resource base and control of demands on its output that will insure against its depletion. Consequently, ecologically minded people also tend to monitor population size and its per capita consumption levels. Since most estimates of sustainable levels of world populations place them in the range of one to four billion people,[18] and since world population almost certainly will grow for the next fifty to seventy-five years, most members of the stewardship school favor doing everything possible to restrict the size of the maximum population and to conserve the resource base on which the sustainable population ultimately must depend. They tend to take seriously calls for moderation in levels of living.

III. Sustainability as Community

A third group of people subscribe to yet another set of views that increasingly is being referred to as "radical" agriculture. Perhaps the most distinguishing feature of the movement is its focus on the values of community. A community is made up of individual living things, including human beings, whose lives most deeply affect one another.[19] The identity of agricultural communities traditionally has been based on the geographic proximity of individuals, reinforced with ties of kinship and patterns of common agricultural experiences. But as agricultural specialization has spread with the introduction of industrial farming techniques, the identification of these communities has been blurred by shifts in the locus and scale of decision-making and by the proliferation of new kinds of communities based more on class distinctions, common economic interests, participation in voluntary associations, or shared ideals.

Members of the radical agriculture movement are interested in these changes in the nature of agricultural communities because they imply fundamental changes in the quality of relationships within each community. The unusual richness of relationships within some communities produces a richness of experiences for individuals constituting such communities, and this richness of experiences, even more than conventional measures of success, such as wealth, prestige, and power, is what radical agriculturalists regard as the primary means of individual fulfillment and happiness. In this sense, the community school of agricultural sustainability has come to be called radical.

Radical agriculturalists believe that the richness of relationships within a community depends on the readiness of its members to acknowledge and promote a mutuality of concern and interest among its participants, human and non-human.[20] Social relations within the human community should be cooperative rather than competitive. Also they must not regard land, water, and growing things as resources to be tamed and brought under their control—this attitude of dominance over nature is what has led to the depletion of natural resources and the destruction of stable social structures. Rather, by becoming the "trustees of the life of the topsoil,"[21] community members show respect for the complexity of natural processes and relations, for natural variety, and for the forms of human community that stabilize and live at peace with nature's ecosystems.

To illustrate the adverse effects on sustainable communities of modern energy-intensive agriculture, radical agriculturalists point out that many small American rural communities have withered and died needlessly. Citing Walter Goldschmidt's 1978 classic study and other evidence, they note that family-type farming communities seem to support more people at measurable higher levels of living and with smaller income disparities than in communities dominated by larger operations;[22] they apparently provide better community facilities and services such as school, parks, paved streets, sewage disposal, newspapers, civic organizations, and other public services; and they appear to encourage more institutions for democratic decision-making involving all the citizens. Significant too is evidence that most adults in family-type farming communities are independent entrepreneurs, whereas less than 20 percent of adults in industrial farming communities has an entrepreneurial stake in the community. This fact led Phil Raup to conclude that the migration of key technical, financial, and organizational decisions to larger farming entities, some with headquarters far removed from local communities, has stripped non-family sized farming communities of decision-makers with power to affect the life of the community in significant ways.[23]

In short, the agricultural crisis is a crisis of culture, according to radical agriculturalists:

> A healthy farm culture can be based only upon familiarity and can grow only among a people soundly established upon the land; it nourishes and safeguards a human intelligence of the earth that no amount of technology can satisfactorily replace. The growth of such a culture was once a strong possibility in the farm communities of this country. We now have only the sad remnants of those communities. If we allow another generation to pass without doing what is necessary to enhance and embolden the possibility now perishing with them, we will lose it altogether. And then we will not only invoke calamity—we will deserve it.[24]

IV. A Reformed Approach to Sustainability

Having reviewed three schools of thought about agricultural sustainability, our next task is to ask whether there is anything in the values and commitments of our Reformed tradition which should influence our judgment of their possibilities or appropriateness for dealing with the problems of feeding the world for the indefinite future. Thus, we need to clarify what might be characteristically Reformed elements in a contemporary ethic.

In his two volume work on *Ethics from a Theocentric Perspective,* James Gustafson expresses a preference for the Reformed tradition. It is distinguished from other traditions, he proposes, by its strong affirmation of (1) the sovereignty of God, (2) the centrality of piety, by which he means an attitude of reverence and awe and a felling of obligation before God, and (3) a disciplined ordering of human activities to accord with what are understood to be God's purposes. Gustafson sees affinity between his own thought and Calvin's, where one gets a sense

> of the powerful Other, of that on which all things ultimately depend, to which all are ultimately related, which both limits and sustains human

activities. That Other evokes piety; a sense of awe and reverence, the senses of dependence, gratitude, obligation, repentance, possibilities for action, and direction. Piety is, in a sense, the hinge which joins the frame of the moral and natural ordering of life to the door of human duties and obligations.[25]

Though Gustafson finds these characteristics a useable structure for ethics, he expresses his dissatisfaction with other aspects of the tradition, one of which is anthropocentrism, a conviction that the world exists for the sake of humanity and that God's governing of the universe is for the sake of the ultimate well-being of humanity. Gustafson has in mind, for example, Calvin's view that natural disasters, famine, or plague are God's punishment of human sinfulness, and that there is divine purpose in the fact that one nursing mother has ample milk for her infant and another does not.[26]

Gustafson's selection of Reformed characteristics, though certainly not beyond debate, seems a very useful place to begin discussion. It brings into focus Calvinism's highly theocentric orientation, its insistence on personal religious experience and the response of worship of God, as well as its demonstrated capacity to produce activists who pour their life energy into transforming human society so that the kingdom of God is more visible. Put in other words, it reminds us of the characteristically Reformed third use of the law: the Christian who is saved by God's grace alone willingly undertakes to do the will of God as it has been revealed in God's commandments. The only proper response to God's gracious activity is grateful worship, defined both as devotion and as obedience to God's will. The feelings or gratitude and devotion are quite naturally connected to obedient action. Despite the liberality of God's mercy and the fact that salvation in no way depends on human action, nonetheless humanity is accountable before God for obedience.

These elements of Reformed thought can be strikingly illustrated by Calvin's summary of Chapter I of the Book of Genesis:

After the world had been created, man was placed in it as in a theatre, that he beholding above him and beneath the wonderful works of God, might reverently adore their Author. Secondly, that all things were ordained for the use of man, that he, being under deeper obligation, might devote and dedicate himself entirely to obedience towards God. Thirdly, that he was endued with understanding and reason, that being distinguished from brute animals he might meditate on a better life, and might even tend directly towards God, whose image he bore engraven on his own person.[27]

Criticism of the Calvinistic focus on humanity at the expense of the rest of the created order must be examined in the light of the purposes of this paper. Two aspects of the criticism deserve special attention: first, the idea that the functioning of the created order reflects God's judgment on human sin; second, the seeming concern for human welfare at the expense of the rest of creation.

First, there is nothing peculiarly Calvinistic about the idea that natural disasters such as drought and famine, presumably not under human control, should be seen as the punishment of God for sin; this idea has been drawn out of biblical teaching all through the church's history. But modern people have had ample opportunity to observe the self-righteous way in which many Americans and western Europeans have seen their prosperity as a sign of God's approval and the poverty of the third world as a sign of God's displeasure. Since we now know that some aspects of drought-and-famine cycles are the result of mismanagement of the land, contemporary Christians cannot simply write them off as "acts of God." Calvin is very clear that where God makes human help available, we are expected to use it. In the midst of his discussion of God's providential activity which is so characteristic of his thought, Calvin warns against the scorning of prudent planning:

> For he who has set the limits to our life has at the same time entrusted to us its care; he has provided means and helps to preserve it; he has also made us able to foresee dangers; . . . he has offered precautions and remedies. Now it is very clear what our duty is: thus, if the Lord has committed to us the protection of our life, our duty is to protect it; if he offers helps, to use them; if he forewarns us of dangers, not to plunge headlong; if he makes remedies available, not to neglect them. . . . God's providence does not always meet us in its naked form, but God in a sense clothes it with the means employed.[28]

Though surely we are called today to use all means available to manage land wisely, we are left with the theological and ethical problem that many innocent people today suffer from the mismanagement of the land by their foreparents. The very positive aspects of a strong Reformed doctrine of providence must be liberated from any temptation to use it as a club in the hands of the healthy and comfortable against the weak and poor.

The second form of criticism has to do with putting humanity too exclusively at the center of the created order. Western Christianity, to a greater extent than eastern Christianity, has emphasized that the creation was made for humanity and is to be used for human welfare. Theological focus on the welfare of the creation apart from its usefulness to humanity appears infrequently. Consider, for example, the Book of Confessions where the doctrine of creation is surprisingly rare. The Nicene and the Apostles' creeds identify God as "maker of heaven and earth" but have nothing more to say about creation. The Scots Confession repeats this, refers to "the creation of man" in a peculiarly anthropocentric way (Chapter 11), and leaves it at that. The Heidelberg Catechism does slightly better, making reference to God's creation in relation to God's providential care for humanity in three of its one hundred twenty-nine questions and answers (questions 26–28 on the creed). It is not until one gets to Chapters VI and VII of The Second Helvetic Confession that one finds serious attention to the creation story, again in the context of the doctrine of providence; even so, one searches in vain within this chapter for explicit references to nature or the earth as part of God's creation; angels and "men" are declared most excellent among all creatures. Two other characteristic points are made here. In Chapter VI on providence, a concluding section reiterates Calvin's point about the importance of making use of the means available to us to preserve life, so far as they are recommended by Scripture. The confession explicitly disapproves of the attitude that belief in God's providence permits human beings to relax and do nothing. Chapter VII in its few lines on the creation story chooses to point out that God placed a human being (homo) in Paradise and made all things subject to him.

In the Westminster Confession of Faith, Chapter IV makes clear that God created the world "and all things therein, whether visible or invisible;" the chapter also acknowledges that "all" God's creation is "very good." But still again, virtually nothing is said about the natural environment or the way it should be cared for. This confession is unusually explicit, however, in pointing out that God's providence does extend to all creatures, though God takes special care of the church. Finally, even the two twentieth century confessions say little about non-human nature. The Theological Declaration of Barmen, written as it was in response to the German Nazi regime's attack on church authority, is mute on the subject. And The Confession of 1967, preoccupied with the theme or reconciliation, has only a few lines. This brief section clearly views nature as simply the context for human life:

> God has created the world of space and time to be the sphere of his dealings with men. In its beauty and vastness, sublimity and awfulness, order and disorder, the world reflects to the eye of faith the majesty and mystery of its Creator. . . . [God] has endowed man with capacities to make the world serve his needs and to enjoy its good things. . . . Man is free to seek his life within the purpose of God: to develop and protect the resources of nature for the common welfare, to work for justice and peace in society, and in other ways to use his creative powers for the fulfillment of human life. (9.16–17)

Once again we find a call to make use of all means available to liberate the world's needy and exploited from enslaving poverty, "an intolerable violation of God's good creation." (9.46) A final section mentions that God's redeeming work extends to the natural environment, which has been damaged by sin. (9.53)

Gustafson's criticism of the Reformed tradition's anthropocentrism must be taken seriously. Our Reformed confessional documents are so preoccupied with questions of human sin and redemption that the doctrine of creation receives only passing nods. Where non-human nature is mentioned at all, it is in the context of its relation to humanity.

The importance of this observation for questions of agricultural sustainability is that ecologists for nearly twenty years have been blaming the degradation of the environment on western Christianity's faulty teaching on the doctrine of creation. In his 1966 lecture on "The Historical Roots of Our Ecologic Crisis," Lynn White noted that exploitative attitudes towards nature became widespread in the Middle Ages, encouraged by a growing anthropocentrism of the prevailing religion. These attitudes helped shape modern thinking about science and technology—thinking, he says, that led us into the environmental crisis. Thus "Christianity bears a huge burden of guilt" for the crisis, he concluded, and now must redouble its efforts to "liberate" nature by reconstructing its theology of creation.[29]

Central to the environmentalists' objections to Christian teaching has been the interpretation of Genesis 1:26–30, where God gives humankind "dominion" over the earth and a command to "subdue" it. This debate was intensified recently when Pope John Paul II in his encyclical Laborem Exercens said that ". . . man is the image of God partly through the mandate received from his creator to subdue, to dominate, the earth." Again, "the expression 'subdue the earth' has an immense range. It means all the resources that the earth (and indirectly the visible world) contains and which, through the conscious activity of man, can be discovered and used for his ends." At a Notre Dame colloquy on the encyclical, Stanley Hauerwas commented:

> John Paul II's stress on 'domination' seems particularly insensitive in that we live at a time when many Christians and non-Christians alike are recovering a sense of our unity with nature and the animal world. We are learning that our task is not so much to dominate as it is to learn to live in a covenant with God's good creation. As James Gustafson has recently suggested, our task is not to control but to consent to God's good order. While I am certainly not suggesting that the Pope should underwrite the ecological romanticism so prevalent today, at the very least he should have felt some discomfort with any theological legitimation of the arrogance of our species' superiority, and the correlative assumption that we have the right to rape, or as John Paul II puts it, to 'master' the world.[30]

In the light of this discussion it is interesting that our survey of the Book of Confessions turned up only one reference to subduing the earth (II Helvetic Confession 5.034), and there either the author follows Genesis 2 where there is no direct command or the text of Genesis 1 has been paraphrased so as to eliminate the command: ". . . God placed him in Paradise and made all things subject to him." The Confession of 1967 assumes that the earth is at human disposal, but only "within the purpose of God: to develop and protect the resources of nature for the common welfare . . ." (9.17) Both in Calvin's commentaries on Genesis and the Book of Confessions the point made seems to be God's providential provision for humanity and human appointment as steward of creation rather than human domination of creation. These impressionistic observations suggest it might be fruitful to do further research to see whether the Reformed tradition may be less guilty of fostering exploitation of the land than White suggests, despite its clear anthropocentrism within the created order.

What then does the Reformed approach have to say to our three schools of thought about agricultural sustainability? To the food-sufficiency school, it communicates agreement that there is a moral obligation to share the bounty of creation with all human beings made in the image of God, and to assure that the means of preservation of life are available to all. It also enthusiastically endorses the use of human imagination, creativity, science and technology to make sufficient food available. Indeed, generally accepted human values and ethical principles dictate that science and technology (among the important attributes of humankind's culture) be used in the moral quest for an adequate food supply in both the short- and long-range future. We have seen the confessions insisting that we must use available means to protect life. Calvin sees science and technology as gifts of the Spirit for the common good and urges that they be used and not despised.[31] The Confession of 1967 is very explicit:

> The church cannot condone poverty, whether it is the product of unjust social structures, exploitation of the defenseless, lack of national resources, absence of technological understanding, or rapid expansion of populations. The church calls every man to use his abilities, his possessions, and the fruits of technology as gifts entrusted to him by God for the maintenance of his family and the advancement of the common welfare (9.46)[32]

But a simple affirmation of science and technology is an insufficient guide for action, since it is widely known that science and technology can be both blessings and curses. Not only can the development of new techniques enhance crop yields; it also can waste or damage natural resources, and it can impose unreasonable demands on individual and community relationships. Thus to the stewardship school of agricultural sustainability, Calvin himself identifies a connection between his respect for the goodness of God's creation and the need for careful management of the land. In his commentary on Genesis 2:15 he says:

> Moses adds, that the custody of the garden was given in charge to Adam, to show that we possess the things which God has committed to our hands, on the condition, that being content with a frugal and moderate use of them, we should take care of what shall remain. Let him who possesses a field, so partake of its yearly fruits, that he may not suffer the ground to be injured by his negligence: but let him endeavor to hand it down to posterity as he received it, or even better cultivated. . . . Moreover, that this economy, and this diligence, with respect to those

good things which God has given us to enjoy, may flourish among us; let every one regard himself as the steward of God in all things which he possesses. Then he will neither conduct himself dissolutely, nor corrupt by abuse those things which God requires to be preserved.[33]

The idea of the Christian as "steward" of god's gifts in order to put them at the disposal of others in need has come to be a particularly Calvinistic emphasis. Precisely because God's world is good, it should be used with care and moderation in order that all God's children can enjoy its bounty. Closely related to this of course is the Cavlinistic tradition of a simple lifestyle, without ostentation, to conserve resources for sharing with others.

One further point can be made: Calvinists have characteristically been open to the future, rebuilding institutions and society if need be to make the kingdom of God visible. Calvin never shared Luther's sense that the world was about to come to an end, though the world is not eternal. Cavlinists expect God to fulfill his work in creation someday, in God's own good time, but in the meantime they plan for the future. This would be further incentive for affirmation of the stewardship school.

It is difficult to respond to the community school of agricultural sustainability because until recently no one ever envisaged that the rural community could disappear. Whereas Luther tended to romanticize himself as a farmer with manure on his boots, affirming good solid rural German values over against those who lived by trading luxury goods from abroad, Calvin is unabashedly a city dweller. Though the Reformed tradition certainly attracted strong rural following, as in France, it flourished in cities. Nonetheless Calvin preached to his Genevan congregation the kinds of values of mutual responsibility, stewardship, and interdependence which the community school is eager to preserve.

To all three schools the Reformed tradition would say that human knowledge is finite and human motivations are mixed. Surmounting all obstacles rationally and continuously is not possible. Even well-intended projects sometimes produce bad results. Thus a Reformed view of sustainability would take fully into account both the promises of an increased supply of nutrients for the world population through scientific and technological innovations, and the potential hazards for the ecological and social environment of adopting some innovations rather than others. While some of these "externalities" may be global in scope, for example, the impact of acid rain on soil and water resource availability, others such as soil erosion and pesticide poisoning or community dislocation are more limited in immediate geographic effect. Policies directed at sustaining a future human population must be constantly monitored and changed whenever it appears that the side effects of further technological interventions begin to undermine the capacity of nature to sustain other forms of life. As noted by Gustafson, "while man, by virtue of human capacities, has a special dominion, nonetheless all things are 'good,' and not just good for us. Special dominion implies special accountability as much as special value."[34]

V. Sustainability as Seen in Recent Church Pronouncements

Two church documents published in 1985 offer a unique opportunity to assess the churchs' biases about sustainable agriculture. The first, an additional chapter on "Food and Agriculture Policies" issued in May, 1985, by the U.S. Catholic Bishops, amends the first draft of their pastoral on "Catholic Social Teaching and the U.S. Economy" released in November, 1984. The other document, a "Resolution on Rural Community in Crisis," was approved by the 197th General Assembly of the Presbyterian Church (U.S.A.) in June, 1985.

Chapter 5 of the Catholic Bishops' pastoral identifies most directly with the community school. Its defense of family-sized farming is justified not on ecological grounds—indeed, it studiously avoids references to family farmers as good stewards of nature—but on the argument that family-sized farms promote meaningful participation by owners and laborers in the structure of production and that the economic and political decisions made by family farmers nurture healthy rural communities. It says virtually nothing about producing enough food for the world's people.

The latter point deserves emphasis. By ignoring altogether the arguments made by the food-sufficiency school, the Catholic Bishops seem either to dismiss the problems of balancing supply and demand of nutritious foodstuffs as unworthy of their time and effort, or, more likely, to be assuming that their strong affirmation in other portions of the pastoral of the importance of fulfilling the basic needs of the poor will somehow lead to a "working out" of these macroeconomic concerns. At only one isolated point do they seem aware of the potential effects on productivity of a radical restructuring of American agriculture: "Beyond the present crisis," they say, "small- and moderate-sized farms will remain in operation only if they continue to be efficient and economically competitive." (para 31) To help them be so, the Bishops recommend a reordering of federal and state research and development expenditures in favor of technologies and management practices suited to medium-sized farms (para 31). The question of whether this would be enough to assure their survival is not taken up in the chapter.

The Bishops' lack of attention to the concepts of sustainability found in the stewardship school, though understandable, is nonetheless shocking. There are only two references in the chapter to the importance of encouraging resource preservation. The first catalogues the primary kinds of resource depletion (para 15) and the second says that society as a whole is responsible for the stewardship of natural resources (para 34). No effort is made to identify agroecological differences between alternative farming practices, or even to hazard a guess about the impact on renewable and nonrenewable resource supplies of differing structures of farm ownership. Alternatives to conventional farming practices that limit petrochemical uses, promote crop rotations and diverse plantings, and optimize output decisions over a longer time period than most industrial farms are not even mentioned—despite dramatic improvements in their plausibility recently. In short, the Bishops simply don't seem interested in ecological questions.

Their interest in the questions of human communities, on the other hand, is very high indeed. After summarizing the "human distress" associated with recent changes in the structure of American farm ownership (para 2–4), the Bishops declare that "we cannot stand by while thousands of farm families caught in the present crisis lose their homes, their land, and their way of life." (para 17) Thus they propose a series of actions—access to emergency credit for both family farmers and rural lending institutions in distress (para 28); reassessment of federal price support, tax, labor, and research policies that now favor large operations at the expense of small- and medium-sized farms (para 29–31)—that they hope will bring vitality back into the traditional family farm system in the United States. More interesting than these proposals, though, are the reasons stated by the Bishops for supporting them.

For example, "wide distribution in the ownership of productive property . . . provides incentives for diligence and is a source of an increased sense that the work being done is truly one's own." (para 19) Powerful firms, it is alleged, are more self-conscious about the rate of return to invested capital than are family farmers; in times of distress, therefore, family farmers are more likely to tough it out in hope of better times, "and thereby enhance national and global food security." The life of rural communities also benefits, according to the arguments of this chapter, because full-time family farmers tend to spend more locally and relate more closely to local social and political and cultural institutions. Note, however, that these are human institutions; the Bishops have nothing to say about the habits and traditions of full-time farmers that link their human existence to other forms of community, viz., the animals and organisms and natural phenomena that make up the richness of experiences in rural communities. "Trustees of the life of the topsoil" the Bishops are not!

The "Resolution on Rural Community in Crisis" approved by the 197th General Assembly is not as easily identified with a particular school or agricultural sustainability as is the Catholic Bishops' pastoral. Since it dwells primarily on the damage being done to farm families and communities by the radical changes now underway in American agriculture, it too can be thought of as affirming the vision of agricultural sustainability found in the Community School. Its theological focus, on the other hand, is on the Old Testament understanding of land as a gift, a trust, a covenant from God, suggesting instead a serious identification with the stewardship school. Yet no more is said in its description of the rural crisis about the need to husband scarce agricultural resources than is mentioned by the Catholic Bishops. As found there too, nothing is said about the compelling need to assure adequate nutrition for the world's ballooning population.

The most plausible explanation for why the resolution seems to be less clear about the meaning of sustainability (even though it uses the term repeatedly), is that its primary purpose is to tell a story about the immediate crisis of rural America—about the "bitter reality of impending doom" (28.823) manifest in lowering farm prices, high energy costs, rising debt, falling land values, and worrysome rates of farm and farmer bankruptcies. One of its techniques of story-telling is to let those experiencing the pains of adjustment speak for themselves. Thus the paper is a mosaic of quotations far more than an analysis of the causes and lasting consequences of the crisis. It communicates feelings more than understandings; accordingly, it is never very clear why the authors favor family farming compared to other structures of production, or why they think particular recommendations will improve its chances of survival.

A sure sense of what the paper means by sustainability may be missing also because it lacks a coherent theological and ethical point of view. Most attempts by the General Assembly to establish positions on issues of public moment begin with thorough reviews of biblical teachings, theological understandings, and ethical norms relevant to each issue at hand. This is especially important in the Reformed tradition that draws so heavily on biblical and creedal understandings to discern the proper ordering of human life. Yet this paper begins with a description of human suffering without reference to its religious significance. The prophetic vision is not encountered until the end of the descriptive material, and then seemingly more as a means of justifying what has been said than of giving direction to the analysis of the rural crisis. It is not a very Presbyterian approach to social witness.

"Who Will Farm?" a report approved by the 190th General Assembly (1978) of the predecessor United Presbyterian Church in the U.S.A., in contrast, is abundantly clear about the meaning and significance of sustainable agriculture. To the argument that bigger is better, the report takes note of numerous studies that show family farms to be as efficient as larger farms; accordingly, the trend towards larger producing units and concentrated farm ownership need not yield higher levels of production. Large industrial farms also encourage development of crop varieties that weaken taste, change texture, and lower nutrition, it observes, compared to crops typically cultivated by smaller operators. Family farmers also are said to have a more "genuine" concern for their land and a more responsible approach to resource conservation than larger industrial operations. Then, too, the retention of traditional family farming structures is essential to preserve the vitality and stability of rural communities, the report avers. "The family farm is both a viable economic unit and a valuable part of our national life," the report concludes: "a diversified system of agriculture, with control dispersed among many persons, is more conducive to equity and justice in our society than a system where control is increasingly concentrated in relatively few hands." (22)

Perhaps the most interesting feature of this testimony is the assertion that family farming promotes both ecological balance and community stability without sacrificing productivity. Rather than identifying trade-offs among the objectives of different schools of agricultural sustainability, "Who Will Farm?" seems to be saying that a diversified system of farming enterprises—including a dominant family-farming segment—can achieve economic efficiency, biological equilibrium, and social equity simultaneously, without the need to sacrifice some of one to get more of another. This is an interesting assertion which we shall take up in the final section.

VI. Reformed Faith and Public Policies for Sustainability

The purpose of this final section of the paper is twofold: First, we attempt with the aid of our understandings of the Reformed tradition to integrate into a single conception the three dominant visions of agricultural sustainability developed in the opening portions of the paper. And second, we explore the degree to which the fashioning of such a conception requires the sacrifice of important values held by one or another of these sustainability schools—that is to say, whether the trade-offs potential in such an exercise are real. This exploration leads us to summarize some recent findings, primarily from the literature and experience of economic development, that suggest ways to alter public policies for the purpose of minimizing the trade-offs among sustainability objectives.

Our first stylized school of agricultural understanding—that agriculture is sustainable when farmers produce enough food to meet reasonable projections of global market demand—leads immediately to the question: At what economic, environmental, and human costs? One way to begin reconciling this understanding with alternative views is to insist that future agricultural systems meet reasonable future demands for foodstuffs without imposing on society real increases in social costs of production. Social costs, as the term is used by some economists, would include economic costs (the outlays natural resource economists tend to call "externalities"), and the costs of community dislocation (outlays rarely if ever considered by economists in calculating project costs and benefits). Real social costs would be nominal social costs adjusted for changes in the general price level. In this preliminary and general way, we might begin to account for the concerns of people allied with the stewardship school and community school of sustainability.

To be sure, this conceptual compromise begs almost as many questions as it answers. What does it mean to limit future demands for foodstuffs, for example, to "reasonable" levels? What changes in social institutions and processes are implied by efforts to limit future demands to reasonable levels, and are these changes plausibly attainable given prospective arrangements of decision-making power at home and in the world at large? Does the measure of reasonableness also suggest a degree of vigor in population control that is either infeasible or improbable? Might one component of real social costs be allowed to rise and still judge systems to be sustainable as long as other components of cost are expected to fall enough over time to offset tendencies for real social costs to rise? What specific techniques of production, processing, and distribution should be chosen under given circumstances to minimize economic, environmental, and human costs and given projections of future demands for foodstuffs? What forms of incentives or commands ought society to institute in order to ensure appropriate technological choices? To what extent should nations try to become self-sufficient in the production of basic foodstuffs? What roles for international trade in foodstuffs and food security assistance would be likely in a more sustainable agricultural system? Can a system of social accounting be devised to identify when society suffers increasing or decreasing real social costs of production? These are important questions that deserve systematic attention.

Knowledge of the Reformed tradition is helpful to a limited degree in constructing specific answers to some of these questions. Reformed judgment surely reflects the ethical principle that every human being, no matter how poor, should have sufficient nourishment and therefore that whenever markets price adequate nutrition for the poor prohibitively, other means must be found to meet their basic needs for food. Reformed thought also is reasonably clear that in circumstances where well-off Christians consume and pollute at a rate which is greater than would be possible for all the people of the world, they should be ready to sacrifice their interests for the sake of the needs of others. Thus the principle of modesty in lifestyle has a place in the determination of reasonable levels of food demand. But Reformed thought is not operational in the sense that it would be helpful in setting precisely the level of basic nutritional needs or in constructing particular policies to restrain the appetites of higher-income people for needlessly rich diets of food. Those are matters best left to the markets, technocrats and body-politics of the world.

Similarly, a Reformed perspective makes clear that any rule of reason about the level of prospective food demand ought to include practical limits on the rate of population growth as well as concern with the adequacy of nutritional standards. Reformed Christians disagree with the Roman Catholic Church in this regard by suggesting that artificial means of conception control are morally justified in some circumstances, especially when population is pressing hard on available resources. For Catholics who believe there are no such circumstances, technological innovations that increase food production become the primary, if not the only, morally approved course of action;[35] and this action runs grave risks of undermining the capacity to produce for future generations. Reformed Christians, on the other hand, while affirming appropriate technological advances, also emphasize the importance of human individuals understanding their interdependence with the "wholes" of life and making adjustments in their own behavior to better serve the communities of which they are part. Ethical principles derived from Reformed thought have preferences for voluntary restraints in matters such as birth control,[36] but they nonetheless could sanction collective action in circumstances of intense imbalance between food and population. What particular policies to follow, however, would have to be decided within the community.

Yet again, the Reformed tradition offers significant guidance in the matter of technological choice, but only up to the point of confronting the facts of particular circumstances. A properly Reformed view of scientific investigations and technological developments is that they are potentially a means of preserving and enhancing nature's own gifts. They offer enormous opportunities for raising the productive capacities of economic systems over time. But they also can disrupt or destroy the environment and community life. The key to choosing the right kind of technology, therefore, is to make sure that it yields the best kind of economic, environmental and human results—in short, that the technology that is chosen is "appropriate." What is appropriate, of course, depends on the objectives to be served. Economic efficiency calls for techniques that husband the scarcest resources in order to minimize costs; ecological and environmental balance requires techniques that conserve the natural order; human and community vitality suggest techniques that encourage human interaction and opportunity. These objectives, as they are sought by alternative processes, may or may not lead to technological conflicts. The processes that create new technologies must be aware of potential conflicts and try to adapt and adjust prospective designs to achieve as many objectives as possible in selected systems. Since there is no political or economic power bloc serving the common good of nature and future generations of the human species, the critical moral concern from a Reformed point of view is to help assure that the monitoring and correcting of new technologies are not subverted by economic and political special interests operating outside the limits of life's ordering in the world.

Our composite definition of agricultural sustainability raises still other questions that deserve more attention than we can give them here. Let us conclude instead with some comments about the design of public policies that can help to minimize the extent of trade-offs between the objectives of food sufficiency, ecological balance and community stability.

Jan Tinbergen, the noted Dutch economist and Nobel Laureate, drew upon a familiar mathematical theorem when he observed that policy-makers faced with several objectives they want to achieve simultaneously must harness to the task at least an equal number of policy instruments; otherwise, he said, policy-makers will have to trade-off one or another objective to achieve others—unless they turn out to be very lucky.

Tinbergen's insights have been put to good use recently among people seeking ways to limit the trade-offs of development in the Third World. How should the strategies of agricultural development be altered to yield results that better accord with the performance standards of our composited definition of agricultural sustainability? Indeed, are there any ways at all to reduce the trade-offs of ecological stability and social equity for abundant supplies of foodstuffs without undermining our capacities to meet reasonable demands for food and fiber in the future? We believe that a key to answering these questions in the affirmative is a strategy of integrated rural development applied both in the developing countries where its logic already is being explored[37] and in developed countries where rapid structural changes have placed the entire agricultural enterprise at risk.

For the developing countries, integrated rural development implies a three-pronged development strategy including (1) broad-based, unimodal approaches to output and employment growth using human labor more efficiently, thereby generating incomes that enable the poor to improve their level of consumption; (2) improved programs of education, health, nutrition, and family planning that reduce fertility, enhance productivity, and improve income distributions; and (3) increased attention to the institutional infrastructure and managerial skills needed for rural development, including those that encourage the ecological soundness of agricultural practices. A further word about each of these strategies may be helpful.

The first prong of integrated rural development depends upon the important insight that food consumption, development, and employment are tightly interdependent. The level of food consumption in developing countries is closely related to income that is available, since 70–85 percent of family incomes among the poor ordinarily is spent on food.[38] Family income, in turn, is highly correlated with the availability of gainful employment and the productivity of employed workers. And levels of employment and productivity are usually a function of the structure and vigor of development in late developing countries.[39] A unimodal rather than bimodal approach to development—especially in agriculture—is recommended because it has been shown in varied settings that smaller-scale, more labor-intensive producing units in both agriculture and industry tend to be more successful at generating employment and raising productivity as well as more likely to improve the distribution of income and opportunity than bimodal or dualistic structures of production that often cater heavily to export markets.[40] Additional confirmation of the usefulness of a unimodal strategy is found in the story of the "Green Revolution": Countries that continued to employ labor-using, capital-saving technologies, relying heavily on divisible innovations such as the high-yield, fertilizer-responsive crop varieties of the Green Revolution, grew faster and with less adverse effects on income distribution than those that continued a bimodal strategy.[41]

The second prong of an integrated rural development strategy involves programs to strengthen education, health, nutrition, and family planning. While mounting major efforts in these complex areas is difficult while promoting rapid economic development, they are important means of assuring equity with growth. Measures to improve nutrition and health, especially among the poorer parts of the population of developing countries, have very desirable effects on workers' productivity and, indirectly, on fertility rates. Primary education, especially of girls, also has been found to give favorable effects on the next generation's health, fertility and education. Policies to lower fertility rates are essential, lest continuing rapid rates of population increase aggravate the task of expanding employment opportunities fast enough to absorb additions to the labor force. Unless family planning spreads among low-income rural households, the widespread oversupply of unskilled labor is bound to depress labor incomes and therefore worsen the chances of assuring adequate nutrition for all.[42]

Integrated rural development also requires careful effort to enhance institutional infrastructure and managerial skills needed for rural development. Organizational requirements are not easily fulfilled; indeed they are not likely to be satisfied unless major energy is put into the design and implementation of governing structures. These structures or "frameworks" provide the means by which individuals can undertake collective actions—identifying claims, distributing resources, improving resource productivity, capturing additional resources—which improve the well-being of the rural poor. National and regional governments, cooperative associations, informal groups of volunteers all may be involved at one time or another; effective rural development requires that they be trained for the task and increasingly that the rural poor have a dominant voice in their direction. Only then can one really expect "trickle-down" to work.

Thus integrated rural development requires simultaneous concern for production, consumption, and organization—rather than preoccupation with production as commonly practiced. This is not easy because attaining multiple objectives simultaneously is difficult in most policy settings. Even taking the first step of trying to develop a concensus favoring a particular set of objectives is harder than it seems. But in one respect, a strategy of integrated rural development helps to avoid the difficulties that have plagued the economics profession over the perceived trade-off between growth and equity. By focusing on the complementarities among rather than the competition between objectives, this strategy has helped to reconcile some of the conflicts seen in achieving sustainable agriculture.

The key requirement, in our judgment, is that rural development programs be chosen with due regard for both the rate of technical change and the biases inherent in technical change. Foregoing technical change and advances in productivity would be disastrous for developing countries because the output and income they produce are desperately needed by the vast majority of their people. But if those technical advances are biased in a labor-saving, capital-using direction, most people in rural areas will not share the fruit of productivity's advance. Indeed, there is an unsettling accumulation of evidence that rural areas suffer worsened conditions in the implementation of bimodal, industry-first strategies of development.[43] Efforts simultaneously to accelerate the growth of farm output (a prerequisite, many believe, for generalized development) and to expand employment opportunities require simultaneous concern for the rate and bias of technical change. To concentrate only on its rate or its bias is an inefficient means of reducing poverty and improving nutrition in low-income countries.

If, in addition, methods of technical advance in agriculture can be chosen with an eye for long-range ecological balance, another giant step towards more sustainable agricultural systems will be taken. We are pleased to report that genuine signs of progress have been made towards this objective recently. It has resulted from new research initiatives by the network of international agricultural research stations coordinated by the United Nations-linked Consultative Group on International Agricultural Research (CGIAR). The research initiative we speak of is called farming systems research. It is concerned not with the maximization of production of a particular commodity but with the optimization of outcomes of the entire farming system. Accordingly, it tends to redirect research away from disciplinary and commodity orientations and towards the complex interdependence of people, crops, soil, livestock, environment, and communities. Preliminary findings suggest that implementation of farming-systems techniques do not necessarily lower productivity in specific crops. That the international agricultural research and training institutes have been the first to develop these techniques speaks well for their orientation towards sustainable outcomes.[44]

A similar three-prong strategy of agricultural development would greatly aid the transition in America from a production-oriented, resource-exploiting, dehumanizing agricultural system to one that cares about the quality of its output and its rural life. Hard thinking about consumption and institutional strategies has been as lacking here as in many parts of the developing world, yet integrated rural development in America requires it—if we are to achieve agricultural sustainability in the foreseeable future.

Endnotes

1. Gordon K. Douglass, *Agricultural Sustainability in a Changing World Order* (Boulder: Westview Press, 1984).

2. K. O. Campbell, *Food for the Future: How Agriculture Can Meet the Challenge* (Lincoln: University of Nebraska Press, 1979), p. 58.

3. M. E. Abel, "Growth in Demand for U.S. Crop and Animal Production by 2005," in P. R. Crosson, ed., *The Cropland Crisis: Myth or Reality?* (Baltimore: The Johns Hopkins Press, 1982).

4. John W. Mellor and Bruce F. Johnston, "The World Food Equation: Interrelations Among Development, Employment, and Food Consumption," in *Journal of Economic Literature*, vol. 22 (June 1984).

5. Pierre R. Crosson and Anthony T. Stout, *Productivity Effects of Cropland Erosion in the U.S.* (Washington, D.C.: Resources for the Future, 1983).

6. Pierre R. Crosson and Sterling Brubaker, *Resource and Environmental Effects of U.S. Agriculture* (Washington, D.C.: Resources for the Future, 1982).

7. Yujiro Hayami and Vernon W. Ruttan, *Agricultural Development: An International Perspective* rev. ed. (Baltimore: The Johns Hopkins University Press, 1985).

8. Robert E. Evenson and Yoav Kislev, *Agricultural Research and Productivity* (New Haven: Yale University Press, 1975). Vernon W. Ruttan, *Agricultural Research Policy* (Minneapolis: University of Minnesota Press, 1982).

9. Crosson and Brubaker, 1982.

10. *Ibid*, p. 138.

11. P. Hazel, "Sources of Increased Variability in World Cereal Production," (Washington, D.C.: International Food Policy Research Institute, 1984).

12. Lester Brown, *Building a Sustainable Society* (New York: W. W. Norton & Co., 1981).

13. William Lockeretz, ed., *Environmentally Sound Agriculture* (New York: Praeger, 1983).

14. Gil Friend, "The Potential of an Alternative Agriculture," in D. Knorr, ed., *Sustainable Food Systems* (Westport: AVI Publishing Co., 1983).

15. Thomas C. Edens and H. E. Konig, "Agroecosystem Management in a Resource-Limited World," in *BioScience* 30:697–701. Thomas C. Edens, et al., eds., *Sustainable Agriculture and Integrated Farming Systems* (East Lansing: Michigan State University Press, 1985).

16. Garth Youngberg, "Alternative Agriculture in the United States: Ideology, Politics, and Prospects," in D. Knorr and T. R. Watkins, eds., *Alterations in Food Production* (New York: Van Nostrand Reinhold Co., 1984).

17. William Lockeretz, G. Shearer, and D. H. Kohl, "Organic Farming in the Corn Belt," in *Science* vol. 211 (Feb. 1981).

18. A. H. Ehrlich, "Feeding the Transitional Society," in J. C. Coomer, ed., *Quest for a Sustainable Society* (New York: Pergamon Press, 1981).

19. Charles Birch and John B. Cobb, Jr., *The Liberation of Life* (Cambridge: Cambridge University Press, 1981).

20. Wes Jackson, Wendell Berry, and Bruce Colman, eds., *Meeting the Expectations of the Land* (San Francisco: North Point Press, 1984).

21. Wendell Berry, "Where Cities and Farms Come Together," in R. Merrill, ed., *Radical Agriculture* (New York: Harper & Row, 1976), p. 18.

22. Walter Goldschmidt, *As You Sow: Three Studies in the Social Consequences of Agribusiness* (Montclair: Allenheld, Osuman & Co., 1978).

23. Phil M. Raup, "Societal Goals in Farm Size," in A. G. Ball and E. O. Heady, eds., *Size, Structure, and Future of Farms* (Ames: Iowa State University, 1972).

24. Wendell Berry, *The Unsettling of America: Culture and Agriculture* (San Francisco: Sierra Club, 1977), p. 81.

25. James M. Gustafson, *Ethics from a Theocentric Perspective* 2 vols. (Chicago: University of Chicago Press, 1981, 1984), vol. 1, p. 167.

26. *Ibid.*, pp. 165f, 178–182, 188, 190f.

27. John Calvin, *Commentaries on the First Book of Moses Called Genesis*, vol. 1, tr. The Rev. John King, (Grand Rapids: Eerdmans, 1948).

28. John Calvin, *Institutes of the Christian Religion*, ed. John T. McNeill, tr. Ford Lewis Battles (Philadelphia: The Westminster Press, 1960), I:xvii, 4.

29. Lynn Whtie, Jr., "The Historical Roots of our Ecological Crisis," *Science* vol. 155 (1967).

30. Stanley Hauerwas, "Work as 'Co-Creation'—A Remarkably Bad Idea," in *This World* no. 3 (Fall 1982), pp. 92f.

31. Calvin, *Institutes*, II:ii, 15–16.

32. cf., Calvin, *Institutes*, III:x, 5.

33. Calvin, *Commentary Genesis*, p. 125.

34. Gustafson, vol. 1, p. 109.

35. Gustafson, vol. 2, p. 229.

36. *Ibid.*, pp. 247ff.

37. Johnson and Clark, *Redesigning Rural Development;* Ruttan, *Agricultural Research Policy.*

38. World Bank, World Development Report, 1980 (Washington D.C.: World Bank, 1980), p. 61.

39. Mellor and Johnson, "The World Food Equation."

40. *Ibid.*

41. M. Prahladachar, "Income Distribution Effects of the Green Revolution in India: A Review of Empirical Evidence," in *World Development*, vol. 11, no. 11 (November, 1983).

42. World Bank, *Reports 1980 and 1984.*

43. Hayami and Ruttan, *Agricultural Development.*

44. Douglass, *Agricultural Sustainability.*

Chapter Nine

An Order in Crisis, and the Declaration of New Things

William E. Gibson

Behold, the former things have come to pass
And new things I now declare . . . (Is. 42:9)

The Necessary, Offensive, and Radical Question

As I was thinking about writing this paper, my radical young friend
dropped by. (I think of him as young, even though he was a 19-year-
old college student in 1968). Abruptly, I asked, "What do you think
of the economic system?"

"It creates vast disparities of wealth," he replied without hesitation.
"It destroys the ecology and is not viable in the long run. It makes
gross demands on resources . . ."

He went on for quite some time. Many Presbyterians would be put
off by his analysis. Nevertheless, most of it is unexceptional. Disparities between rich and poor *are* great. Capitalism depends on growth,
and that is contradictory to conservation. If the economy shrinks, it
means depression and lots of people lose their jobs. The wage-
earner's situation is precarious indeed.

But what about the benefits of the modern capitalist economy?
Certainly no previous system ever came close to being so productive.
Surely we prefer the problem of distributing to that of stretching
scarcity.

But does the present system have the capability of ever solving the

distribution problem—especially if its global dimensions are acknowledged? Why is the United States so hostile to revolutions? Do the
essential characteristics of the present system make it prone always to
block the equitable distribution of goods, the prudent conservation
of resources, and the full participation of "surplus" workers and
"excluded" peasants? Can it be made to serve the deepest values of
our faith, or can those values generate only a rearguard action against
the fallout from the economy's inherent dynamic?

Presbyterians must ask the question: Does the Reformed faith lead
them *to affirm the existing economic order in its essentials* and to work
within that order for the reforms and improvements that might make
it better serve the purpose of justice, peace, human freedom, and
convenantal community, *or* does it lead them *to become participants in
the shaping of an essentially different order* which may be more in keeping
with the will of God for these times?

The question has been made necessary by the unprecedented crisis
of this historical moment. It will be offensive or at least threatening,
because many, probably most, Presbyterians have been well served in
material terms by the existing order. And the question is appropriately radical, for it cuts to the very heart of the capability of Presbyterians to be led by God as servants in a time of extraordinary danger
that now becomes almost impossible not to see, and also perhaps
extraordinary possibility that can still only dimly be perceived.

The Economic Order in the Plan of God

The basic view of the economic order in the Reformed tradition
was well stated by Swiss theologian Emil Brunner. The purpose of
economic activity, said Brunner, is "to provide the individual and the
community with the material goods that are necessary for life"—not
just that people may eat and survive but "that [their] *human* life may
be preserved." This formal purpose, while it applies to every economy, is only introductory to the understanding of what drives and
shapes a particular economy:

> . . . the motive force of every economic system is the 'system of values' of
> the economic community, and its dynamic and its structure finally issue
> from its 'general outlook on life': its faith or its superstition.[1]

Economic order, according to Brunner, belongs to the plan of the Creator for human beings. They cannot exist without material goods; by their labor they obtain or create them.

> Since God has created man as a corporeal being, He has also created him as a being needing an economic order, and capable of creating an economic order. Thus the economic order forms part of the original Divine order in creation; as such, like all Divine order, it is at the same time a Divine law. Man is commanded to create an economic order.[2]

And with that commandment comes naturally the obligation to participate in the economic community, not only by enjoying economic goods but also by contributing to their creation.

John Calvin in the *Institutes* regards a person's participation in the economic community as "what he owes to others according to the responsibility of his own calling." To withhold this—that is, not to work in accordance with one's calling—violates the commandment against stealing. We obey that commandment properly, says Calvin.

> if, content with our lot, we are zealous to make only honest and lawful gain; if we do not seek to become wealthy through injustice, nor attempt to deprive our neighbor of his goods to increase our own; if we do not seek to heap up riches cruelly wrung from the blood of others; if we do not madly scrape together from everywhere, by fair means or foul, whatever will feed our avarice or satisfy our prodigality.[3]

While Calvin regarded human labor as under the curse consequent upon the Fall, he saw the origin of labor as prior to the Fall. "The Lord God took the man and put him in the Garden of Eden to till it and keep it." (Gen. 2:15) This custody of the garden as given to Adam shows us, says Calvin, not only that we are "to employ [ourselves] in some work" but also that we possess the things which God has committed to our hands, on the condition, that being content with a frugal and moderate use of them, we should take care of what shall remain." Let the possessor of a field "hand it down to posterity as he received it, or even better cultivated." ". . . let everyone regard himself as the steward of God in all things he possesses."[4]

But of course all actual work is carried on "after the Fall" within a system permeated by sin. In every economic order, says Brunner, there is an "alienation from its Divine purpose." The alienation, inherent in the order itself, is two-fold:

. . . on the one hand, it has been spoilt by its false tendency to become an end in itself, and on the other by egoistic exploitation by the individual which always works out both as sin and as a curse.[5]

The sinful corruption of the order, however, does not constitute justification for a refusal to take part in it. It remains true that by means of this order, and only by means of it, God gives us life. Therefore, the first question for the Christian is not how to get out of it or even how to change it, but how to serve within it. Corrupt as it is, it remains the sphere and the instrument, not only for preserving one's own life, but for serving the neighbor and practicing love.[6]

More than any more recent theologian, I believe, Emil Brunner draws taut the tension between the commandment of God that we participate in the order necessary for life *and* the ethical problem of resisting conformity to the order's sinful spirit, seeking to make it relatively better as a sphere of service, and all the while remembering that our own justification is by faith alone. Adaptation to the existing order, broken and sinful as it is, is the first point but never the last. Obedience to God, whom we know not only as Creator but also as Perfecter and Redeemer, means that "the believer will be found now in the camp of those who maintain and justify the existing order, now in that of those who protest and demand a new order." The existing orders (family, state, culture, and church as well as economy) constitute a "framework" or "vessel" which "we are to fill with the content of love." But "there are vessels which are contrary to this content of love, and it is quite possible that such vessels ought to be smashed."[7]

Though Brunner's abhorrence of disorder makes him a very unlikely rebel against existing order, his critique of capitalism is penetrating and severe. The principle of profit obscures the qualitative understanding of appropriate "livelihood." The glorification of individualism denies the need for community. Economic rationalization introduces "a kind of calculating necessity," whereby

the economic sphere becomes one vast mechanical monster, which runs with a sort of apparently natural necessity, and leaves to the creative and personal element scarcely any other scope than the discovery of the chance of gain.[8]

Labor is robbed of its dignity, for the worker becomes something to be bought and sold in accordance with his or her numerical significance for the calculation of profits. The service of God and neighbor "is made almost impossible for the individual," because the spirit of the system is "contrary to the spirit of service . . . : [capitalism] is irresponsibility developed into a system."[9]

Even so, there remains some scope for exercising love. It is still possible to resist infection by the system's spirit. Christians are called to search for a *better* order, one with a *different* economic spirit.

> It is the duty of the Church—not of the Church alone, but still of the Church above all—to revive the idea of the responsibility of all for all, the idea of concrete responsibility in mutual unity; for only out of this thinking and willing can a new order be created, which—while it certainly is not the Kingdom of God—does deserve to be called a 'better' economic order.[10]

The Reformed tradition thus understands the economic order as necessary for life, though sin permeates every actual order. If the order continues to preserve life, the faithful servant/steward participates in it. The law of love compels and guides participation, even as it presses for a better system. The actual order is always to be reformed. In special moments of history it may be subject to replacement.

The Crisis of the Present Order

The attention given to economics or political economy in the mid-1980's by the Presbyterian Church (U.S.A.) and its predecessor bodies, as well as by other communions, notably the Roman Catholic Church[11] and the United Church of Christ,[12] indicates a dawning realization that Christian concern for justice demands a fresh and penetrating analysis of the contemporary situation. The reports and study papers issued thus far provide the beginning of such an analysis from the perspective of biblical faith, but they do not offer the definitive word of the church on economics. The historical context within which the concrete meaning of Christian faithfulness must be determined is startlingly new and for the most part still dimly grasped.

I believe that the contemporary situation is one of major crisis. The church today has the task of understanding historically and theologically the present time as *a time of turning*—a change of course from one historical era to the next. The announcement of this time of turning is seldom made in church. My own conviction that it must be proclaimed and heard comes in large part from relating the theology of Jeremiah and Second Isaiah to the nontheological but holistic and forward-looking analyses of various keen observers who see in the present situation profound implications of a very different but still undermined future.

Physicist Fritjof Capra, for example, holds that the world is now entering "one of the great transition phases" that occur at extraordinary times in the course of centuries. The transition may be "more dramatic than any of the preceding ones," such as the slow switch from hunting to agriculture or the transition from the medieval period to the industrial, scientific age. The changes now underway occur more rapidly than ever before, involve the entire planet, and represent the coinciding and interacting of several momentous developments.[13]

Let us consider briefly some components of the crisis in the economic order.

1. Insufficient Sustenance

The primary aim of the economic order as willed by the Creator is the preservation of life. How many lives lost through nonparticipation in the economy do we need to count in order to demonstrate failure in that primary aim?

The global scope of the economy is a new fact of our time. All nations have been incorporated as interdependent members into a global economic system. An ethical and "reformed" evaluation of the U.S. economy must consider the leadership role of the United States in the world economy and the effects of various U.S. policies upon other nations, particularly those in the Third World.

The most basic requirement for the preservation of life is food. The average daily caloric requirement for health is 2,400. The average worldwide daily consumption is 2,600. So far so good. But the average intake in the developed countries is 3,300, while in the developing countries it is 2,200. In other words, the average diet for something like two-thirds of the world's people is insufficient.[14]

According to the Food and Agriculture Organization and the World Bank, almost 500 million persons—one-tenth of all people—regularly consume less than the "minimum critical diet" without which it is impossible to maintain body weight and stay healthy. In sub-Saharan Africa the amount of food available per person has declined steadily since 1970. In rural Kenya 40 percent of the people suffer a daily caloric deficit that hovers around 640. In periodic times of widespread mass famine, as in the mid-70's and again in 1984–85, the cases of severe malnutrition soar. In 1974–76 some 435 million people had less than 1,500 calories daily. It is estimated, however, that every year 40 million people die from hunger and hunger-related diseases. Nearly half of them are children.[15]

People are hungry, of course, because they are poor. And they are poor and hungry because they have no land, or too little productive land, on which to grow the food they need, or because they have no employment to get the money to buy it. The global economy is affected widely by a work famine. In the developing countries of the South only sixty-four percent of the working-age people are in the workforce, according to the International Labor Organization; in the North the comparable figure is eighty percent.[16]

The Presbyterian report entitled "Toward a Just, Caring, and Dynamic Political Economy" takes considerable note of poverty in the United States. As of 1983, some 35.3 million Americans—one out of every seven people—were poor according to federally defined standards. Close to a quarter of all children were living in poverty. Blacks and Hispanics were suffering disproportionately.[17]

For the world as a whole the sweeping but widely accepted generalization is that it is divided into the one-third of its people who are affluent and the two-thirds who are poor. Of the affluent a small percentage are super-rich; of the poor a large number are miserably impoverished.

The point here is simply to ask whether the economic order realizes its primary aim. More than half the human family lack an equitable and sufficient share of the good things of God's creation. Hundreds of millions are badly undernourished. Because they have neither land nor work, they are effectively excluded from participation in the economy. Even in the United States there are millions of nonparticipants. The *prima facie* case is very strong for handing the economic order a failing mark with respect to its primary aim of sustaining life.

2. Inordinate Power

Another recent Presbyterian report came from a special task force appointed to review the church's "policies, strategies, and programs . . . related to transnational corporations." The task force discovered that in the denomination one in five of the members and elders, or their spouses, worked for or were retired from a transnational corporation (TNC). The report assured this large contingent of the church of the "legitimacy" of their economic activity. It pointed to the denomination's Committee on Mission Responsibility through Investment:

> The entire basis of MRTI, in fact, rests upon a clear recognition of a stake in the system, a responsibility for it. . . . [This] commitment to reform and improve rather than to destroy and replace rests on the assumption of basic positive value, of essential legitimacy.[18]

The task force claimed that this affirmation of legitimacy "does not blunt criticism or thwart improvement."[19] I disagree. The report fails to lay bare the enormity of the power wielded by TNC's in the present global economy. Their power profoundly affects the well-being of virtually everybody in the world but is exercised in accordance with decisions made by a handful of corporate executives without representation of the masses affected and without effective restraint by any government. The task force admitted that, ". . . had the world Christian community been proportionately represented in [its] review . . . the report submitted would have been very different."[20] Without ample attention to the suffering of Third World victims of excessive power, any critique of the TNC's will necessarily be blunted.

For an objective account of the power of the modern corporation I recommend Charles Lindblom's *Politics and Markets*. His analysis entails more than I can summarize here, but some statements from his concluding paragraphs are worth quoting.

> . . . That the corporation is a powerful instrument for indoctrination we have documented. . . . That it creates a new core of wealth and power for a newly constructed upper class . . . it also reasonably clear. The executive of the large corporation is, on many counts, the contemporary counterpart to the landed gentry of an earlier era, his voice amplified by the technology of mass communication. . . .
>
> It has been a curious feature of democratic thought that it has not faced up to the private corporation as a peculiar organization in an ostensible democracy. Enormously large . . . the big corporations, we have seen, command more resources than do most government units. They can also, over a broad range, insist that governments meet their demands, even if those demands run counter to those of citizens expressed through their [democratic] controls. . . . And they exercise unusual veto powers. They are on all these counts disproportionately

powerful, we have seen. The large private corporation fits oddly into democratic theory and vision. Indeed, it does not fit.[21]

In the fiercely intensifying global competition of the 1980's, the TNC's have entered a new phase. A new set of management precepts reflects an overriding concern for survival. Ruthlessness has become the order of the day. The *New York Times* reports:

> The new order eschews loyalty to workers, products, corporate structure, businesses, factories, communities, even the nation. All such allegiances are viewed as expendable under the new rules. With survival at stake, only market leadership, strong profits and high stock price can be allowed to matter.[22]

Particular TNC's may go under in the competition, but the dominance of TNC's over the global economy is greater than ever. Their aim is not the preservation of life; it is not the common good; it is not the stewardship of the Creator's gifts. Their aim is market leadership, strong profits, and a high stock price.

3. Institutionalized Selfishness

The Chief Executive Officers who manage according to the new precepts are doing what the system requires them to do. They did not suddenly become less civic-minded, less responsible and humane than their predecessors in earlier decades. Ruthlessness may be rising to a new level of intensity and sophistication in the late-twentieth century battle for expanding market shares, but it is not an aberration. The modern industrial, capitalistic order did not invent greed, but it institutionalizes and encourages it.

This is not to suggest that the managers of TNC's are basically more "greedy for unjust gain" (Jer. 6:13) than other people. In the competition with TNC's based in West Germany or Japan, the question truly is a matter of corporate survival. The alternatives are grow or perish; get ahead or lose out! The "gain" that the managers seek may be perfectly or at least technically legal, even if it is "unjust" by a biblical standard that gives priority to the overall well-being of the community, with special concern for the needs of the poor. The Presbyterian elders who serve in the upper echelons of TNC management and crave the church's stamp of legitimacy are not to be singled out as bad. In a fallen world, where "[it] is not possible for the individual to engage in economic activity without sin,"[23] they may, however, be especially vulnerable to being drawn seductively into rationalizing and taking for granted a relentless focus upon self-interest or corporate interest that exceeds the bounds of the legitimacy based on the necessity of economics.

Doubtless these churchmen and churchwomen have often correctly felt that their work was their form of service, meeting the need for products and jobs. They have engaged, moreover, in the kind of business and business-related philanthropy that would benefit the local community together with their employees. But that kind of business always had to be "good for business"; in all fairness it never could be at the cost of jeopardizing company survival. In the restructuring of the 1980's that kind of business is expendable; efficiency for productivity and profitability is all that finally counts. This may be painful to many business executives who nevertheless find it a hard fact with which they must come to terms. *Time* reports:

> At many once paternalistic companies, the cost cutting has produced stunning changes in the business culture. Eastman Kodak, which has always prided itself on being a home away from home for its workers, has closed its employee bowling alleys and billiard rooms. . . . Reluctantly abandoning its virtual guarantee of job security, the company trimmed away 13,000 of its 129,000 employees last year as a part of a program to save $500 million annually. Says Kodak Chairman Colby Chandler: "The principal object is to make the company more agile, more competitive and more flexible."[24]

In this restructuring much more is at stake than bowling alleys and billiard rooms. Whole communities have been devasted by plant closings. Long before the newly heightened preoccupation with efficiency, TNC plants abroad paid wages in the range of $3.00 per day. Advertising exploited sex and promoted covetousness and envy. Small farming was made unprofitable; peasant land-holdings were taken away. Governments were subverted, land reforms aborted, and military interventions undertaken in the name of free enterprise and anti-Communism. Soil, water, and air were poisoned. Measures to mitigate the disruption and damage from such phenomena sometimes resulted from individual conscientiousness, people's protest, and legislative action. But measures and policies of restraint were and are against the stream—contrary to the essential dynamic of a system driven by the desire, indeed the greed, for gain.

4. Environmental Degradation and Exhaustion

In the economic order human beings have used nature as instrumental to the preservation and enrichment of human life. This is consistent with God's plan; we as humans must depend upon the nonhuman creation for sustenance. Nevertheless, Christian theology, including the Reformed tradition, has been seriously amiss in generally treating the nonhuman as though its role in God's plan could be understood *solely* in terms of its relationship to humans. This anthropocentrism, pervasive in Western civilization, has reached a culmination in the modern economic order. Treating nonhuman nature only as an instrument, without respectful regard to its own integrity, "economic man" is rendering it unfit to continue as that instrument which he/she has for so long taken for granted.

In contrast, biblical writers by no means confine the significance of the earth to its usefulness to human beings. They assume and express God's high valuation of, and delight in, the nonhuman creation, for its own sake as well as its sustenance of human life. "The Lord is good to all, and his compassion is over all that he has made." (Ps. 145:9) Similar passages are found throughout the scriptures. Nowhere are they contradicted.

The biblical sense of the intrinsic worth of the whole creation is largely overlooked in the dominant theological traditions and is virtually obliterated in the main thrust of the modern industrial economic order. Caring or caretaking that is merely selfish is always fragile. Mutual love that cherishes another person only to the extent that the other gives pleasure to the self remains on shaky ground until transcended by a love that forgets about self in truly caring about the other. Similarly, regard for nature only as instrumental to human pleasure and prosperity tends to turn into the abuse of nature unless it is transcended by a respect and reverence that celebrates the handiwork of God and balances self-interest with the appreciation of nature for nature's sake. When we do not care about nature for its own sake, we lack the wisdom to take care of it in our own best interest. The tendency then to abuse nature undermines its capacity to continue to provide the sustenance that humans need. Hence the economy now is plagued by the problem of its own sustainability.

The spectacular economic growth of the quarter century following World War II could not sustain itself through the 1970's and still has not resumed at comparable rates in the 1980's. Report after report—from the first report to the Club of Rome in 1972, to the *Global 2000*

Report to President Carter in 1980, to the Worldwatch Institute's *State of the World* series beginning in 1984—has presented massive evidence that economic growth is destroying the ecological foundation of its own continuation. These reports, ignored by most economists and insufficiently recognized and interpreted by theologians, still have not shaken the conventional wisdom's devotion to growth as the definition of economic health and the only way of overcoming poverty.

The first Worldwatch report on the state of the world concluded, ". . . we are living beyond our means, largely by borrowing against the future." Not only do governments practice deficit financing to get the funds to maintain consumption, especially of food and oil, and to enlarge their armies and their armaments, but "the world is engaging in wholesale biological and agronomic deficit financing." In other words, the world is consuming the natural "capital" that can only be rebuilt very slowly, if at all.

> As the demand for products of the basic biological systems—grasslands, croplands, forests, and fisheries—has exceeded their sustainable yield, the productive resource bases themselves are being consumed . . . [but with] biological systems, as with income-earning endowments, this is possible only in the short run.[25]

The modern economy runs on fossil fuels. Energy from oil or some other source is the key to its continuation. We depend on energy, not only for heat, transportation, and manufacturing, but for the mining and refining of the ores from which come the various minerals and metals used by industry. The Complex Systems Research Center at the University of New Hampshire recently modeled the energy future of the United States, including implications for agriculture. The results, reported in a volume entitled *Beyond Oil,* are sobering.[26] By the year 2000, and perhaps as early as 1995, we shall no longer explore for new oil and gas in the United States. It takes energy to get energy, and we would use up more energy than we could get. We will go on pumping from old wells awhile longer, but they will be effectively empty by 2020. World oil and gas supplies will last perhaps another three decades—longer than that only if Third World economies remain stagnant. A transition to an economy based upon renewable (i.e., solar) resources appears inevitable.

Still, neither corporations nor governments are purposefully undertaking that transition with the seriousness appropriate to the situation. The longer they wait, the more disruptive and painful it will be.

. . . the price of oil is bound to rise sharply and pressure for gas rationing and oil cutbacks . . . during the late 1990's will grow. The skyrocketing price of oil will no longer seem an equitable solution to dwindling oil supplies. And although the rush to renewable resources will by then be well under way, it will be far too late for a relatively painless transition to a world beyond oil.[27]

The decision-makers in the present economic order have demonstrated that they are incapable of making the decisions and pursuing the policies that would serve even the long-term best interest of economic institutions, let alone the common good of the whole society. The economy is driven by the pursuit of immediate and relatively short-term profit. The problems being generated for the late 1990's do not weigh heavily in the late 1980's. Perhaps the problems will not materialize. The coming situation cannot be predicted with precision. Science, technology, and market mechanisms may somehow devise and stimulate solutions before it gets too late. Besides, the corporate managers cannot think of the long-term when they are embroiled in fierce competition for survival in the short-term. The executive who is determined to maintain or advance his or her position cannot succeed by being more environmentally responsible than the company's competitors, any more than by subordinating profitability to the needs of workers or the unemployed.

On the one hand, poverty and unjust distribution, power and its abuse, and the selfishness of individuals and institutions have never been absent from human history. The difference in our time is one of magnitude and scale: the massive extent of hunger and the chasm between wealth and poverty; the extreme concentration of power and the global dimensions of its use and abuse; the weakening of religious, moral, face-to-face, and even governmental restraints on selfishness, even as the scope of its rationalized, impersonal institutional operation extends around the world. On the other hand, the environmental implications for legitimacy and justice in economics are dramatically new. More precisely, the magnitude of difference even from the recent past is so great that we have nothing with which to compare the present plight of nature.

Never before our own time did the human population threaten to exceed the carrying capacity of the planet. Only very recently have science, technology, and industry, which have vastly extended the planet's carrying capacity, begun to cause damage to life-support systems that threatens to reduce it. In the past few decades industry has manufactured and sold thousands of synthetic substances whose impact upon the environment and human health is only slightly understood, substances that do not break down and cannot be absorbed back into the environment. An uncertain but significant number of these have poisonous and often cancerous effects and require safe, permanent storage that we do not know how to provide. Despite all the warnings, producers and consumers continue to burn fossil fuels and destroy forests on a scale that accelerates the "greenhouse effect" and leads to climate changes that will affect agricultural productivity all over the globe. These and other strains on ecosystems and threats to life are not accidents or aberrations. They are the standard consequences of economic activity and growth.

Considering the unacceptable poverty of a majority of the human family, I suggested earlier that there appears to be a *prima facie* case for judging the existing economic order a failure with respect to its primary aim. If considerations of environmental degradation and exhaustion are added to our examination, it would appear that those who now are well served by the present system, the large affluent minority, face threats even to their own survival and well-being and certainly to that of their children and their grandchildren. The structures of power that claim a disproportionate share of the earth's finite abundance for the minority are built on sand. By not respecting, cherishing, and protecting the ecological foundation of a viable economy, they operate suicidally. Even their short-term "health" depends upon the further oppression of both the earth and the poor.

The Challenge to the Reformed Faith

Does the Reformed faith in this time of crisis lead us to affirm the existing economic order in its essentials or to participate in the formation of an essentially different order?

It is, of course, possible—and for most of us not only unavoidable but obligatory—to participate in the existing order, even if we refuse to affirm it as it is and insist that in its essentials it must be changed. The existing order is all that we now have. For those who can participate it does fulfill the aim of preserving life. For me it may fulfill that aim quite well, but that is not all I have to think about. I cannot escape the admission that it does not fulfill that aim for millions in the United States and over half the people in the world. The economic system perpetuates poverty, abuses natural systems, and jeopardizes the future. I believe it is imperative to work for its replacement by an essentially different order.

This does not necessarily mean that the system can and must be "smashed." Fundamental change, however, will not occur without conflict, extended struggle, and occasions and seasons of "plucking up" and "breaking down," even as the work of "planting" and "building" the better order goes forward. (See Jer. 1:10) It is time to revive the idea of the responsibility of all for all, the thinking and willing out of which a new and better order can be created.

This thinking and willing would point the community of faith and the larger community to a changed system of values as the motive force of the economic system, a transformed outlook on life that would alter the dynamic and the structure of the economy. The church must wrestle with the question of the practical relevance of the biblical ethic of love, justice, and community to the realm of economics. In so far as that ethic, rooted in faith, can empower and direct behavior within the economic order, the order itself will begin to express something very different from the individualistic self-interest it now reflects. E. F. Schumacher states well his view of the evil and the obsolescence in the attitudes that currently prevail:

> Systems are never more nor less than incarnations of man's most basic attitudes. . . . The *modern* private enterprise system ingeniously employs the human urges of greed and envy as its motive power. . . .
> Can such a system deal with the problems we are now having to face? The answer is self-evident: greed and envy demand continuous and limitless economic growth of a material kind, without proper regard for conservation, and this type of growth cannot possibly fit into a finite environment.[28]
> . . . present-day industrial society everywhere . . . has produced a folklore of incentives which magnifies individual egotism in direct opposition to the teachings of the Gospel.[29]

Standing in the Reformed tradition, we know the changed system of values cannot be one in which self-interest has no place. But self-interest need not be glorified and exploited. Properly informed, it draws back from self-destruction. It can embody the realization that the self is fulfilled only in community, together with the recognition that material accumulation beyond the level of sufficiency brings diminishing satisfactions and has less to do with happiness than loving relationships and involvement in activity that serves one's neighbors and the common good. A changed system of values can view both poverty and pollution as unacceptable in a world where all could have enough if the sustenance of earth were obtained carefully and shared equitably. It can acknowledge seriously the validity of the claim of the poor and the marginalized to full participation in the economy, the claim of nature to respect, protection, and restraint, and the claim of future generations to a habitable, life-supporting environment.

As part of the task of promoting the thinking and the willing that are basic to the creation of a new order, the particular challenges to the Reformed faith that I want to stress are the following four.

1. To Observe and Criticize

> Who is blind but my servant,
> or deaf as my messenger whom I send?
> He sees many things, but does not observe them;
> his ears are open, but he does not hear. (Is. 42:19a, 29)

Can the Reformed faith enable Presbyterians to look at this world and see it as the arena of the continuing activity of the Creator-Deliverer whom they know from the biblical story? The Reformed faith is second to none in its emphasis upon Scripture as containing God's word. But the word in Scripture is not God's word to people in this world until it becomes contemporary. The biblical story has to connect with our story, so that we recognize our story as the same story at the beginning of a new chapter.

The God whom we know from the biblical story "made heaven and earth" and "executes justice for the oppressed." (Ps. 146:6 f.) Steeped in the biblical story, we look at the world in which that story continues and seek to discern what the Creator-Deliverer does, declares, and commands in the midst of the conditions and events of our own time. And we seek to hear what the Word asks of us as participants with God in the ongoing story. In a world in which the whole creation, both human and nonhuman, is endangered and in crisis, the distinctive feature of the contemporary Word may be that it speaks to the meaning of involvement with the Creator-Deliverer in protecting and restoring the vulnerable and the oppressed, understood now as including the earth along with the poor.

The challenge, then, to the Reformed faith is to help people to observe the world as biblical people, seeking to know what is going on and what they must do. More particularly, it is to help people to know what is going on in the economic order and what they must do there. It is precisely there that the vulnerable and the oppressed need protection and restoration.

To know what is going on and what to do, we must be critical of the existing order. We must seek to understand what it is about this system that causes or permits the large-scale oppression of earth and people.

E. F. Schumacher, Lester Brown, Herman Daly[30] and many others criticize the existing system for its intense preoccupation with growth. Here the Presbyterian Church might well become more critical. The 1985 report, "Toward a Just, Caring, and Dynamic Political Economy" in its discussion of growth is deficient on two counts. First, while stating that the committee submitting the report "believes in growth," it fails to undertake any serious examination of the kind of growth which is so central to the functioning of the existing order. It does not probe the issue of whether such growth is in fact sustainable for the long term without, as Daly and Brown suggest, costing more than it is worth. The report acknowledges "some critics" who point out that growth causes pollution and resource depletion, but blandly states that "this does not have to happen"[31]—showing no appreciation of the magnitude of the problems of depletion and pollution nor any understanding that they occur, not as minor, avoidable "blips," but as products of the essential dynamic of the system.

Second, the report correctly observes that a decline in the rate of growth in the United States can have damaging effects on Third World economies; but it prematurely uses this observation as an argument for growth without looking critically at the global economy. It shows no recognition of the absurdity of a system in which further consumption by the affluent of things they really do not need is required in order to keep the poor from losing basic necessities. According to the authors, "Growth is the only way to feed, clothe, and shelter adequately the poor of this country and the world."[32] But the decades of greatest growth left the majority in many countries more impoverished than before. Growth has failed to feed, clothe, and shelter adequately the poor, not because the world's productive capacity is too limited, but because the economy's mechanisms of distribution are not designed to accomplish that objective. Production responds to effective demand, and the desperate demands of the poor are ineffective. It is not profitable to gear production to the basic necessities of those who suffer want. The comfortable may not consciously intend for the poor to remain impoverished, but they tolerate a system ill-designed to wipe out poverty. Simply to endorse growth as the solution to poverty not only dodges the issue of sustainability but shows blindness to the system's fundamental incapacity for distributive justice.

I use this as an example of the need for criticism that penetrates to the root causes of persistent poverty and mounting pollution. My own critique in the preceding paragraphs is of course subject to further criticism, for the search for truth requires dialogue and respectful attention to many points of view. Still, the penetrating critical endeavor, to which the church is challenged, belongs to the role of a servant truly seeking to shed his/her blindness and deafness, that the servant may see the realities of these times and hear what God commands.

2. To Transcend Personal Interest

I have given you as a covenant to the people,
a light to the nations,
to open the eyes that are blind,
to bring out the prisoners from the dungeon,
from the prison those who sit in darkness. (Is. 42:6 f.)

According to the Reformed tradition, the Christian man or woman, having been justified by God's grace, and therefore freed from "perpetual dread" of the law's condemnation, is now "disposed with eager readiness to obey God."[33] For Calvin this new readiness, while always a response to grace and not a means to salvation, necessarily entails a strenuous striving after righteousness in the life of the world. The person and redemptive act of Jesus Christ, who "has been set before us as an example" provides the motivation for the Christian life.

For we have been adopted as sons by the Lord with this one condition: that our life express Christ, the bond of our adoption. Accordingly, unless we give and devote ourselves to righteousness, we not only revolt from our Creator with wicked perfidy but we also abjure our Savior himself.[34]

For Calvin in Geneva in the sixteenth century and for the Presbyterians in the United States in the twentieth, the connection of the

Reformed faith to economics means that the arena of work and business becomes a critical field for the testing of the Christian's devotion to righteousness.

The connection of the biblical story to the contemporary story must surely be that God's servant people are again called to be agents of light and liberation. In a world of massive oppression, poverty, and pollution does this not point to the task of protecting and restoring the earth and the poor? What does this mean for Christians who are not poor and who strive for righteousness in economic life?

These are hard questions for most Presbyterians. They are particularly hard for the 20 percent of the members and elders who have benefited directly from identification with transnational corporations. How can they raise basic questions about a system in which they have played willing, leading roles and in whose continuation they have a large personal stake? How can they view the system "from below"—from the perspective of the excluded and the victimized?

To do so, they must transcend their personal interest. The Reformed faith is challenged to free and empower them to do just that. The task for the church is both prophetic and pastoral. As a prophetic task, it will be controversial; "prophets" and critics, preachers and teachers will be pressured to desist. Those who apply the pressure may be prominent members of the congregation.

> If the teacher allows himself to be impressed with any sort of superiority in men, he will not dare to offend those whom he thinks distinguished by power or wealth, or by some reputation for wisdom or honor. There is no remedy against such fears, except for teachers to keep God before their eyes and to be assured that he is the author of their words.[35]

The teacher, without claiming God's authorship for his or her critique of the economic order, can ascribe to God the call to live and work in the economic arena as a participant with God in bringing light to dark places and setting at liberty the oppressed.

3. To Envision a New Order

> For you shall go out in joy
> and be led forth in peace;
> the mountains and the hills before you
> shall break forth into singing,
> and all the trees of the field shall clap their hands.

> Instead of the thorn shall come up the cypress;
> instead of the brier shall come up the myrtle;
> and it shall be to the Lord . . .
> for an everlasting sign which shall not be cut off.
>> (Is. 55:12 f.)

Second Isaiah envisioned the Second Exodus. The people of God would go home. Released from captivity, they would go out in joy and be led forth in peace. And nature itself would rejoice in their liberation. At first look the prophet's vision may seem too utopian or too eschatological to suggest the new economic order that our contemporaries struggle to conceive. As Brunner insistently cautioned, that order would not be the kingdom of God; it would only be a better order. Still, if God acts in human history, God's rule breaks fragmentarily into time. In a time of ecological responsibility the deserts may quite literally be reclaimed, so that shade trees replace the brier and the thorn. In a sustainable economic order the mountains and hills will have reason to sing for joy and the trees of the field to clap their hands. The church in the Reformed tradition is challenged to participate in the conception of a better order.

Actually, the envisioning of that order is proceeding apace, with or without the church's participation. The watchwords of a new economics are justice, decentralization, democratization, and ecological sustainability. The new economics assumes that there will be a redistribution of power, to come not always by wrenching from the existing centralized concentrations but sometimes by mobilizing people for cooperative initiatives and new forms of entrepreneurship at the local community level.

The Living Economy: A New Economics in the Making is the title of a recently published volume from TOES, The Other Economic Summit. TOES defines itself as "an independent, international initiative, seeking to develop and promote a New Economics, based on personal development and social justice, the satisfaction of the whole range of human needs, sustainable use of resources and conservation of the environment."[36] The name derives from the TOES conferences held in conjunction with the annual economic summit meetings of the major industrial powers.

The TOES people in formulating a theoretical framework for the New Economics base their work on five principles, laying out a paradigm for economic development that was advanced by the Dag Hammerskjold Foundation in 1975 and 1977 as a clear and distinct alternative to conventional development theory. The Foundation

coined the term "Another Development" to stand for the new paradigm. Another Development would be (1) "need-oriented, that is,
geared to meeting human needs, material and non-material"; (2)
"endogenous, that is, stemming from the heart of each society"; (3)
"self-reliant, that is, implying that each society relies primarily on its
own strength and resources in terms of its members' energies and its
natural and cultural environment"; (4) "ecologically sound, that is,
utilizing rationally the resources of the biosphere in full awareness of
the potential of local ecosystems as well as the global and local outer
limits"; and (5) "based on structural transformations . . . in social
relations, in economic activities and in their spatial distribution, as
well as in the power structure, so as to recognize the conditions of
self-management and participation in decision-making by all those
affected by it. . . ." The five principles are "organically linked"; unless
they are taken together the paradigm is ineffective.[37]

Erik Damman, the Noreweign founder of the "Future in Our
Hands" movement, in the title of his most recent book calls for
Revolution in the Affluent Society. This title expresses the conviction that
"the problems that have been created by the development of industrial
society are too deeply rooted to be overcome by reforms on the
system's own terms." In addition, the title stresses the "transformation
of the *affluent society,*" which would be "a revolution without historical
parallel," but one that would be nonviolent and generated "from
below." "What is brewing in today's pyramidal society is . . . a revolt
for the right of the majority to responsibility and for the legitimacy
of the common sense and the values of ordinary people."[38]

As *counteraction* to the maximization of production and consumption, Damman calls for "antimaterialism combined with active solidarity." Unless this motive becomes "a new and fundamental driving
force," the system will not be transformed. "But if, on the other hand,
an increasing number of campaigns and actions based on this motive
develop in society, they will inevitably dissolve the basis of the existing
system and, at the same time, pave the way for a new one."[39] Damman
is not overlooking essential material needs. For him *solidarity* is the
key for getting production focused on what is "socially useful," for it
entails "the common will of society to pay for those lacking the
necessary purchasing power."[40]

Similarly, Australian sociologist F. E. Trainer calls for a radical
abandonment of excessive materialism. Anticipating a global population of 11 billion by 2050 and analyzing the prospects for the
availability of global resources, he concludes that there is no chance

that the developing world can ever achieve the American level of material affluence. The affluent world is affluent only because it is "hogging scarce and dwindling resources"; and this is "grossly immoral" and "extremely dangerous."[41] The thesis of Trainer's book *Abandon Affluence!* is summarized in a paragraph:

> The reasons for Third World poverty are complex . . . but the main reasons derive from the determination of the developed countries to pursue ever-rising standards and from the logic of the global economic system that provides them with their affluence. . . . Their superior effective demand enables them to secure many of the resources produced in the Third World and to ensure that the industries built there are industries that will produce the things we want, rather than the things the world's poor people need. If the underdeveloped nations were able to pursue a more self-sufficient development model, gearing their usually quite adequate resources directly to producing what their people need rather than to export markets, the rich countries would suffer the disastrous loss of most of their resource consumption and one-third of their export markets. If on the other hand we were content with material living standards that were reasonably comfortable and convenient . . . and if we had an economy that would allow us to cut total production and resource use to perhaps one-fifth of what they are now, enough resources would be freed to enable the Third World to provide for itself the basic goods and services that would eliminate its most serious problems.[42]

The key then to global economic justice is the *de-development* and the abandonment of affluence by the world's rich countries. Since they are quite unprepared for such a strategy, the most urgent task for the next couple of decades, says Trainer, is educational—to raise awareness and transform values—in order that the required structural changes may eventually follow.

Barry Commoner in a recent *New Yorker* article expresses more optimism than Trainer about the long-term availability of resources. He relies on the potential of solar energy for collecting and refining the minerals that the economy requires. "The issue is . . . how to create a system of production that can grow and develop in harmony with the environment."[43] Drawing upon the experience of the environmental movement that the significant improvements in environmental quality have come far less from cleaning up pollution after it occurs than from changing the technologies of production to keep pollution from occurring in the first place, Commoner concludes that social rather than private governance of production decisions, particularly those that determine production technologies, has become imperative. The fact that decisions are predominantly private accounts for the very limited results from the considerable effort that has been made to improve the environment.

> This effort, however forceful, meets a politically immovable object: the conviction, powerfully embedded in American society, that the decisions that determine what is produced and by what technological means ought to remain in private, corporate hands. In the United States there appears to be a powerful taboo against even public discussion, let alone criticism, of this principle.[44]
>
> [But] social guidance of technological decisions is vital not only for environmental quality but for nearly everything else that determines how people live: employment; working conditions; the cost of transportation, energy, food and other necessities of life; and economic growth.[45]

Because here there is common ground for environmentalism with the various other movements for justice and peace, Commoner sees some hope for basic change—if these movements can come together in effective political action.

And what has all of this to do with the Reformed faith? All of this envisioning is profoundly rooted in *values*—in *caring* about people, the poor, the earth, and the future. Christians nurtured in the Reformed faith have something to share—about justice and compassion and freedom, about the stewardship of God's creation, about sin and hope and patience and courage, about the will and the grace of God—that *belongs* in all the places where a new order is envisioned and anticipated and fragmentarily made real. They are called to involvement in planning and working for changes in values, structures, policies, and practices directed toward the well-being of all humankind on a thriving earth.

4. To Get With the New Things That God Declares

> And I will lead the blind
> in a way that they know not,
> in paths that they have not known
> I will guide them.
> I will turn the darkness before them into light,
> the rough places into level ground.
> These are the things I will do,

and I will not forsake them. (Is. 42:16 f.)

Massive, unnecessary poverty calls into question the legitimacy of the present historical form of economic order. Disregard for ecological limits and for the integrity of natural systems suggests that the system would have to be judged unsustainable, indeed suicidal, even if it were otherwise acceptable. The measures that have been taken to reduce poverty, pollution, and resource depletion run counter to the essential dynamic of the system and therefore can never be expected to have more than very limited effectiveness. It may be that the new things that God declares are the emerging elements of a very different system.

The path to the new order is dark, and the way is not clear. We do know that there will be rough places all along the route. Can Reformed Christians venture nevertheless onto it with a sense of involvement in God's new things? Can they participate *theologically* in the struggles for justice, sustainability, community, democracy, and peace? Can their involvement be faithful in the quite literal sense that it is full of faith? And will this give them some special strength, some special insights to offer, as they walk and stumble along the path with companions not nurtured in the same tradition? Will their "equipment" of radical realism about the human condition enable them to see and expose the blatant and the subtle sin in powerful individuals and institutions, and also the naivete of expecting sheer goodness from "the people?" Will the radical hope inherent in their faith enable them to keep going when some falter and turn back? Will the radical goodwill that "expresses Christ" enable them to transcend the interests of self and class, and even to relinquish possessions and power, in their solidarity with the impoverished and the oppressed?

The proposals and possibilities of the new economics may be unclear, unrefined, incomplete, and inconsistent, but that does not keep them from being in some limited but important sense guideposts that can keep us moving along the path. The final challenge to us who are informed by the Reformed tradition is whether we can draw on our heritage to see signs that do point to paths that we have not known—whether we will follow the lead of God in the story of our time, seeing, hearing, accepting, and moving with, the new things that the Creator-Deliverer declares.

Endnotes

1. Emil Brunner, *The Divine Imperative*, trans. Olive Wyon (Philadelphia: Westminster Press, 1947), pp. 397 f.

2. *Ibid.*, p. 398.

3. John Calvin, *Institutes of the Christian Religion,* trans. Ford Lewis Battles, The Library of Christian Classics, Vol. XX (Philadelphia: Westminster Press, 1960), Bk. II, ch. 8, secs. 45 and 46, pp. 409f.

4. John Calvin, *Commentaries on the Book of Genesis,* trans. John King (Edinburgh: The Calvin Translation Society, 1847), p. 125.

5. Emil Brunner, *The Divine Imperative,* p. 399.

6. *Ibid.*, pp. 399–401.

7. *Ibid.*, p. 218.

8. *Ibid.*, p. 419.

9. *Ibid.*, p. 423.

10. *Ibid.*, p. 430.

11. National Conference of Catholic Bishops, *Economic Justice for All: Pastoral Letter on Catholic Social Teaching and the U.S. Economy* (Washington, D.C.: United States Catholic Conference, 1986).

12. Audrey Chapman Smock, ed., *Christian Faith and Economic Life* (New York: United Church Board for World Ministries, 1987).

13. Fritjof Capra, *The Turning Point: Science, Society, and the Rising Culture* (New York: Bantam Books, 1983), pp. 32f.

14. Norman Myers, ed., *Gaia: An Atlas of Planet Management* (Garden City, N.Y.: Anchor Press/Doubleday, 1984), pp. 48 f.

15. *Ibid.*

16. *Ibid.*, pp. 182 f.

17. Advisory Council on Church and Society, "Toward a Just, Caring, and Dynamic Economy," *Minutes,* 197th General Assembly, Presbyterian Church (U.S.A.), Part I (New York and Atlanta: Office of the General Assembly, 1985), pp. 344-352.

18. "Report of the Task Force to Review Policies, Strategies, and Programs of the United Presbyterian Church Related to Transnational Corporations," *Minutes,* 197th General Assembly, United Presbyterian Church in the U.S.A., Part I (New York and Atlanta: Office of the General Assembly, 1983), p. 224.

19. *Ibid.*, p. 225.

20. *Ibid.*, pp. 232 f.

21. Charles E. Londblom, *Politics and Markets: The World's Political-Economic Systems* (New York: Basic Books, 1977), p. 356.

22. Steven Prokesch, "Remaking the American C.E.O.," *The New York Times,* January 25, 1987, Sec. 3, p. 1.

23. Brunner, *The Divine Imperative,* p. 399.

24. George Russell, "Rebuilding to Survive," *Time,* February 16, 1987, p. 45.

25. Lester R. Brown *et al.*, *State of the World 1984,* A Worldwatch Report on Progress Toward a Sustainable Society (New York: W. W. Norton and Company, 1984), pp. 13 f.

26. John Gever *et al.*, *Beyond Oil: The Threat to Food and Fuel in the Coming Decades* (Cambridge, Massachusetts: Ballinger Publishing Company, 1986).

27. *A Summary Report of Beyond Oil* (Washington, D.C.: Carrying Capacity, Inc., 1986), p. 8.

28. E. F. Schumacher, *Small Is Beautiful: Economics as if People Mattered* (New York: Harper Torchbooks, 1973), p. 147.

29. E. F. Schumacher, *Good Work* (New York: Harper & Row, 1979), p. 27.

30. See Herman E. Daly, *Economics, Ecology, Ethics* (San Francisco: W. H. Freeman and Company, 1980).

31. Advisory Council on Church and Society, "Toward A Just, Caring, and Dynamic Economy, p. 353.

32. *Ibid.*

33. Calvin, *Institutes,* Bk. III, ch. 19, sec. 4, p. 836.

34. *Ibid.,* Bk. III, ch. 6, sec. 3, p. 687.

35. John Calvin, *Calvin: Commentaries,* trans. and ed. Joseph Haroutunian, The Library of Christian Classics, Vol. XXIII (Philadelphia: Westminster Press, 1958), p. 378.

36. Paul Ekins, ed., *The Living Economy: A New Economics in the Making* (London and New York: Routledge & Kegan Paul, 1986), p. xv.

37. *Ibid.,* p. 44.

38. Erik Damman, *Revolution in the Affluent Society,* trans. Louis Mackay (London: Heretic Books, 1984), pp. 11 f.

39. *Ibid.,* p. 114. Original in italics.

40. *Ibid.,* p. 117.

41. F. E. Trainer, *Abandon Affluence* (London: Zed Books, 1985), p. 3.

42. *Ibid.,* pp. 8 f.

43. Barry Commoner, "The Environment," *The New Yorker,* June 15, 1987, pp. 64 f.

44. *Ibid.,* p. 64.

45. *Ibid.,* p. 68.

Chapter Ten

Celebrating Embodied Care: Women and Economic Justice

Bebb Wheeler Stone

In Toni Morrison's recent novel *Beloved,* a brutal incident occurs just as the black heroine, Sethe, is liberating herself from slavery. Several years later, Sethe, reunited with one of the men from the plantation, remembers the incident and describes it for him: Sethe had sent her three children, one a nursing infant, on ahead with other friends before she, breasts bursting with milk and pregnant with her fourth child, was violently abused. She reported the abuse to the sympathetic, but dying mistress of the plantation. Somehow Sethe's having told reached the ears of the abusers, and Sethe sustained a whipping from them that left a scar in the shape of a tree on her back. Here is the key passage:

> 'After I left you, those boys came in there and took my milk. That's what they came in there for. Held me down and took it. I told Mrs. Garner on em. She had that lump and couldn't speak but her eyes rolled out tears. Them boys found out I told on em. School teacher made one open up my back, and when it closed it made a tree. It grows there still.'
> 'They used cowhide on you?'
> 'And they took my milk.'
> 'They beat you when you was pregnant?'
> 'And they took my milk!'[1]

Hear Sethe's repeated insistence that the first abuse, the stealing of her milk, was the greater outrage, the more profound indignity. In the distinction that Sethe makes—in that prioritization—is a critical clue to understanding women's relationship to economic justice, especially when the socio-political context of economic justice is understood to be nothing less than global.

Sethe, as a nursing mother, is living-as-part of a relationship; she is living in interdependence with a suckling child. A nursing mother is a metaphor of human care-in-relationship, with her milk, which is regenerated by the demand of the hungry babe, a tangible symbol of power to care-in-relationship, the power to sustain life materially.

Sethe has been inhumanly abused twice, but she is more indignant about the theft of her milk than the theft of her dignity. She is more outraged about the violation of her power to care-in-relationship than the violation of her power to care for herself. That is not to say that she is not outraged about the violation to her person: note well that her responses to her friend begin with "And." Paul D's outrage for Sethe is appropriate too, but as women struggle the world over for economic justice, defined here as appropriately shared access to the materials necessary to sustain life, women do not want words put in their mouths; they do not want to be told what they need; and they do not want to be told what their complaints should be. They are naming their own pain, and often that pain is over powerlessness to extend life-sustaining care to another, the inability or incapacity to care-in-relationship. Yet the stories of incapacity, or powerlessness, must not be the only stories we tell as we struggle "to do justice." The stories of women's power must also be told, and it is some of these stories that will be told and celebrated here as paradigms.

The debate about the meaning of the word "justice" has engaged philosophers and theologians for centuries. In a discussion of women and economic justice, to enter the theoretical line of reasoning about "justice" is to postpone entering lines of reasoning about women's relationship to justice and, in particular, economic justice. Nevertheless a few words about theological assumptions are in order. The vision of justice that is so compelling is the vision witnessed to by the community of faith grounded in the Old and New Testaments as that community has journeyed with God through the centuries. As Beverly Harrison expresses it, justice is constitutive of the community:

> justice . . . is the central notion of what constitutes all rightly related communities under God. . . . A biblical sense of justice focuses on concrete human need and is therefore substantive, not merely procedural.[2]

Substantive justice is the central strand of a braid of theological reflection whose other two strands are feminist theology and Christian realism. Within this understanding of substantive justice, priority is given to women's experience, particularly women's experience in community; women's engendered reality is no longer included; and the utopic vision of justice is understood to have inherent power for informing present social change. These priorities all nod to an ethic based on liberation theology.

At the same time, the anthropology is taken from a Christian realist perspective: female human beings cannot be abstracted from the reality of human sin. Should anyone wish to romanticize maternal love and fail to acknowledge its potential for human evil, Lamentations 4:10, where witness is given to maternal cannibalism in the midst of the fall of Jerusalem, will end any illusions. Further, the realities of social, economic, and political power must be considered as women attempt to structure economic justice. Christian realism has insisted on the limits and constraints which prevent human sin from overwhelming reality. Women's search for justice has insisted on the possibilities in spite of the limits, and on the enhancements in the face of constraints, even in the context of pervasive human sin.

Admittedly there is real tension here, but instructive tension: Christian realism has within itself a prophetic, self-critical voice which has the potential to constrain its own practitioners. At its best it bears fruit in self-limitation. Appropriate self-critical limitation, in contrast, is not a virtue of liberation theology, and a first-world woman seeking justice is well advised to heed Christian realism's warnings against pride before she claims a simplistic equality of gender oppression with her third world sisters. Listen to an Asian Christian sister:

> Unlike individualistic bourgeois women, poor working women are in solidarity with other women on the basis of their shared strength, not their shared oppression.[3]

This voice insisting on shared strength must be celebrated given that the historical context of global injustice can be so easily established.

Documentation of Injustice

At the 1985 United Nations End of the International Decade on Women Conference in Nairobi, more than half of the women were African, and the concreteness of their agenda was heard:

To be poor, black, and female in South Africa or in Uganda or in Ethiopia, and whether one's enemy is supplied by the West, the East, or simply the weather, is to have no future but pain and death, the pain of watching one's children die, the death of hope, then life.[4]

The last phrase is haunting: "the death of hope, then life."

For women around the world economic injustice is deepening:
    In the Third World, where three-fourths of the world's people live, rural women account for more than half the food produced, and for as much as 90 percent of the family food supply of rural Africa.[5]
    As a rule, women work longer hours than men. Many carry triple work loads, in their household, labor force and reproductive roles. Rural women often average an 18-hour day. Nutritional anemia is a serious health problem for women in the Third World.[6]
    Relatively few women have entered occupations traditionally dominated by men. Most women remain highly segregated in low-paid jobs.[7]
    Women are a minority in the conventional measures of economic activity because these measures undercount women's paid labor and do not cover their unpaid labor. The value of women's work in the household alone, if given economic value, would add an estimated one-third to the world's GNP.[8]
    In the U.S., one of the most prosperous countries on earth, two out of three adults living below the poverty line in 1983 were women.[9]

This global documentation of injustice is all too familiar. The statistics no longer shock. What should be heard as a distortion of reality has become reality itself:

A mirror held up to our world reflects the rupture of justice and the reign of injustice. That is why injustice must be the beginning point.[10]

Statistics and stories of injustice are the beginning point, but to the community of faith that worships God as the ground of justice, those stories are not and cannot be the ending point. Karen Lebacqz has provided a typology of injustice in her book *Justice In An Unjust World* in order to bring justice into focus by implied contrast. In like manner I intend to articulate a paradigm of women's power in the face of economic injustice in contrast to protestations of powerlessness.

Paradigms of Women's Power

There are stories of women in the Old and New Testaments which need to be re-examined for their narrative celebration of women's power to care-in-relationship. Biblical writers also reflected theologically on economic justice, and their model gives us authority to reflect theologically on the socio-economic events of our day. We must begin to celebrate more intentionally our tradition of justice and to collect more avidly contemporary stories of justice.

My approach is to alternate the contemporary good news with the scriptural good news in a litany of women's victories of embodied, relational care. I will assume a socio-economic perspective of global interdependence and will reflect on local, personal experiences in that light. I make no pretence of objectivity: the goal of being "objective" is inherently unobtainable since there is no place to stand outside of one's own history, tradition, culture and experience. Therefore, I write as a positioned subject—as a white, western, middle-class Christian woman with a particularity of vision.

I also acknowledge my commitment to social change as a feminist, and I intend to be accountable to women's lived experience. Even if it is not women's universal experience, it is women who biologically experience the power to sustain another's life physically. We have bodily housed, carried, delivered, and usually nourished every female and male who has ever lived. This power to sustain life is uniquely women's experience; it is uniquely women's power. But it has not yet informed theological ethics in more than a marginal way, and even when it has, it has often been sentimentalized to the banality of most Mother's Day sermons. Yet all over the world women are beginning to act intentionally out of their power to care-in-relationship.

Finally, my approach is global. According to Roland Robertson, "we live in the midst of the process by which the world is becoming a single place."[11] From that summer day in 1969 when Neil Armstrong turned the camera in his space ship back toward Planet Earth, we could see our physical and social environment as one place. The whole world, not the nation-state of our birth, is the horizon that orients us to the possibilities and limits of our lives as individuals and as societies. It is no longer sufficient to develop economic policy for a nation as if that economy were self-sufficient and that nation an island. Justice demands that we recognize our interdependence with other nations, with our ecosystem, and with our future. And while shared inequality may have put women in touch with each other globally, what has bonded them is the shared and poignant desire to sustain lives and thereby life itself. Women are calling to other women to model or embody new ways of living symbiotically within the universe so that nations may learn the benefits as well as the risks of interdependence.

While living in India for several months in 1985, I heard Devaki Jain, an Indian development consultant, lecture at an International Women's Day celebration.[12] She told of being hired by the United Nations to evaluate a development project in a tribal village of northern India in the foothills of the Himalayas. It took Ms. Jain an entire day to reach this remote village. She had to clamber up a narrow, rocky path which is the only access to the village. The Himalayas have abundant chalk deposits readily available to quarry. In the late 1970's a private developer went to New Delhi and then Calcutta to gain a governmental license to quarry chalk in this village. He came with hundreds of pack burros and erected a huge machine to process fine chalk powder from the quarried stone. The powder was then packed out of the village by burro-train along that single narrow path.

The women also used the path for access to the fields where they labored, and to the well from which they hauled water. At first when women would encounter the long pack trains, they stepped off the path and waited until the pack trains had passed. Since the pack trains were very long, this occasionally consumed hours of time! The women of the village went to the men of the village *panchavat* (council) and told them of their problem, but the men said, "He has a license from the government. It's all legal. What can we do?" So the women decided on a course of action. They narrowed the path even further by adding rocks and soil in some places and carving it out in others. The burros began to slip off the path!

So many accidents occurred with spillage of chalk and injury to burros that the chalk mining became unprofitable. The man abandoned his machine, his quarry, and the village. Ms. Jain reported that in front of the chalk quarry are now rows of small trees which represent an effort at reforesting the denuded area. She also reported that the machine sits rusting and that life in the village has returned to normal. She went on to discuss the fragility of the Himalayas as an ecosystem. The mountains are being rapidly stripped of forests, and India is in danger of losing an important water and weather regulator. Finally, she reported that the end use of chalk powder is cosmetics, a product which can be afforded only by the wealthy of India.

Thus the short-term self-interest of the women villagers coincided with India's long-term self-interest of reforestation and resource preservation. Not all "development" is good, as the word itself seems to imply. According to Ms. Jain, the short-term self-interest of women has become for her an important criterion by which development projects should be evaluated. Her use of this criterion is echoed in Ruth Leger Sivard's *Women . . . A World Survey,* in which she writes: "The Link between women's advancement and socio-economic progress in general begins to be more widely recognized. What is good for women is also good for society at large."[13] Women have become an heuristic category: to determine if an economic development project will benefit the common good, consider whether it is good for women.

In the City of Pittsburgh in 1984, Mayor Richard Caligiuri appointed a Task Force on Women which had several subcommittees, one of which was on housing. After two years of work, the Housing Sub-committee submitted its "Action Plan" to the mayor.[14] One of its policy recommendations was that the Mayor direct city departments and authorities to develop a "female impact statement" so that housing policy, production, and funding would first be evaluated by how those decisions affected women's lives. Modeled after the environmental impact statement, a female impact statement is an attempt to eliminate the often unintended consequences of ill-conceived policies. It is an example of women's lives as a standard of the common good. A further refinement of this point with regard to technology came out of the Nairobi Forum: "technology is not appropriate if it's not appropriate for women."

In Exodus 1:8–21 is the story of the Hebrew midwives who took matters of sustaining life into their own hands, and God, we are told, was pleased. Karen Lebacqz finds here an illustration of appropriate subversive rebellion on the part of the oppressed.[15] While Lebacqz is correct, the purpose of their action was pro-active, not merely reactive. The text says "the midwives feared God . . . and let the male children live." Their theological understanding established a direct connection between knowledge of God and norms for behavior. The women in awe of God overcame their fear of Pharoah. Putting their own lives (rights) on the line, the women used their embodied power to sustain life. "And because the midwives feared God, God gave them families." (v. 21) The midwives were rewarded with relationships!

This is a rich narrative. There is oppressive authority, resistance, faith, biophilic courage, and liberation in the midst of oppression. Dr. Christopher Duraisingh, an Indian theologian, noted that this text points to women as liberators of the Hebrew people prior to Moses.

Just outside of Seoul, South Korea, a group of Korean Christian women have come together to liberate young Korean women caught in systemic prostitution. The women call themselves The Voice of Han. "Han," in Korean, is an oft-used word which refers to the accumulation of anger and deep resentment over years of unrelieved suffering and oppression. In this particular case, The Voice of Han seeks to give cathartic expression to women's anguish and to give constructive direction to the socio-economic realities of prostitutes.

The Voice of Han is led by three women: a former prostitute, a Maryknoll sister, and a Presbyterian missionary. These women are searching for models of economic development with which to create new jobs for women. Prostitution in Korea can be equated in our culture with indentured servitude: one must buy one's freedom out of ever-deepening indebtedness, as entrapping as fly-paper. It is impossible to escape by oneself. Sisters have found each other, and through the Voice of Han they are liberating themselves economically and spiritually. The Voice of Han speaks of women creating jobs for other women. It asks us to consider using our power to do the same.

In Matthew's genealogy of Jesus we find Tamar, a woman whose life story is told in Genesis 38:1–30. Tamar, married and widowed twice by sons of Judah, is denied the economic security of a levirate marriage to Judah's third son. Disguised as a prostitute, Tamar has sexual relations with her father-in-law. Before Judah leaves her, she asks from him and receives a pledge of his signet, cord, and staff as a promise to pay her. When Judah later threatens to burn his pregnant, widowed daughter-in-law, she discloses the pledged objects. Judah immediately recognizes the redress of an earlier injustice he had perpetuated, and he exclaims, "She is more righteous than I, inasmuch as I did not give her to my son Shelah." (v. 26)

Morality is not the issue in this narrative; economic justice is. The levirate marriage, in which a man married his brother's widow, perpetuated the productive capacity of the family as an economic unit. Widows were impoverished persons in this culture, a paradigm of the disenfranchised throughout the Old Testament. Tamar's action not only realized her rights under the levitical code, but also embodied her power to care-in-relation by providing heirs for her family. That she bore twin males would have been strong legitimation in that patriarchal culture of her bold action. Righteousness, *tsedeqah*, is right relationship acknowledged by all parties to the relationship. When

Judah had used his power to subvert righteousness, Tamar embodied her power to achieve it. Embedded in this Old Testament narrative is a victory of economic justice accomplished by a woman.

The structures of power must be confronted by women for the sake of economic justice. In the hill area of northern Uttar Pradesh, India, a conflict arose in the early 1980's over development projects which earned cash income but also involved deforestation, such as planting fruit trees and clearing land for potatoes. The women who continually collect from the forest dry twigs for fuel and green leaves for fodder opposed the land clearing. After learning of the connection between deforestation and the floods and landslides that had occurred in the area, a regional group of women formed what came to be called the Chipko ("to embrace") Movement. As a tactic to save the trees from the bulldozers, the women hugged the trees, embraced them, and resolutely prevented attempts at deforestation. In the face of threats and abusive behavior, the women hired watchwomen, paid in kind, to guard the forest. The women of the Chipko Movement have learned the significance of the forest in their lives and have been awakened to their role in saving it. A leader of the Chipko Movement estimated that ninety percent of the women and ten percent of the men of the region were supportive of the Movement. The women's energy, which in rural India is concentrated in subsistence, reproduction, and childrearing, was collectively transformed into power to sustain the material necessities of life.[16]

Justice and Human Rights

The women of India were the first to teach me that our human rights thinking needed to be relativized. When I entered a discussion with Christian women one evening, I spoke of women having a "right" to speak out against the ill-treatment of Indian women at the hands of the police. "You've got a first-world notion of justice," someone quickly retorted. "Your talk of rights means that your idea of justice is access to a political and economic system. Our idea of justice is food, fuel, shelter, and water." The debate over human rights that I thought would translate into an Indian cultural context was said by my Indian friends to be a luxury which women of the "two-thirds world" (as I was taught to say in India, reflecting accurate demography) could ill afford as they struggled to sustain life materially.

The concept of human rights is western and originated in the seventeenth and eighteenth century struggles against absolutism.[17] To John Locke the term meant an entitlement by virtue of one's humanity. In our human rights discourse both the common and the individual good are implied. Yet many non-Westerners think that Westerners understand only one of the meanings—that of individual good. In addition, cross-cultural dialogue about justice often remains confused until the discourse of human rights and human dignity is clarified. Non-western political and cultural traditions lack not only the practices of human rights, but also give the concept different meaning. In a western context the concern is for human dignity, and human rights are seen as but one path to the realization of that human dignity.[18]

Our discourse on rights has been more parochial than we have realized. We have universalized what was particular to our western culture, and subsequently we have had to listen carefully in order to learn that our concern for rights was not always the same as what others meant in their concern for justice. The concern for justice in a global context must be deindividualized and disaggregated so that the substantive content of justice can be heard as having a higher priority than procedural justice. Bread is as important as a trial by jury.

But now a further debate has emerged from feminist scholarship. Carol Gilligan, tracing the moral development of women and men, has challenged earlier conclusions (particularly Kohlberg's based on studies of males) that the highest stage of moral development "derived from a reflective understanding of human rights."[19] According to Gilligan, the fact of relationship precedes the fact of individuation.[20] The former gives rise to an ethic of care, first of others, but eventually inclusive of self; the latter gives rise to an ethic of fairness, expressed in terms of rights, which are often asserted against the other.[21]

While these two ethics are not pitted dualistically against each other, it is clear from her studies that women are more apt to develop a mature morality that originates with relationship, becomes an ethic of care, and enters into dialogue with an ethic of rights. Just the reverse is the case for men. Finally the two moralities complement each other:

> We know ourselves as separate only as we live in connection with others and that we experience relationship only insofar as we differentiate other from self.[22]

To the extent women have been excluded from societal decision-making and socio-economic power, women's complementary morality of care has been lacking. That lacuna, poignantly expressed in Sethe's story, must be redressed not only because women's embodied care continues with or without celebration of it, but also because our biblical understanding of justice is one of mutual responsibilities and duties within the covenant with God.[23] Hear a Christian sister from the Philippines reflecting on the Asian struggle:

> Women's ultimate goal is not just to gain more rights or a better status for themselves but the liberation of both women and men in a transformed society. It is that "all may have life and have it in abundance." (John 10:10)[24]

In this instance, Christian realist assumptions in tension with liberationist assumptions yield a balance which tips toward the conclusion that women's power to care-in-relation is salvific. Women the world over are using their power in life sustaining ways for others. An economic ethic of care, formulated out of women's lived experience, takes seriously a woman's biological bias towards life, her experience of symbiosis with life, and her power to sustain life materially.

Luke tells of Jesus on the road to Calvary with Simon of Cyrene carrying the cross behind:

> And there followed him a great multitude of the people, and of women who bewailed and lamented him. But Jesus turning to them said, "Daughters of Jerusalem, do not weep for me, but weep for yourselves and your children. For behold, the days are coming when they will say, 'Blessed are the barren, and the wombs that never bore and the breasts that never gave suck!' Then they will begin to say to the mountains, 'Fall on us'; and to the hills 'Cover us.' For if they do this when the wood is green, what will happen when it is dry?" (Luke 23:27–31)

Women have been weeping for themselves and their children. And for 2,000 years the days have come, again and again, when they have endured anguish at "the death of life" which they conceived, bore, and suckled. But not yet have they abandoned their power to care-in-relation. The days have now come in which all of us can celebrate self-consciously the value and meaning of this power. Pray God the wood stays green.

Endnotes

1. Toni Morrison, *Beloved* (New York: Alfred A. Knopf, 1987), pp. 16–17.
2. Beverly Harrison, *Making The Connections: Essays in Feminist Social Ethics,* Carol S. Robb, ed. (Boston: Beacon Press, 1985), p. 177.

3. Soon-Hwa Sun, "Women, Work and Theology in Korea," *Journal of Feminist Studies in Religion*, vol. 3, No. 2, fall 1987, p. 132.

4. Inge L. Gibel, "The Women of the World Have Won." *Christian Century*, vol. 102, Sept. 11–18, 1985, p. 802.

5. Ruth Leger Sivard, *Women . . . A World Survey* (Washington, D.C.: World Priorities, 1985), p. 7.

6. *Ibid.*, p. 11.

7. *Ibid.*

8. *Ibid.*

9. *Ibid.*, p. 16.

10. Karen Lebacqz, *Justice In An Unjust World* (Minneapolis, Minn.: Augsburg Publishing House, 1987), p. 11.

11. Roland Robertson, "The Sacred and the World System," *The Sacred in a Secular Age*, Philip E. Hammond, ed., (Berkeley: University of California Press, 1985), p. 348.

12. Devaki, Jain, "Development As If Women Mattered or Can Women Build A New Paradigm?", Institute of Social Studies Trust, New Delhi, India, 1983.

13. Sivard, *Women . . . A World Survey*, p. 7.

14. "Action Plan," The Housing Committee of the Mayor's Task Force on Women in Renaissance II, Pittsburgh, 1986.

15. Lebacqz, *Justice In An Unjust World*, p. 94.

16. Shobita Jain, "Women's Role and the Chipko Movement," *Asian Women*, Vol. 9, No. 28, Lucknow, India, March 1984, pp. 1 and 6–8.

17. Jack Donnelly, "Human Rights and Human Dignity," *American Political Science Review*, 76:2, 1982, p. 303.

18. *Ibid.*

19. Carol Gilligan, *In A Different Voice* (Cambridge, Mass.: Harvard University Press, 1982), p. 19.

20. *Ibid.*

21. Lebacqz, *Justice In An Unjust World*, p. 155.

22. Gilligan, *In A Different Voice*, p. 63.

23. Lebacqz, *Justice In An Unjust World*, p. 155.

24. Virginia Fabella, "Asian Women and Christology," *In God's Image*, Sept. 1987, Christian Conference of Asia, Hong Kong, p. 18.

Chapter Eleven

Capitalist Virtue

Lee C. McDonald

The question I wish to address is whether there is something that may properly be called capitalist virtue and, if there is, how it may relate to virtue in general, to present-day American society, and to Christian virtue.

Socrates raises the question of whether virtue is one thing or several things in the *Protagoras,* and the issue surfaces in several other Platonic dialogues. The different virtues—courage, moderation, piety, etc.—may be aspects of some common core that can be called virtue in general, or, Socrates rather surprisingly suggests, these may simply be different names for the same thing. Even to suggest this unity probably requires something like Socrates' belief that virtue is the same thing as true knowledge. Ultimately, for him, to know the good is to do the good. Christians, if they believe in original sin, cannot go along with Socrates. They believe that many times we can know—really know—what ought to be done and still not do it. Moreover, most of us, Christians or not, assume that the separate virtues are indeed separable. We can think of courageous fools, or generous cowards, or immoderate but compassionate souls.

My aim here is not to probe the depths of Socratic theory. Our concerns, I take it, are more practical. Nevertheless, a word must be said about moral wholeness, for on the one hand it may be that the problem of capitalist virtue is not that it does not exist, but that it does not connect with other virtues. On the other hand, it may be that what we have come to conceive as Christian virtues are conceived in too narrow and specialized a way. We do speak of persons as having "integrity." When we do this we are not ascribing to such persons a specific virtue, but implying a congruence of personal moral traits.

Some important traits do appear and stand alone. As even Socrates admitted, courage in particular has the earmarks of a detachable virtue. But, could we properly say of someone that she has a basic moral integrity, yet is cowardly? Courage, we should remember, is not incompatible with being afraid. It is the capacity to act in certain ways even when afraid. It may also be the case that certain dispositions we call virtues are so minor in the moral catalog—neatness, or eagerness, for example—that they do not belong in the company of the major virtues we are talking about. The capacity to take risks may be part of courage, as courage may be part of wisdom, but risk-taking itself could still be a minor virtue. Risk-taking, like neatness, or agreeableness, can become pathological. We are not accustomed to seeing major virtues like courage or compassion or justness or moderation become pathological. The capacity to take risks is often thought to be one of the capitalist virtues, so perhaps it is now time to look at some of the other commonly understood virtues of capitalist man and woman.

Good Capitalists

Although American society is, most people would agree, thoroughly capitalist, and has, if anything, become ideologically more so in the last few years, a phrase like "good capitalist" is morally ambiguous. Unless we know the speaker, we do not know whether the phrase is meant as a compliment or an insult or a mere description. Does 'good" mean skilled in certain ways, or believing certain things, or being morally good?

Virtues are human excellences. An Aristotle tells us, they are not emotions, for emotions are not under our control and we cannot always be praised or blamed for our emotions as we can our virtues and vices. They are not capacities, for capacities may lie latent and unused. They are characteristic dispositions of some durability, displayed over time. The positive dispositions most people would identify with capitalistic achievements include: resourcefulness and hard work (these two together often are called enterprise), determination, practical judgment, intelligence, imagination, adaptability, self-discipline (meaning especially willingness to forego short-run gratifications), and, finally, the aforementioned willingness to take risks. Less often mentioned today, but of considerable historical significance is service, the willingness to put customer's needs ahead of other needs. There are, of course, many other dispositions that some would call capitalist virtues, but others would call capitalist vices: ruthlessness, toughness, shrewdness, and the ability to focus on the "bottom line."

The sources for these ascriptions include the popular press, literature, autobiographies such as Lee Iacocca's best-seller, books written *for* capitalists such as Peters and Waterman, *In Search of Excellence,* and conversations. Political candidates who have founded their own businesses advertise that fact, hoping to convert what will be perceived as capitalist virtue into what will be perceived as political virtue. In addition to these current, often implicit ascriptions of capitalist virtue, we can go back to the early theorists of capitalism, such as Adam Smith, and see whether they had anything comparable in mind.

Adam Smith and Capitalist Virtue

Adam Smith is well-known for the paragraph in which he uses the term "invisible hand." It is not so well-known but that it cannot usefully be quoted here:

> . . . every individual necessarily labors to render the annual revenue of the society as great as he can. He generally, indeed, neither intends to promote the general interest, nor knows how much he is promoting it. By preferring the support of domestic to that of foreign industry, he intends only his own security; and by directing that industry in such a manner as its produce may be of the greatest value, he intends only his own gain, and he is in this, as in many other cases, led by an invisible hand to promote an end that was no part of his intention. Nor is it always the worse for society that it was no part of it. By pursuing his own interest he frequently promotes that of the society more effectually than when he really intends to promote it. I have never known much good done by those who affected to trade for the public good. It is an affectation, indeed, not very common among merchants, and very few words need be employed in dissuading them from it.[1]

If one naturally works to advance his own interest and if conscious attempts to serve the public good in economic activity are not only ineffective but probably contrary to the public good in their effect, it would seem that the whole question of virtue as I have been using the term is irrelevant. Several things can be said about this. In the first place, we must look at the context of Smith's statement. The whole of the chapter in which this statement appears is devoted to the question of governmental restraints on imports. The argument is not directed at individual merchants and how they should run their businesses, but it is a defense of a national policy of free trade. The target is the statesman who would "attempt to direct private people in what manner they ought to employ their capitals."[2] The pretension of "trading for the public good" is criticized; but this does not imply an endorsement of avarice. The invisible hand is not patting the greedy on the back, but watching over international trade. It is patting the prudent on the back:

> What is prudence in the conduct of every private family, can scarce be folly in that of a great kingdom. If a foreign country can supply us with a commodity cheaper than we ourselves can make it, better buy it of them with some part of the produce of our own industry, employed in a way in which we have some advantage.[3]

Nature, it appears, in the economic sphere can convert self-interest to a social good. We would have to agree that this does happen—up to a point. In my gratitude for the pleasure and enlightenment my VCR brings me, I can acknowledge that the maker of the VCR probably cared not a whit about the social good and certainly cared not a whit about me, but was only out to make a few bucks. Smith's faith in a benevolent nature, says Joseph Cropsey, "makes it unnecessary to look beyond nature—to a divine will above it as Scripture teaches, or to a human will alongside it, as Kant teaches."[4] But this does not mean Smith was complacent about selfishness in human nature or uninterested in the question of virtue. Indeed, in the *Wealth of Nations* itself he displayed a precocious concern for public education. He thought private education was superior to public education, but recognized that the very division of labor he advocated could condemn industrial workers, confined to wholly repetitive tasks, to becoming "as stupid and ignorant as it is possible for a human creature to become." The worker's dexterity at his trade would "be acquired at the expense of his intellectual, social, and martial virtues."[5] The remedy was the establishment of public education at state expense.

More fundamental was the consideration of virtue in Smith's *Theory of Moral Sentiments,* the very first sentence of which begins:

> How selfish so ever man may be supposed, there are evidently some principles in his nature, which interest him in the fortune of others, and

render their happiness necessary to him, though he derives nothing
from it except the pleasure of seeing it.[6]

This book is a defense of the idea of natural sympathy, but natural
sympathy was not simply a function of biology. "I consider what is
called natural affection as more the effect of the moral than of the
supposed physical connection between parent and child."[7] Again,
Smith sounds almost Aristotelian in discussing how natural sympathy
relates to friendship, for the highest form of this kind of sympathy
and this kind of friendship "can exist only among men of virtue."[8]

Adam Smith's invisible hand is often compared to Bernard Mandeville's famous formula "private vices, public benefits," the notion that
the vices of commercial society—greed, envy, desire for recognition—
are necessary to produce prosperity. But Smith considered Mandeville's work "ingenious sophistry." He accused Mandeville of perni-
ciously destroying the very distinction between vice and virtue. Mandeville, Thomas Horne tells us, "was alone among his contemporaries
in being able to live comfortably with the idea of "private vices, public
benefits."[9] The crucial moral distinction is that "Smith agreed that
men desire to be praiseworthy against Mandeville's argument that
men desire only to be praised."[10] The importance of sympathy in *The
Theory of Moral Sentiments,* moreover, shows that Smith did not think
the operations of self-interest in economic life would come to dominate all areas of life, as Mandeville did. Mandeville thought "calm
virtues" only "qualify a man for the stupid enjoyments of a monastic
life.[11] To make people work hard required more than positive ideals.
Commercial prosperity depended upon an economic system that
could stimulate pride, envy, and greed in a whole population.

The question remains very much alive for us: however strong may
be the entrepreneurial virtues of industry and imagination, are other
virtues, including Christian virtues, antithetical to commercial prosperity?

A similar question is raised inferentially by economist A. O. Hirschman in *The Passions and the Interests,*[12] a fascinating historical study of
how, with the decline of aristocratic values and appeal of the principle
of glory after the Renaissance, and with subsequent loosening of
religious restraints, thinkers were alarmed by the possibility of unre-
strained passion in the mob and the despotism of the power-hungry
who could exploit the mob. Montesquieu in France and Sir John
Steuart in England, as well as Mandeville and Smith, argued that,
though lowly, commercial interests could replace higher and more
dangerous passions and lead to peace.

Whatever else it was, money-making was regarded as "innocent." Hence, the most powerful arguments for capitalism were not economic, but political, and were made for political reasons. Without quite refuting Max Weber's argument that capitalism was one of the unintended consequences of Calvinism, Hirschman stresses the *intended* but largely unrealized consequences of advocates of capitalism. Even in the twentieth century, he notes, economists as eminent and diverse as Keynes and Schumpeter, against plenty of historical evidence, still believed that capitalist enterprise is a reliable remedy for warlike passions. John Calvin would not have put that much faith in any economic system. In his view, even the church was bound to have difficulty controlling the errant passions deep in the human soul. "In this church," he said, "are included many hypocrites, who have nothing of Christ but the name and appearance; many persons ambitious, avaricious, envious, slanderous, and dissolute in their lives, who are tolerated for a time, either because they cannot be convicted by a legitimate process, or because discipline cannot be maintained with sufficient vigor."[13]

Current Capitalist Heroes

Joseph Schumpeter also argued that a possibly fatal flaw of capitalism was that capitalists, guided above all by prudence, could not be heroic enough to capture the admiration of a mass public. Had he lived into the 1980's, the time of Lee Iacocca, Peter Ueberroth, and Ted Turner, he might have changed his mind. Heroism is not itself a virtue, however, but only a display of certain well-received virtues. In the early days of capitalism, those called heroes were founders of new enterprises. Today, they are apt to be those who "turn around" a floundering, profitless company and put it into the pantheon of companies with good earnings ratios: Iacocca at Chrysler, William S. Anderson at NCR, John R. Opel of IBM. Corporate raiders (the term "raider" is a heroic borrowing from military terminology)—Saul Steinberg, T. Boone Pickens, the Bass brothers—are heroes to some and villains to others. What is prominent in business lore these days is discussion of leveraged buy-outs ("LBO's"), "greenmail," "white knights," and "golden parachutes," practices that drive up costs, and in the short run the value of stock, without corresponding increases in productivity. This is what Robert Reich calls "paper entrepreneurialism." Productivity-oriented inventors and engineers have been

replaced by balance-sheet-oriented accountants, lawyers, and financial wizards. Virtue in any classical sense seems to have rather little to
do with all of this. The standard of a good manager and the standard
of a good company may not fit what ethicists would regard as a moral
good.

> President after president, honest and less honest, has been turned into
> a hero figure, sometimes even without benefit of assiduous publicity.
> Behind the great collapses of companies and reputations—IOS, King
> Resources, National Student Marketing, Equity Financing, Penn Square,
> Continental Illinois, and so on—are collapsed heroes, feet of clay, now
> mostly forgotten names. Among fallen idol companies, some, like Litton,
> ITT, or Rolls Royce, would be too conspicuous ever to forget even if they
> hadn't survived; others slid so far from grace that nobody remembers
> either their names or the exact astronomical height of their former
> price/earnings ratios.
>   In management, wonders nearly always cease . . . corporate goodness,
> even measured on the standard scales, is infrequent. Any study of
> leading companies will show that few can claim to be good—if you define
> goodness as doubling profits in real terms in a decade, maintaining
> return on stockholder's equity over the ten years, and having only one
> off year.[14]

The "standard scale" of goodness is profitability—making money
for the company and along the way for oneself. This perspective does
not come close to the standard of good-for-humanity, a basic requirement of a genuine ethical good, or even good-for-our-society, which
most often passes for an ethical good.

One of the ironies of the depressed criterion of good we are
considering is that the compensation of managers at the top does not
correlate very well with the company income they generate, despite
the persistence of the idea that pay correlates to some degree with
merit. Before stock options became all but universal for corporate
executives, one study showed that among executives in the hundred
top companies, those with fancy stock options did no better at
managing their companies than those on straight salary. There seems
to be a certain fortuitousness in top salaries. In 1982 the top income
was made by Fred Smith of Federal Express ($51.5 million), about six
times the income of the CEO of Ford Motor Company, who, in 1983,
was top, with $7.3 million. Second place in 1982 was Charles Lazarus
of Toys R Us ($44 million), who in 1983 fell to 25th place with a
simpler salary arrangement of $2 million. That same year the Presi-

dent of IBM was making $2.4 million in salary only (i.e., exclusive of bonuses, stock options, and retirement benefits), while the President of Xerox was making $579,000.[15]

> [I]n 1982, profits at Norton Simon, the dull and tarnished conglomerate headed by David J. Mahoney, rose by a tiny 4 percent. Mahoney collected $2 million for this effort, and then proceeded to reap a richer harvest still when the whole caboodle passed into the ownership of another and better managed conglomerate. At City Investing, to quote *Business Week* 'a management-designed plan of staggering generosity' offered chairman George T. Scharffenberger $16.4 million as his reward for taking the company into voluntary liquidation."[16]

Many of these anomalies occur because top corporate executives come close to having the power to set their own salaries.

Those who have neither high salaries nor stock options do not demonstrate in the streets about these anomalies. Mandeville's principle of envy in a commercial society has done its work. Instead, we buy best-selling books telling us how we, too, can become millionaires. A 1986 newspaper ad for Mark H. McCormack's *What They Don't Teach You at Harvard Business School: Notes From a Street-Smart Executive*, says: "This summer's #1 priority for those most likely to succeed. Ambitious people everywhere will be opening doors and closing deals with Mark H. McCormack's #1 national bestseller—now in paperback for the first time." The Stock Market crash of October, 1987, will probably stimulate a different genre of how-to-do-it literature.

Excellence?

One of the most successful how-to-do-it books of recent years was *In Search of Excellence* by Thomas J. Peters and Robert H. Waterman. It sold more than a million copies in hardcover. This 1982 book was succeeded by their 1985 sequel *A Passion for Excellence*. Peters in the meantime left McKinsey & Co., and set up five consulting companies of his own, while Waterman was touring the country lecturing at up to $12,000 per lecture. Though I oversimplify, the gist of their message was that employers should treat their employees as if they were human beings, which those of us who are students of virtue should take as a good sign, while not giving way to envy of their earnings. Peters and Waterman offer good advice—learn from the customer, keep the structure simple and the staff lean, do what you know how best to do, and perhaps most important: extend the philosophy of the organization to all the workers in an intense but informal communication system ("loose-tight"). Their conclusion is a paean to the value of values and to individual business leaders who *believed* in something: Tom Watson, Sr., J. Willard Marriott, Sr., Roy Kroc, William Hewlett and David Packard, Levi Strauss, and J. C. Penney.[17]

We can celebrate that Peters and Waterman have discovered the value of values, and the economic worth of believing in something, and that they are applauded in the business world. But is this such a remarkable discovery? One is still obliged to observe that not all values are equal, and the authors' basic criterion (I hesitate to say "bottom line") is still business success. Humanizing the workplace for the sake of business success is certainly not to be disparaged, but if it were possible, modifying business success for the sake of humanizing the social order would seem to have an even higher priority.

Professor James Kuhn of Columbia University Business School is an economist who belies the cynicism that political scientists sometimes attribute to economists (e.g.: The Economist's Motto: "To err is human, to be paid for it is divine." e.g., "The leading advocates of the need to subject everything to the test of competitive markets are tenured economists.") In a recent presentation he reported on part of the study he and Donald Shriver have made of business values. He stated that today's managers praise what they call *fair* competition, but not free competition; they are more concerned with profit "satisficing" than with profit maximization; and they prefer to be judged by their effectiveness rather than their efficiency. They find the economists' presumption of "independent individualism" unrealistic. Their managerial style is often more elitist and authoritarian than their language, or than the times require. The ideas by which corporate power is defended are, says Kuhn, "anachronistic." He concluded: "Those involved in the large corporation and those whose lives are significantly affected by its activities need to participate in its governance and discover in its foundations a morally legitimate rationale, if they are to provide it any lasting support and approval."[18]

My research in the field of giving business advice is strictly limited. *Fortune Magazine*'s book *The Art of Success* has some inspirational moments. Alfred Hunt, a retired business consultant for the big accounting firm of Coopers & Lybrand, in 1977 wrote The *Management Consultant,* a wholly bland book that reeks with the most elementary common sense. Raymond Baumhart, a Jesuit, offers in *An Honest Profit* (1968) an interesting study of businessmen's ethics. My favorite discovery was *The Making of an Entrepreneur: Keys to Your Success,* by George C. Ballas, the inventor of the Weed Eater.[19] The format is an interview, with questions propounded by David Hollas, who turns out to be an employee of Ballas Enterprises. Is imagination important? "It's vital. Imagination, viewed from a practical point of view, is the ability to recognize opportunity when it comes up and then seize that opportunity." What does creativity mean to you? "Creativity comes about when you get worked up over something like a big problem that is bothering you. . . . I think imagination is a more practical analysis of things, such as recognizing opportunities. Creativity deals with coming up with solutions to problems after you become worked up over them." Who inspired you to become an entrepreneur? "I would have to say Howard Hughes. I think he probably did more for entrepreneurship in this country than any other man." (A little earlier Ballas said he had been inspired by *Think and Grow Rich,* by Napoleon Hill.) Do you think a college education is important? "I don't think it is important at all. Too many people go to college and waste precious years. I am against college unless someone wants to go into a career that requires a college degree. If someone wants to become a doctor, he has no choice . . ." What is your basic business philosophy? "The basic one is an absolute must for every entrepreneur and for everyone in life, for that matter: In every adversity there is a seed of much greater advantage. Not in some adversities, not in most, not just sometimes, but in every adversity, there is a seed of much greater advantage every time!. . . . [However,] when people say 'Everything happens for the best,' and then sit back and wait for good things to happen—that ain't going to get it done. For example, if I hadn't had an adversity with an irate lot owner named Tom Geist, who knows, there might never have been a Weed Eater."[20]

My aim is not to ridicule Mr. Ballas. He is certainly not as dumb as his book. Indeed, despite his remarks about the uselessness of college, he has been an adjunct professor at Rice University. Moreover, we own a Weed Eater and my wife frequently uses it. Further, finding good things in adversity is quite consistent with Christian doctrine, though such good things should not be exclusively identified with million dollar incomes. Business decisions are not amoral. Appeals to moral standards are not only typical, they are inevitable. The question is always: which moral standards? A partner of Goldman, Sachs was quoted in *Fortune* as saying there is no longer a "stigma" attached to selling off a productive and profitable division of a conglomerate just to get the cash for other purposes. "Stigma" is a moral concept, and the implication of his remark was that there is a moral community somewhere out there which at one time stigmatized deals like this but now approves them. "Business success" is itself a moral standard and its meaning changes over time. It is a moral standard that pervades the whole culture. My suggestion is not so much that this standard is pernicious, though it no doubt can be that at times, but that it is often pathetic. It cuts off worthy instrumental virtues from their most worthy ends. This consideration takes us back to the consideration of the wholeness of virtue first raised by Socrates, back to broader questions of business ethics, and to the self-image of Americans as they are affected by the competitive ethos of capitalism.

This ethos has recently been illuminated by the study of Robert Bellah and his associates as reported in *Habits of the Heart.* They interviewed some two hundred largely white, middle-class, upwardly mobile Americans and discovered in them a significant tension between their "first language"—the language of competitive individualism, striving for success, making it on one's own—and a less choate, even subconscious "second language"—a language of community and sharing. "One response to this situation is to make occupational achievement, for so long the dominating focus of middle-class individualism, no longer an end in itself, but merely an instrument for the attainment of a private lifestyle lived, perhaps, in a lifestyle enclave."[21] The psychological tensions created in American experience by the sharp separation we make between "private" values, those things *for which* we earn a living, and "public" values, including political judgments about the *way* we earn a living, has been observed for some time. One of the more vexing questions raised by Bellah is suggested by this comment: "Perhaps the notion that private life and public life are at odds is incorrect. Perhaps they are so deeply involved with each other that the impoverishment of one entails the impoverishment of the other."[22] Regrettably, very few ethicists have faced this question head on, perhaps because the political, economic and cultural implications are so vast.

There is much moral confusion abroad in our industrial or post-industrial society, and a certain part of it arises from an ill-fitting individualist ideology. We try to make what is public inferior to what is private. In fact, we do value our communities, but we only celebrate the achievements of individuals. We hold our politicians to a higher personal standard than we do our business leaders, as Gary Hart and

Joseph Biden have well come to know. This is as it should be. But having in practice erected this higher standard for politicians, in popular theory we continue to say the reverse: politicians are bums, while business leaders are . . . well, leaders, even if we don't know who they are. Politicians are pilloried for saying what may be obvious to thoughtful persons—for example, that taxes may have to be raised to cure the budget deficit—while Lee Iacocca is able to give himself twenty million dollars in salary as Chrysler profits fall and remain a success story.

Virtue Ethics

There has recently been a growth of business ethics programs within corporations. It is clear, however, that the concern with ethics as such is sporadic. The aim of some of these programs is better communication so that employees will know what is expected of them. Others seem aimed at higher productivity through improved morale. Still others are driven by the desire to avoid government regulation. Almost all of the many books on business ethics involve abstract theorizing about ethical principles and how they might be applied to business; or they are concerned with applied ethics, taking principles and seeing what implications they might have for specific problems such as conflict of interest, whistleblowing, kickbacks, inside-trading, sexual harassment, or discrimination.

One of the very few exceptions to these approaches is a chapter written by Joseph Des Jardins, "Virtues and Corporate Responsibility" in a book entitled *Corporate Governance and Institutionalizing Ethics*.[23] Des Jardins argues, as I have elsewhere,[24] that traditional ethical theorizing, which aims to provide general answers to the question "What should I do?" is often less relevant to real-world situations than the analyses of virtue-ethics, which aim to provide general answers to the question "What kind of person should I be?" Des Jardins notes that principle-based ethical theorizing is bound to seek impersonal standards which leave the motivational questions unaddressed. He defends Aristotle's conception of practical wisdom (phronesis) as it might apply to business personnel, and looks at Alasdair MacIntyre's notion of the good life as each individual's conception of the good shared with others who are partners in a historical and social narrative. This, in turn, leads to examination of the deleterious effect of roles as they are assigned in the business corporation, or, indeed, in any bureaucratic structure. For MacIntyre, the difference between a workplace role and a profession is that professions (doctor, teacher, counselor) are assumed to have "internal goods," such that the meaning and value of the activity connected with the profession is not at variance with the meaning and value an individual seeks in life as a whole.

> Unlike jobs, professions do not ask individual participants to suspend their pursuit of the good life at work. On the instrumental view, work is what one does to earn money needed to pursue what is valuable. Since value is determined by money, the individual is left to assign his or her own value to anything at all. According to the professional view, one pursues what has been established as valuable in itself by the social history of the profession.[25]

Finally, for Des Jardins the pursuit of excellence so conceived suggests that business ethics is better approached from the side of political theory than from ethical theory, for the narrative history of what a community most values is preeminently a question for the history of religions and for political philosophy.

Military Virtues and Capitalist Virtues

The Latin origin of the word virtue was vir or man, from which it was clear that early understandings of virtue came close to manliness, which in turn came close to military virtues of strength, virility, athletic skill, courage, and later, honor and obedience. We still rely on these dispositions in military organizations and semi-military organizations like police. Indeed, on patriotic occasions we tend to praise and overpraise these traits. Such virtues *are* virtues, but they may be incomplete by themselves unless part of a larger pattern of virtues. In the same way the dispositions we have identified with capitalist achievements—industry, imagination, determination, etc.— are genuine virtues, but may be seen as incomplete unless part of a wider pattern of virtues.

There is danger in overpraising a single virtue, because a single virtue, carried to excess becomes a vice. Good taste becomes vanity. Dignity becomes pride. Affection becomes lust. Unless we are pacifists we think it proper to pay soldiers to be effective killers. But that does not mean we pay them to have an inordinate affection for killing, or to become brutal, even though that may be a result of excessive concentration on the primary mission. Likewise, entrepreneurs should be rewarded for hard-driving management skills, but not for greed or economic rapacity, even though that may sometimes be a result of the single-mindedness that emerges in the most hard-driven. It is simply wrong to assume that encouraging the bad guys is one way to help the good guys. We must reject Bernard Mandeville: private vices are not public benefits. Private vices become public vices.

But does it follow that public virtues are identical with private virtues? Not necessarily. Compassion and generosity more easily animate private actions than they do public actions simply because public figures cannot be as generous with or compassionate about other people's interests as they can be with their own. States and large organizations exist by virtue of formal structures. As to Christian agape, we can more easily sacrifice ourselves in love than we can sacrifice others. Is this the final disproof of Socrates' unity of virtue theory? Perhaps. But even if we are not able to bring all virtues under the same philosophic tent, that does not mean we should ever stop trying. If we say to soldiers and businesswomen and politicians: "We know you have to do your own thing and we know that your own thing violates higher and more refined moral standards," we are asking for it. For the good of the community, a politician may sometimes have to do ruthless things; but that does not mean we should recruit the most ruthless types to be politicians. As Bernard Williams points out: ". . . only those who are reluctant or disinclined to do the morally disagreeable when it is really necessary have much chance of not doing it when it is not necessary . . . a habit of reluctance is an essential obstacle against the happy acceptance of the intolerable."[26] In similar fashion, we may want entrepreneurs to be hard if necessary, but *only* if necessary and not at an unacceptable cost in human dignity.

Conclusion

If, in fact, greed, envy and pride, are, as Mandeville thought, the motivational fuel of our economic system, we surely have today enough anthropological knowledge to know that they are not the motivational fuel of all economic systems. We should, if this is the case, change our economic system. To be more precise, we should change our social system, for it is not capitalism as a system of investments, ownership, or production per se that is the culprit, but the system as run by people with defective motives and defective imagination. The same defects can be attributed to almost any socialist economic system that we know of. It is largely a waste of intellectual energy to argue in the abstract, cut off from specific cultural contexts, whether capitalism or socialism is "better." Not many useful lessons can be drawn from the simple fact that China, Finland, and Cuba may be called socialist and Japan, Pakistan and Paraguay may be called capitalist. Judge not that you be not judged. Sufficient unto the day is the evil thereof.

We need, rather to understand ourselves better, which is what virtue ethics is all about. We need to recognize how certain possessive motives are reinforced by ideological influences of a subtle and not so subtle kind of advertising, the mass media, schools and the workplace. Lesser virtues are encouraged, which is not bad, but often at the expense of higher virtues, which is bad. In this case the lesser virtue of industriousness is encouraged at the expense of the higher virtue of generosity of spirit, which in economic terms could find expression in a refurbished ideal of service. The religious ideal of service as sacrificial helping has been corrupted into the most empty of commercial slogans, as a stop at many "service stations" or "service centers" will confirm.

The better illumination of what our society actually teaches us to want does not imply the censorship of ideas or indoctrination in the schools. Quite the reverse, it should aim at more openness and spontaneity. Such illumination probably occurs far more often today through the arts—drama, literature, the visual arts, avant-garde comedy—than it does in the press, the schools, or the churches. But all these institutions can help people discover the satisfaction of good work set against the kind of work that only finances a desperate search for personal gratification. Having made that discovery, people still, of course, need to find meaningful jobs. Even ascetics have to eat. Meaningful jobs will be created only by political action, for only through political action does a whole community work out what is most important to itself. An individualistic, competitive, apolitical, profit-oriented industrial system can, perhaps, produce jobs, but cannot allow itself to be concerned with meaningful and personally fulfilling jobs. In an age that seems to despise politics, how could this transformation occur? At the end of the chapter on religion in *Habits of the Heart,* after tracing America's recent tendency for "withdrawal

into purely private spirituality," Bellah and his cohorts quote a
significant passage from Parker Palmer's *Company of Strangers:*

> Perhaps the most important ministry the church can have in the renewal
> of public life is a "ministry of paradox": not to resist the inward turn of
> American spirituality on behalf of effective public action, but to deepen
> and direct and discipline that inwardness in the light of faith until God
> leads us back to a vision of the public and to faithful action on the
> public's behalf.[27]

This call may require more patience than some of us have, especially
those of us who are continually tempted to make political action itself
into a religion. And yet, it is consistent with my earlier assumption
that an ethics of virtue aimed at changing motivations is to be
preferred to the construction of formal principles that must then be
imposed on reluctant subjects. The moral injunctions of Christian
scriptures are, I think, more easily identified with an ethics of virtue
than with deontological principles or utilitarian outcomes.[28]

To sum up:

1. Private vices are not public benefits; private vices become public
vices.

2. Private virtures are not necessarily public virtues.

3. Capitalist virtues are real, but like military virtues, they are
instrumental rather than fundamental.

4. American culture, like most cultures, generally confuses non-
virtues like power and size with virtues, and confuses minor virtues
like industriousness with major virtues like wisdom and charity.

5. How the line between public and private should be drawn,
including the proper place of ethics in corporate life, is a political—
that is to say, a moral—question and not an economic question.

6. The distinction between the satisfaction of good work and work
that finances a search for personal gratification needs to be illumined
in our society.

7. An ethics of virtue can illumine the foregoing distinction.

8. Christian ethics is an ethics of virtue.

Endnotes

1. Adam Smith, *The Wealth of Nations* (New York: Modern Library, 1937),
Bk. IV, Ch. 2, p. 423.

2. *Ibid.*

3. *Ibid.*, p. 424.

4. Joseph Cropsey, *Political Philosophy and the Issues of Politics* (Chicago: University of Chicago Press, 1980), p. 84.

5. Adam Smith, *The Wealth of Nations,* Bk. V, Ch. 1, Part 3, Art. 1. Loc. cit., pp. 734, 735.

6. Adam Smith, *Theory of Moral Sentiments,* Part I, Sec. 1, Ch. 1 (Glasgow edit., 7th ed., 1792. Indianapolis: Liberty Classics, 1982), p. 9.

7. *Ibid.*, V, 2, 1, p. 223.

8. *Ibid.*, p. 225. The apparent conflict between *The Wealth of Nations* and *The Theory of Moral Sentiments,* most scholars agree, can be dissolved; for the theory of self-interest in the former (not to mention the sharp comments about some aspects of commerce) does not contradict the approval of prudence guided by the rules of justice in *The Theory of Moral Sentiments.*

9. Thomas Horne, "Envy and Commercial Society: Mandeville and Smith on 'Private Vices, Public Benefits' ", *Political Theory,* IX (November, 1981) 551–69, at 559.

10. *Ibid.*, p. 560.

11. *Fable of the Bees,* Vol. I, quoted in Horne, op. cit., p. 557.

12. A. O. Hirschman, *The Passions and the Interests* (Princeton: Princeton University Press, 1977).

13. John Calvin, *The Institutes of the Christian Religion* (1559 edit.) IV, i, 7, in H. T. Kerr, ed., By *John Calvin* (New York: Association Press, 1960), p. 49.

14. Robert Heller, *The Naked Manager: Games Executives Play* (New York: E. P. Dutton, 1984), p. 5.

15. *Forbes Magazine,* June 4, 1984.

16. Heller, *The Naked Manager,* p. 136.

17. Thomas J. Peters and Robert H. Waterman, *In Search of Excellence* (New York: Harper and Row, 1982), ch. 12, pp. 318–25.

18. James W. Kuhn, "Values Implicit in the Business System" (unpublished manuscript), p. 5–45.

19. George C. Ballas, *The Making of an Entrepreneur: Keys to Your Success* (Englewood Cliffs, New Jersey: Prentice-Hall Spectrum Books, 1980).

20. *Ibid.*, Quotations from pp. 170–175. Emphasis in original.

21. Robert N. Bellah, Richard Madsen, William M. Sullivan, Ann Swidler, and Steen M. Tipton, *Habits of the Heart: Individualism and Commitment in American Life* (Berkeley and Los Angeles: University of California Press, 1985).

22. *Ibid.*, p. 163.

23. W. Michael Hoffman, Jennifer Mills Moore and David A. Fedo, eds., *Corporate Governance and Institutionalizing Ethics* (Lexington, Mass.: Lexington Books, 1984).

24. Lee C. McDonald, "Three Forms of Political Ethics," *Western Political Quarterly,* XXXI (March, 1978), pp. 7–18.

25. Des Jardins in Hoffman, Moore and Fedo, op. cit., p. 141. He is paraphrasing Alasdair MacIntyre in *After Virtue* (Notre Dame, Ind.: University of Notre Dame Press, 1981).

26. In Stuart Hampshire, ed., *Public and Private Morality* (Cambridge, Eng.: Cambridge University Press, 1978), p. 64.

27. Quoted in Bellah, et. cal., op. cit., p. 248.

28. See, among other passages: Matt. 5:21–30, 44; 6:14–15; 12:9–12; 22:37–40; Mark 7:14–23; 9:47–50; 10:15.

Part Four

Church Responses

Chapter Twelve

Learning Reformed Theology from the Roman Catholics: The U .S. Pastoral Letter on the Economy

Carol Johnston

The U.S. Roman Catholic Bishops' pastoral letter[1] on the economy has established itself as *the* church statement on the ethical issues of our economic system. Densely yet beautifully written, it draws heavily upon biblical and church sources as it tries to consider how the U.S. economy affects lives in the U.S. and throughout the world. It has been hotly debated both in the public press and in the Catholic and Protestant churches. It has been accused at one pole of being uncritically supportive of capitalism while at the other pole it has been attacked as anti-capitalist or dismissed as simplistic and merely reaffirming the outworn ideas of the long gone New Deal era. The critics are partly right on all of these counts, but not fully because they have focused attention on only one or another aspect of what the bishops are trying to accomplish.

When the letter is read primarily for its policy recommendations, confusion is understandable because the policy recommendations are deliberately tentative. They are meant to be suggestive of promising directions that might be taken as we struggle to incarnate the theological and ethical vision proposed by the bishops (paragraphs 126, 130). It is this vision that is the heart and soul of the letter, and the foundation for everything else.

The Bishops' Strategy

It is also crucially important to understand the strategy which the bishops have adopted and their intended audience. They very much want to do more than "address" their people: the millions of Roman Catholic Americans. The bishops want to reach their people. They want to motivate them to wrestle with these ethical issues in relation to the economy. They want to help their people to understand their vocations as both intensely personal and social, so that people do not feel alone in their struggle to be faithful, and realize that faithfulness has social consequences. And they want to inspire their people with a sense of hope and adventure, so instead of being paralyzed by the difficulties of realizing justice in society, they feel invited to join in a great ongoing work. This strategy is rooted in the theology of the letter, especially in the theology of vocation, which the bishops acknowledge was learned from Protestants. We might do well to relearn it from the Catholics!

While the primary audience is Roman Catholics, the bishops are clear about entering the public debate about economic systems (27), and influencing non-Catholics who share their vision. This is easier for them to do than for many Protestants because of the complementarity in Catholic thought of revelation and reason. They are concerned to articulate the solidarity of all human beings and to invite everyone to join in realizing justice. They base their position in the doctrine of the creation of each person in the image of God, but they are not thereby individualistic. They insist that "human dignity" is "realized in community with others and with the whole of God's creation." (Preface) This fundamental conviction leads to the rejection of both radical individualism at one extreme, and at the other a communalism that sacrifices the individual for the sake of society.

The bishops' strategy has advantages and disadvantages. By concentrating on developing a theological and ethical vision for the economy, and not on possible policy consequences, they are able to leave more room for wide participation in an ongoing debate about policy. Their statement will also be relevant to the discussion for much longer, since it does not depend so much on recommendations about matters that can change rapidly.

A major disadvantage is evident in the reaction to the letter. Those who are looking for **answers** based on sophisticated and thorough analysis find the policy recommendations inadequate, and they are right. It is unfortunate that the very good reasons for their inadequacy are overlooked. From a Protestant point of view, the reluctance of the bishops to pronounce in hierarchical manner on difficult issues for which they have no special competence, and over which they want to encourage wider discussion and participation, can only be applauded.

When we understand the strategy of the bishops and their emphasis on the theological and ethical starting point for the discussion of economic policy, the letter begins to look more radical: not in its conclusions, but in its implications. I believe that the theological and ethical vision has consequences that, if realized, would do much more than "reform" the U.S. economic system. The bishops seem to be gambling that those who accept the vision and learn how to act out its implications will, in the process of incarnating it in our society, take it much farther. Rather than imagining a concrete end, a "utopian" outcome, and trying to conform society to it, the bishops have chosen to articulate a stance from which to begin the transformation of the concrete reality in which we live. They have given us some clear ways to judge our policy proposals and to measure the health of the transformations we achieve, but for the most part have left the specifics for us. They have chosen a pragmatic strategy that arises out of an incarnational theology.

The strategy of the bishops is illustrated in the very first paragraphs and is consistently carried out. First comes the careful inclusion of everyone and the presentation of the economy as a positive sphere of human life, and then the focus on the most vulnerable as the test of the health of the whole:

Every perspective on economic life that is human, moral and Christian must be shaped by three questions: What does the economy do for the people? What does it do to the people? And how do people participate in it? The economy is a human reality: men and women working together to develop and care for the whole of God's creation. All this work must serve the material and spiritual well-being of people. It influences what people hope for themselves and their loved ones. It affects the way they act together in society. It influences their very faith in God.

The Second Vatican Council declared that "the joys and hopes, the griefs and anxieties of the people of this age, especially those who are poor or in any way afflicted, these too are the joys and hopes, the griefs and anxieties of the followers of Christ." (paragraphs 1, 2)

Inclusiveness and Working People

Once this strategy is set the letter perceptively shifts to the daily struggles of working people:

> Many fathers and mothers skillfully balance the arduous responsibilities of work and family life. There are parents who pursue a purposeful and modest way of life and by their example encourage their children to follow a similar path. (3)

Although the bishops are not going to waver for a moment in their insistance on the "preferential option for the poor," they are also not going to fall into the trap of setting the poor apart and thus forcing non-poor working people to identify with the rich and powerful. Again and again through the letter they show their sensitivity to the great mass of middle-class working people who struggle daily to live faithful lives.

I raise this as a key issue because I have seen how the working of church statements frequently serves to alienate people who might otherwise be sympathetic. We often speak as if all white Americans are inherently rich oppressors. While it is true that all middle-class Americans do participate in the U.S. economy, it is not true that they benefit equally, or that they exercise any real power. The bishops are working to distinguish the injustices of a system from the individuals who participate in it. They believe that many, if given a chance to participate in a more just system, would prefer to do so. How well-founded their belief is, is another issue. I only wish to point out that an added feature of their strategy is to reach a broad spectrum of individuals rather than alienate them by **a priori** damning them along with the system.

This strategy arises from their theological vision. The bishops consistently affirm the intrinsic worth of each and every human being, and insist that all "human life is fulfilled in the knowledge and love of the living God in communion with others," (30) and that "no dimension of human life lies beyond God's care and concern." (31) But it is precisely because God's care and concern is for **all** that the condition of the most vulnerable and powerless becomes **the** test of justice. Where else would Christians begin, but with those most at risk? Given the strong concern for the poor in the tradition, it simply is not good enough to measure social health by an average that ignores those left on the margins. And since people who are benefitting by a social system are often unable to experience the sting of injustice, it is necessary to insist on measuring policy with the eyes of the poor, who alone can see clearly what is happening to them. This is the context into which the bishops set their insistence on the "preferential option for the poor." (52)

A Theology of Grace

The salvation of us all is effected through the identification of God with "the least." The bishops point out how the covenant tradition of the Old Testament held up the Law, not as "arbitrary restriction" but as codes that "made life in community possible." (36) At the heart of the Law was protection for the powerless: "the widow, the orphan, the poor, and the stranger in the land." (38) The bishops go on to show how throughout the Old Testament God hears the cries of the oppressed and acts to save them again and again. They show the link between experiencing redemption and acting on behalf of justice:

Because God loves Israel, he rescues them from oppression and summons them to be a people that "does justice" and loves kindness. The quest for justice arises from loving gratitude for the saving acts of God and manifests itself in the wholehearted love of God and neighbor. (39)

For Christians the redemption wrought by Jesus has the same result as the Exodus has for Israel. Because of the saving acts of God in Jesus Christ, we in "loving gratitude" are invited "to seek ways in which God's revelation of the dignity and destiny of all creation might become incarnate in history." (41)

This is a theology of grace and is as Reformed as anything Calvin himself ever wrote. Roman Catholics have finally learned what we are forgetting. In too many socially active Protestant churches I have heard people castigated and made to feel guilty for not doing enough for justice and peace. It is true: they are not doing enough, they are guilty, and they do participate in unjust social structures. But all the castigation and all the rehearsal of grim statistics only leave people numb with guilt and paralyzed with hopelessness. The result is severe depression and impotent remorse at best, and abandonment of the church or turning to shallow "feel-good" religion at worst.

We have introduced a new form of "works-righteousness" to people who feel utterly alone in their job situations, unsupported in their families, and barely able to cope with the pressures of our society. This is neither Reformed theology nor an effective strategy to motivate people and empower them for a lifetime of service.

What the bishops are up to here is exactly what a theology of grace implies. They are showing people how the saving acts of God are available to them, and showing them how these same acts inevitably issue in our participation, so that we experience love, forgiveness, and empowerment even as it is shared with others. Implied in the bishops' discussion is an understanding that the love of God arises from the prior experience of grace, is made effective in our lives through the loving acts of others towards us, and issues in love of neighbor "made real through effective action" on behalf of others. (43) Thus grace and works go together. Grace that does not issue in works is shallow, fruitless, and quickly trampled by the harsh realities of the world, like the seed that fell on the path in Jesus' parable. But works cannot last if not rooted in the good soil of grace: like the seed that fell on rocky ground, they spring up like weeds, but wither in the fierce sun.

The bishops are trying to help us to respond to grace by putting down deep roots in our faith in Christ:

> To be a Christian is to join with others in responding to this personal call and in learning the meaning of his life. It is to be sustained by that loving intimacy with the Father that Jesus experienced in his work, in his prayer and in his suffering.
> Discipleship involves imitating the pattern of Jesus' life by openness to God's will in the service of others (Mk. 10:42–45). . . . It is a model for those who suffer persecution for the sake of justice (Mt. 5:10). The death of Jesus was not the end of his power and presence, for he was raised up by the power of God. Nor did it mark the end of the disciples' union with him. . . . When they received the gift of the Spirit (Acts 2:1–13), they became apostles of the good news to the ends of the earth. In the face of poverty and persecution they transformed human lives and formed communities which became signs of the power and presence of God. Sharing in this same resurrection faith, contemporary followers of Christ can face the struggles and challenges that await those who bring the gospel vision to bear on our complex economic and social world. (46, 47)

Identification With the Poor

Having appealed to Christians to respond to the experience of grace by becoming disciples in communities of faith which struggle to incarnate justice while they sustain each other, the bishops then go on to discuss Jesus' identification with the poor and oppressed and the implications of that identification for all Christians. They make a very important promise to all those who join Jesus in so identifying themselves:

> Christian communities that commit themselves to solidarity with those suffering and to confrontation with those attitudes and ways of acting which institutionalize injustice will themselves experience the power and presence of Christ. They will embody in their lives and values of the new creation while they labor under the old. The quest for economic and social justice will always combine hope and realism, and must be renewed by every generation. (55)

The bishops do not minimize the difficulties. Incarnating justice is no easy task. But no matter how difficult, no matter how hopeless it seems, we keep at the task because we are doing so in response to what has already been done for us, and in solidarity with others who have experienced the same grace.

In the section called "A Living Tradition," the bishops lift up those Christian communities that have sought to identify with the poor: the early church, the monasteries that took in those most in need, and the mendicant orders such as the Franciscans. The bishops purposely choose not to deal with the large portion of the church that in every age has supported structures of injustice. In so doing they have chosen a very selective history. Their purpose is to get Catholics to identify with that part of their history which **has** been faithful to Jesus' identification with the poor. The bishops recognize the need of people to feel part of something bigger than they are, to feel that they are joining in a long and resilient history that offers real hope.

Interestingly, the bishops credit Protestantism with teaching them the understanding of vocation found in the letter: "We also have much to learn from the strong emphasis in Protestant traditions on the vocation of lay people in the world and from ecumenical efforts to develop an economic ethic that addresses newly emergent problems." (59) The Catholic bishops have seen in the way Protestants understand vocation an important key to helping people cope with the demands of working for justice. I think they have seen more clearly than we do, and can help us to clarify our own practices and traditions.

For example, often in our churches and seminaries business ethics is approached as a matter of how individual business people make ethical decisions in the course of their daily work. Of course this is an important dimension of the ethics of the workplace, but it is only one dimension. The corporate dimensions of vocation are not as well articulated. In the Reformed tradition we have understood that it is not enough to expect individuals to act ethically when the social structures within which they must work are unethical. And so Reformed Christians have gone to work to change society to embody more just arrangements. As long as child-labor was the universal practice, business people could try hard to treat children fairly, but they could not stop using children and hope to compete with those who did. It was not until child labor was outlawed altogether that it became possible for the individual business person to be 'ethical' in that respect.

Reformed Christians have been dealing with both the individual and the social aspects of vocation all along: social both in respect to the structures in which people work and in respect to joining with other Christians to work **together** for change. We need to articulate these social dimensions of vocation to our people better, to help them realize that they need not and indeed cannot exercise their vocations alone. Vocation is intensely personal, yet is never individualistic. The bishops see vocation as expressed most fully and nurtured most completely in worship, and then taken by the laity into their daily lives not only as individuals, but in the way they join others to deal together with complex issues. (326–332)

The Wider Society

We have seen in some detail how the bishops work to reach Christians, grounding their strategy in a theology of grace which invites all Christians to join Jesus Christ in exercising the "preferential option for the poor." But what about the wider society? They claim that they want to join the public debate about economic policy, and to make common cause with non-Catholics who share their vision of justice.

The way that the bishops reach out to the wider society parallels the way they reach out to Christians. Their strategy is congruent with their theology, and seeks to be inclusive and empowering. Since all human beings are created in the image of God and destined to realize their inherent dignity "in community with others and with the whole of God's creation," (Preface) the bishops appeal to all people, whether

Christian believers or not, to work together. They use American history as their source for building a common vision, rather than the history of Israel and the Christian church, but the strategy is the same. Once again, they are helping people to feel part of a great on-going historic adventure, rather than to feel isolated. They lift up the "liberty and justice for all" strand of American history and call upon Americans to identify with it rather than acquiescing in selfishness and individual license:

> For over 200 years the United States has been engaged in a bold experiment in democracy. The founders of the nation set out to establish justice, promote the general welfare and secure the blessings of liberty for themselves and their posterity. Those who live in this land today are the beneficiaries of this great venture. Our review of some of the most pressing problems in economic life today show, however, that this under-taking is not yet complete. Justice for all remains an aspiration; a fair share in the general welfare is denied to many. (291)
>
> The nation's founders took daring steps to create structures of partic-ipation, mutual accountability and widely distributed power to ensure the political rights and freedoms of all. We believe that similar steps are needed today to expand economic participation, broaden the sharing of economic power and make economic decisions more accountable to the common good. (293)

By placing their economic agenda in relation to our cultural tradi-tions, the bishops claim their proposals are the next logical step in the "American experiment." Because of this continuity, some critics judge that the bishops are merely "reformist" and unrealistic about the extent of injustice in U.S. society. Other critics, such as Michael Novak and members of the self-appointed "Catholic Lay Committee," are not fooled for a moment. They are well aware that if the bishops' proposals about "economic participation," and the sharing of power and accountability were realized, the structure of power in the U.S. economy would be transformed. In this regard they charge the bishops with being highly unrealistic about human sin.

What about this latter charge? In part they are correct. The bishops simply do not meet the pervasiveness of sin head on, and as a consequence the letter has a tone of optimism that will strike some readers as naive. They often sound as if they really think good intentions are enough. But their critics who purport to take sin seriously see it almost exclusively in the coercive power of govern-ment, and are themselves naive about sin in the coercive power of our economic system.

On this issue the Reformed tradition is helpful, because it insists that sin infects every area of life—"in individuals as well as institutions, in good intentions as well as selfishness, in passivity as well as prideful assertion."[2] Because we understand sin as pervasive, we recognize the necessity of accountability in **all** forms of power. We have historically rejected the optimism of both **laissez faire,** free market proponents who place their faith in the workings of the "invisible hand," and proponents of state control who place their faith in government:

> We believe the potential danger is in the pursuit and use of power itself, whether it is exercised by public or private organizations, individuals, or groups, local or distant. All power, whether economic, political, or ecclesiastical, whether personal, corporate or governmental, needs appropriate checks and balances for accountability. Power needs to be restrained by countervailing forces. Such restraint cannot be taken for granted or left to chance; effective mechanisms for the proper constraints must be built in.[3]

This realism about sin and power can provide an important balance to the work of the Catholic bishops.

Justice

Nevertheless, the bishops' emphasis on broadening participation at all levels does lend itself to building in accountability for power. It also broadens the parameters within which the debate about justice has been confined. For years American society has struggled over how to balance individual freedom against social equity. Those who focus more on equity have sought more equitable distribution of wealth through higher wages for labor, progressive taxation, and various welfare programs. Those who focus more on individual freedom feel strongly that programs for redistribution deny basic liberties and provide disincentives to work hard and economic efficiency. There would seem to be an impasse between freedom and equity.

As long as individuals are considered primarily as standing alone, with relationships in community secondary, individual freedom and social equity will be in conflict. But the pastoral letter points toward another way. The bishops place individuals firmly within community. This is not to negate individuality but to see individuals as integrally shaped by and shaping the communities in which they live. When this is understood, then it becomes evident that a healthy community is necessary to the nurture of healthy individuals and that participation in relationships is necessary for the fulfillment of individuality. When people are denied the opportunity to develop their gifts and talents by contributing them to their communities, then their freedom to exercise their individuality is being denied. This is why unemployment, discrimination, and poverty are so intolerable. They are unjust denials of both individual freedom and social equity.

This understanding is the foundation for the expansion in the letter of the concept of justice from a narrow focus on distribution to a wider emphasis on participation. Although the bishops do not deny the importance of a more just distribution, they insist that redistribution of wealth is not enough. Participation at all levels must be improved before justice in terms of both individual freedom and social equity can be realized:

> The ultimate injustice is for a person or group to be actively treated or passively abandoned as if they were non-members of the human race. . . . Exclusion can take a political shape, as when a person or group is denied influence on public decision making through restriction of free speech, through an inordinate concentration of power in the hands of a few or through outright repression by the state. Marginalization can also take economic forms that are equally harmful. Within the United States, individuals, families and local communities can fall victim to a downward cycle of poverty generated by economic forces they are powerless to influence. (81)

The bishops go on to discuss the requirements of justice as they might be worked out in the economy, especially in terms of the priority of labor and the need to structure the economy to enable "minimum levels of participation in the life of human community for all persons." (81) This means working out full employment policies, making economic forces accountable, and re-thinking the way people participate in production. The bishops suggest that such measures as production teams and the participation of workers on corporate boards of directors are possible ways to increase the quality of participation.

Critics of the pastoral letter whose conception of justice emphasizes distribution inevitably miss these implications. It is true that the policy suggestions in the letter hardly begin to sketch the possibilities for realizing greater justice in the economy. This is a weakness of the letter. It has resulted in the charge from both the left and the right that the policy recommendations of the letter amount to nothing more than "the democratic party at prayer," or a rehash of New Deal liberalism. At the other extreme, some who do understand the emphasis on justice as participation jump to the conclusion that the bishop's call for democracy in business would paralyze the economy. The bishops have done no such thing, but neither have they anticipated the question. It would have been helpful if they had included some discussion of the problem of how to optimize participation in relation to economic, personal, and social efficiencies.

The bishops, in accordance with their strategy, have left many issues still to be sorted out, and the difficult policy work to be done by all of us. But they might have placed their discussion more adequately in a global and environmental context. They do not seem to be aware of the link between injustice to people and injustice to the land. In a document that does so much to develop a theology that locates human well-being in healthy communities, this is a major omission. Nevertheless, they have made a great contribution to both the church and the national debates, not so much in developing social policy, but in finding the ground and impulse for realizing economic justice. In a national atmosphere where it is increasingly futile to talk about policies for greater justice, the bishops have refocused our energies.

I believe that the basic theology and strategy of the letter is congenial to the Reformed tradition. We have much to learn from the bishops about the importance of helping people to make sustaining, empowering connections with the past that can lead us more surely into God's future. And we have much to relearn about the intensely personal yet corporate character of our vocations in the world. Finally, I have suggested that we have much in common with the letter through our common heritage of response to the gracious acts of God, who, in bringing about creation, covenant, and community, works to redeem our fragile world.

Endnotes

1. *Economic Justice for All: Catholic Social Teaching and the U.S. Economy*, The Third Draft. *Origins*, National Catholic Documentary Service (June 5, 1986), Vol. 15: No. 3. All further references to the document will be given in the text by referring to the paragraph number of *Economic Justice for All.*

2. *Toward a Just, Caring, and Dynamic Political Economy* (JPE), The Report of the Committee on a Just Political Economy, Advisory Council on Church and Society (ACCS), Presbyterian Church (USA), June 1985, p. 6.

3. *Toward a Just, Caring, and Dynamic Political Economy*, p. 8.

Chapter Thirteen

Reformed Economic Ethics in Presbyterian General Assembly Statements, 1900–1987

Christian T. Iosso

The Reformed tradition has evolved over time and is still growing and reforming in light of current needs and expanding knowledge. The essays in this volume have identified certain Reformed themes in economics. The task of this essay is to correlate these themes and positions taken by twentieth century Presbyterian General Assemblies,[1] and to suggest future work in both economic policy and program for the church.[2]

Isolating distinctive Reformed themes is no easy task since each interpreter describes them differently. Elsewhere in this volume, Ronald Stone sums up the Reformed tradition as follows: "commitment through personal experience to shaping of life toward the discernable will of a powerful, loving God." Benefiting from Luther's lead in bringing Christian life out of the monastery and into the world, Calvin himself, according to Stone, benefited from Geneva's early tradition of citizen government and its 'roughly' middle class outlook. Stone thus follows Andre Bieler and other modern Calvin scholars in seeing a post-feudal approach to money, commerce and government as key to the Reformed ethos.

Along with the formative work of Calvin and the Church in Geneva, many of the Reformed distinctives are also seen in the Puritan experience, as in John Winthrop's oft-quoted statement on the Arabella concerning the ethic of "self-abridgement" for the "city set on a

hill." The Puritan ethic encouraged self-discipline and the contribution of talents and goods to the common good of a model community.
It may also be helpful to remember the slogan, *ecclesia reformata,
semper reformanda* (the Church reformed, and always to be reformed),
with its implication that we have a faith for social innovators as well as
traditionalists.

Elsewhere, Jane Dempsey Douglass has focused on the themes,
'humanity in God's image,' 'restoration of the social order,' 'personal
responsibility for the neighbor,' and 'public responsibility for the
neighbor,' as well as on usury and capitalism.[3] In its study report to
the 1985 General Assembly, the Just Political Economy Committee
chose three key concerns, "power, community and government,"
which build on an idea of God's justice as "the basic criterion by which
we can judge the legitimacy of any economic policy or system."[4]

With regard to the present economic policies and programs of
General Assembly, a helpful summary is found in *Social Teachings of
the Presbyterian Church:*

> Work is good and each contribution to the welfare of God's world for
> the benefit of humankind deserves to be recognized and compensated
> fairly. However, each person has a right to a just share of his or her
> society's economic produce including the means of life—adequate food,
> clothing, shelter and education—regardless of that person's ability to
> work or the availability of good jobs. . . .
>
> Each person has a right and a responsibility to contribute to the
> general welfare to the best of his or her ability. Every economic system
> has the obligation to provide opportunities for its members to do useful
> work or to receive sufficient income support. . . .
>
> Participation in the economy is vital to human dignity and human
> self-worth. A just political economy does not accept significant unem-
> ployment or disregard the health of its workers. . . .
>
> Workers as well as owners and managers have a right to share in the
> profit of productive labor and need opportunities to bargain collectively
> for justice, as well as to have safe working conditions. Even well-inten-
> tioned paternalism robs persons of their dignity and must be opposed . . . .
>
> The church's investments, divestments, and purchases should be util-
> ized to express mission responsibilities, with the goal of being faithful
> and effective in the quest for corporate social accountability.[5]

As this initial survey makes clear, there is no concensus on themes.
For the purpose of this essay five themes have been selected for both
historical continuity and current relevance.

A) Responsibility of Government and Economic Powers
B) Poverty, Equality, and Stewardship
C) The Protestant Ethic, Vocation, and Work
D) Covenant and Community; Racial-Ethnic Groups and Women
E) Eco-justice, the Market, and the Common Good

The Responsibilities of Government and Economic Powers

The responsibilities of government in Calvin's view are well summarized by Ronald Stone: "The governing authorities were the agents of God for the welfare of the people." He notes that "[t]he state had the responsibility of regulating business both for its own efficiency and just management as in the cases of the medium of exchanges . . . and for the protection of the population." W. Fred Graham describes the wide range of economic responsibilities undertaken by the City Council in Geneva, including the organization of a textile business to provide needed work.[6] David Little in this volume insists that there is "a foundation in Calvin's thought . . . for *twin commitments* to safety *and* sustenance as the basic obligations of government."

The issue is the accountability of government for the general welfare. Questions here have to do with the relations between the political and economic spheres, the role and independence of the church, and whether the church has always remembered that political and economic structures are provisional. Particularly important is the distinction between the political and economic spheres in the Reformed tradition.[7] The overall question posed by twentieth century church economic policy is whether there has been a deliberate lessening of this distinction, and support for curbing economic autonomy and some business initiative in order to achieve a more just political-economy.

By and large, Presbyterian General Assembly statements on government's economic role have called for the primacy of the political sphere over the economic, mainly due to its more representative character. If we are going to have a capitalist system of competition and private ownership, the Church has emphasized the government's concern for equality, economic growth and adequate welfare programs.

In tune with the tenor of the times, the church's social and economic policy has emphasized social and moral welfare concerns from the turn of the century through the 1920's, social idealism in the

1930's refined into "Reformed Realism" in the 1940's and 50's, and various empowerment struggles in the 1960's and 70's.[8] In the 1980's the church's statements have been more pointed, but its institutional action more tempered by a desire to prevent outright divisions in the church on social-ethical matters. This twentieth century outline reveals that the church has reflected the mood of the country in each period, standing against the tide at some points, but rarely swimming hard against it.

Positively, even in the more conservative periods, the church has held government accountable. Even when the United Presbyterian Church of North America (UPNA) was concentrating on its fairly conservative moral reform agenda, it did so with direct government lobbying, telegrams, and deputations. While that church did have some strong statements on economic concentration and greed between 1903–7, and 1910–13, it came to have a 'single issue' flavor on the subject of prohibition. But again, those statements were remarkable in their detailed attacks on the economic interests behind liquor and Sabbath breaking, and in their call for government to crush these interests before more were corrupted by "brewers' gold."

A good short history of the Presbyterian Church's economic witness is found in "The Church in Economic Affairs," a part of the report of the Task Force on the Church and Transnational Corporations.[9] It notes the General Assembly's endorsement in 1910 of thirteen Social Principles modeled on the 1908 "Social Creed" of the Federal Council of Churches, which called for an end to child labor, a minimum wage, better working conditions, a shorter working day, and the right to organize unions.[10] Behind this policy action was the energetic work of Charles Stelzle, a self-styled "son of the Bowery," who for ten years headed the church's work with labor. Combining an evangelical approach with social gospel conviction, Stelzle held countless rallies, wrote a column for three hundred labor papers, helped co-sponsor a Labor Sunday with the AFL, and founded the innovative Labor Temple in New York City.[11] His effective work generated considerable controversy, prompting a re-organization of his department and re-assertion of "inviolable presbytery rights and . . . initiative." Stelzle's departure soon afterward in 1913 left the church without as significant an economic witness until 1930, although a long-time National Missions board member, John McDowell, maintained some industrial concern through the 1920's.

From the 1930's onward General Assemblies called on the government to provide full employment and to protect the rights of workers, often coupling appeals for cooperation and good will among all sectors of society. The fullest support for labor came in a major 1944 report on "The Church and Industrial Relations," which praised unions as "a primary agent of democracy," while affirming a vision of social harmony and even shared management. That this was done during wartime reflects both the nation's heightened social solidarity and the staffing skill of a new department head, Cameron Hall. By 1947, the General Assembly's economic reports began to speak of "countervailing" as well as "cooperating" powers, using a power analysis that looked at the differing interests of organized groups in the society.

Then in the 1960's, in a strategy "emphatically ratified in *The Confession of 1967*," the institutional church began to go beyond exhortation of individuals to engagement and conflict as a corporate entity pushing for systemic change. This change in mission theology and strategy put the church in direct confrontation not only with government but with corporations and industries, notably in the J. P. Stevens and Nestle boycotts and the corporate social responsibility movement.

More comprehensive policy treatments of the role of government include *The Church's Responsibility in Society* (1972), which builds on *The Confession of 1967* and on a thorough study of church and state issues in 1963. The statement's section on the Reformed tradition links governmental and economic structures:

> The Church has a saving message for the world, a message which it must advocate and embody. The other structures of the common life have the task of ordering some aspect of the world. The clearest example of this is found in government, though it is also true of economic agencies and of other social structures. . . . The relation of the church to the powers of government, industry, technology, education, the arts and sciences, and society as a whole is to remind them that they are not autonomous, and to help them fulfill tasks of justice and peace, liberation and humanization. . . . Political and economic powers may neither control nor be controlled by the church.[14]

Whatever the church's position on economic accountability, it often lacked the structures for sustained witness. The administrative histories of the three PC(USA) strands illustrate this in different ways. In the UPC since the 1930's, there has been relatively little ongoing organization or structure related to economic life. For example, the joint UPNS-PCUSA work of the Presbyterian Institute for Industrial Relations (PIIR), begun in Charles Stelzle's Labor Temple after WWII, did organize an extensive program of continuing education in economic matters under Marshal Scott. The Institute helped develop the concept of industrial mission, which involved fielding a number of industrial chaplains for a brief period in the 1960's. Yet the work of the PIIR continues now only in the small Institute for the Church in an Urban-Industrial Society (ICUIS) in Chicago.

Similarly, the strong statements of the 1930's on economic responsibility and planning, such as 1938's call for industrial democracy, were primarily the focus of the PCUSA's Department of Social Education and Action. Yet in-depth study and policy work on economic matters did not follow after the War, partly due to the move by SEA staff member Cameron Hall to the National Council of Churches. There he supervised the very respected study program on Ethics and Economic Life (1949–65). Presbyterians took part in this creative mix of theologians and economists, but the eleven volume fruit of that study effort was never institutionalized in the denominations.[13]

The overall PCUS history differs most from that of the two "Northern" branches in relation to unions, and more generally in its insistence on strict separation of church and state, which often also meant church and economics. David Taylor notes the key role of the 1966 Assembly statement, "The Theological Basis for Christian Social Action," in which "the spirituality of the Church and its mission to the world was thoroughly reinterpreted," influencing the creation of the unit on "corporate and social mission" in the 1972 PCUS restructure.[14] An example of the traditional skepticism about unions, collective bargaining, "closed shop," and pro-labor boycotts occurred at the 1980 General Assembly, however, when progressive positions on all these points recommended by the Council on Theology and Culture were turned back by the commissioners.[15]

The lack of structures for sustained economic witness was recognized most clearly in the Task Force on Transnational Corporations, which was to review all relations between the United Presbyterian Church and TNC's, but found little more than the Committee on Mission Responsibility Through Investment (MRTI) and boycotts to investigate.

MRTI has, in fact, been a major structure for the church's economic witness. Its 1971 mandate commits the church to use its billion dollar plus portfolio to further peace, racial, economic, and environmental justice by pushing for changes in corporate policy from "within," in accordance with the idea of a corporate democracy of shareholders. The recent extension of MRTI's strategies to include divestment and investment for direct social benefit indicates the limits perceived in its usual approach of discussions with management, formal proposals at corporation annual meetings, and moral suasion.[16] It should be noted that the PCUS had also developed an MRTI Committee in 1976, five years after the UPC, with a more restricted reach over denominational portfolios. Both denominations worked with the Interfaith Center on Corporate Responsibility, and their operations were functionally united in 1983, shortly after reunion of the two denominations.

Though less structured into the church's central administration, church-supported boycotts have had considerable impact. Starting with Cesar Chavez' United Farm Workers in the late 1960's, task forces associated with the Advisory Council on Church and Society monitored situations where injustice was alleged. In the cases of California grapes and lettuce in 1972 and 1973, and J. P. Stevens textiles in 1979, public endorsement was given to the workers' cause and a boycott recommended to General Assembly against the feelings of those local Presbyterians sympathetic to management.

The church's involvement in boycotts was itself studied at length by the General Assembly Mission Council in 1979 as part of a debate over participation in a boycott against state governments which did not support the Equal Rights Amendment.[17] That report reviewed earlier instances of de facto boycotts against alcohol sale, gambling, products of child labor, and discriminatory businesses, and endorsed criteria for future engagement in boycotts by corporate church bodies. Those criteria helped guide Presbyterian support for the worldwide consumer boycott of the Nestle corporation for marketing infant formula in places where its misuse was inevitable. The effectiveness of that boycott was seen not primarily in its economic impact, but in its "de-legitimation" of both unethical marketing and the Nestle firm itself.

In both the corporate responsibility and boycott strategies, the church was seeking ways to make economic institutions more accountable by joining with other consumer, labor, and investor "stakeholders" to change corporate policies. These admittedly somewhat conservative tactics went directly to the corporations involved, without appealing to the state, and gave new meaning to shareholder "democracy."

The further exploration of corporate accountability and economic democracy can be seen in the 1976 study, "Economic Justice Within Environmental Limits: The Need for a New Economic Ethic." In its own words, "a major underlying theme . . . is an exploration of the prospects for economic democracy in the United States . . . an economy of the people, by the people, and for the people."[18] Where the study argues best for 'economic democracy,' is in relation to economic concentration in its various forms, from oligopoly in industry to a potential "landed aristocracy" in agriculture, against which "adequate checks and balances are needed . . . for a dynamic citizen participation process." Publicly accountable and decentralized economic planning is recommended, providing for "corporate accountability" in the place of corporate responsibility, a concept too voluntary and limited to individual firms and industries.[19] The study's idea of "economic democracy" generally involves extending the role of government, rather than expanding the rights of individuals to include economic rights. There is even the suggestion that the individual rights route is mainly about the right to private property, and as such should be de-emphasized.[20] Overall, the 1976 report focused on new principles and values to guide economic activity, rather than on systems like capitalism or socialism.

The Task Force on Transnational Corporations and the Presbyterian Church might have given more attention to the matter of corporate accountability raised in the church's earlier policy and program efforts. Certainly questions about public accountability through taxes, regulation and incentives, as well as new forms of organization and ownership were well within its scope. Conclusion Two of the task force's report affirmed that TNC's did have a de facto governmental power, and urged more accountability but without giving it specific content.[21] The report, however, focused mainly on the church's own life paying little attention to the need for improved transnational economic structures. The corporate responsibility and boycott strategies were not rejected, but supplementary, less "confrontational" means were recommended to effect change.

In 1985, the Committee on a Just Political Economy showed awareness of a trend toward greater government participation in economic planning in Europe and Japan, but for the most part stayed with moderately progressive industrial policy recommendations for government action. The committee's report is a more moderate sounding document than the Roman Catholic Bishops' Pastoral Letter on the Economy, and is in considerable contrast to papers like the United Church of Christ's *Christian Faith and Economic Life* (1987), which chose economic democracy as a major Christian principle, and economic rights as its corollary.[22] These concepts may be implicit and sometimes mentioned in General Assembly policies and studies, but are not affirmed as unequivocally.[23]

In terms of future study and policy directions in the area of economic accountability and political-economic governance, it may be time for renewed study of economic rights. Various unions have developed their versions, generally stressing the right to good work, as have a variety of economists.[24] While the Church's previous support for economic democracy has been more suggestive than substantial, the direction of the church's witness is clear.

Poverty, Equality, and Stewardship

In a paper on "Calvin's Relation to Social and Economic Change," Jane Dempsey Douglass claims that Calvin viewed attitudes on poverty as key tests of an individual's faith and character. The rich were to share, and the poor were to endure. If 'mutual communication' existed among humanity, "all would . . . give and receive, maintaining an equilibrium." But this equilibrium did not mean equality of outcome. For Calvin, the principle of division was not equality but need.

Concerns for equality and for giving have been the church's two main responses to poverty. A question for twentieth century Presbyterians has been how to hold an ideal of equality without carrying it to egalitarianism and without reducing stewardship to charity.

The Reformed tradition has shied away from egalitarianism. Some Reformed thinkers have embraced socialist understandings of equality, and the tradition generally has given government too important a role to accept a simple model of alms-giving or charity. Andre Bieler emphasizes the "economic solidarity" and even "personalist socialism" of Calvin's thought, in contrast to the capitalism of later followers.[25] Yet the Reformed tradition since Calvin is generally seen as tilted toward the charity approach to equality, often paternalistic in flavor, with stewardship restricted to surplus or even superfluities. Capitalism may be more cause then effect of this "tilt."

There are other options than government imposed egalitarianism and paternalism, for example, charity, and various supports for more equality are present in Reformed thought. Certainly, the relations between spiritual, economic and political equality are as real as they are complex, and equality must be considered with efficiency and freedom as relevant factors in economic ethics. Given the persistent tilt toward inequality of our economic system, however, Reformed concerns for justice and solidarity with the poor would seem to back a more serious look at greater equality than our policy statements have taken.

Of course, even if the church had expressed more appreciation for equality, the social position and self-image of many Presbyterians would keep paternalism alive. Behind the policies opposing poverty and recommending more progessive taxation and economic planning is the reality that most Presbyterians are relatively wealthy and do not want to give up the power which wealth affords.

The recent period of empowerment, self-development, and more inclusive leadership is part of the church's answer to the charge of paternalism. *The Confession of 1967* also contains a strong attack on paternalism. In its most "economic" section, though, poverty is the chief problem and equality is not mentioned:

> Reconciliation of the world through Jesus Christ makes it plain that enslaving poverty in a world of abundance is an intolerable violation of God's good creation. Because Jesus identified himself with the needy and exploited, the cause of the world's poor is the cause of his disciples. The church cannot condone poverty. . . . The church calls us to use our abilities, our possessions, and the fruits of technology as gifts entrusted to us by God for the maintenance of our families and the advancement of the common welfare. . . . A church that is indifferent to poverty, or evades responsibility in economic affairs, or is open to one social class only, *or expects gratitude for its beneficence makes a mockery of reconciliation* and offers no acceptable worship to God.[26]

A similar viewpoint is contained in *A Declaration of Faith*, "a contemporary statement of faith" developed by the PCUS in 1976, though not given confessional status:

> We believe God sends us to work with others to correct the growing disparity between rich and poor nations. . . . We are commissioned to stand with women and men of all ages, races and classes as they struggle for dignity and respect and the chance to exercise power for the common good. We must not countenance in the church and its institutions the inequities we seek to correct in the world. We must be willing to make such amends as we can for centuries of injustice which the church has condoned.[27]

That same year, in the UPC study, "Economic Justice Within Environmental Limits," there is again considerable concern for the poor in the U.S. and overseas, with a general refusal to push egalitarianism as a basic solution. The study favors "distributive justice . . . the equitable sharing of the burdens and benefits of a society. Economic egalitarianism—the theory that the same amount be given to each person—it not the issue. The eradication of human misery is the prime objective." There is an awareness that "great inequities seriously restrict the individual and political freedoms of the have-nots," but greater equity is primarily instrumental in obtaining better political democracy, which in turn will make for better collective stewardship of economic and natural resources.[28]

Equality does appear in various other studies by the church, most notably in the studies of compensation. The discussion in a 1976 document centers on "egalitarian" and "meritarian" ideas of compensation. A compromise is struck between the two approaches, with a weighting scheme for experience, education, and job requirements and a proportion of three to one between ceiling and minimum compensation levels in any given region.

In the early 1980's both predecessor denominations reopened the compensation issue, with more interest in retirement provisions and lay employees. This led to a reaffirmation of the earlier compromise approach, but with a beefed up minimum. At the same time, a study paper by biblical scholar Walter Brueggemann of the United Church of Christ was commissioned by the General Assembly Mission Board.[29]

The Brueggemann paper examines the cultural ethos that affects compensation decisions and attacks directly the "consumer capitalism" that distorts the church's values. In the current "economic disarray," when the false dreams of unlimited growth and affluence are challenged by real and false scarcity, Brueggemann asserts ". . . the Church's own economic arrangements are irrelevant, unless they are an alternative modeling or at least a subversive protest against the ideologies of the day." He continues ". . . the Church and Church members can have almost no direct influence upon compensation matters in large corporate structures." He therefore proposes a "break with those values" or "meritocracy," and favors an "alternative economics" for the church, which would "face the difficult question of some form of equalization among its authorized leadership," and non-financial forms of discipline and connectedness for pastors, congregations and the denomination overall.

A somewhat similar view of equality's importance is found in the 1984 PCUS study paper, *Christian Faith and Economic Justice,* perhaps because its biblical section draws on Brueggemann's work and the sympathetic work of Bruce Birch.[30] According to the paper,

> . . . social and economic equality is the first norm, standard, and ideal by which all economic arrangements are evaluated, but there can be arguments for particular inequalities if they are the result of the pursuit of freedom and work to the benefit of the disadvantaged.[31]

This widely accepted formulation may unfortunately assume too much of a trade-off between equality and economic efficiency and understate the *social* costs of inequality, as ethicist J. Philip Wogaman points out.[32] Fruitfully, however, the paper bases "special concern for the poor" on God loving "all equally." This is linked to a covenantal relationship involving retributive, distributive, and restorative justice. As in the case of the Just Political Economy paper, there is also an instrumental use of equality, not simply for better political democracy, but for life in human community.

Stewardship, however, remains the main conceptual response to poverty and is inevitably related to economic inequality. A 1982 study of stewardship broadened the idea in a number of ways, but did not grapple with a more egalitarian church economics. The denomination's most concrete response to poverty, the Presbyterian Hunger Program, does, however, embody a stewardship model that goes well beyond charity. Money goes not only to direct relief, but also to the "root causes" of hunger, to education and to changing government policy—generally in an egalitarian direction.

A question for the future is whether the church can advocate more egalitarian economics for itself while the society pushes meritocracy. Even if the church were a distinct, alternative minority, the Reformed tradition would seem to suggest an engagement with the world that keeps the tensions on both its own members and the powers that be.

The Protestant Ethic, Vocation, and Work

The original Protestant ethic was simply the attitude toward everyday work of those Christians who believed there was a calling in it. To quote from *The Church and Transnational Corporations*, "the distinction between 'religious vocation' . . . and 'secular vocation' so often made today is decidedly not Presbyterian. There is *one* calling from God—one vocation—to serve the divine purposes of redemption and restoration in *all* the world's life."[33] For early Protestants, this view led to energetic, purposeful action, disciplined to reflect one's sense of election and to overcome self-indulgence. In later generations, though, this approach has been termed "worldly asceticism," "deferred gratification," "inner-directed," "achievement-oriented," even "workaholism," as the sense of being called *by* God has eroded.

What has also eroded is a sense of being called *to* serve a community, as individualism and competition have helped transform a "work ethic" into a "success ethic," with its focus on individual accumulated wealth and no inherent concern for the less fortunate. Without reviewing the scholarly argument over the influences of Protestantism and capitalism on each other,[34] the mid-to-late twentieth century Presbyterian Church has clearly tried to revive the original Protestant ethic among its often success-oriented members. The preeminent instance of this is in *The Confession of 1967*:

> The church disperses to serve God wherever its members are, at work or play, in private or in the life of society. . . . Their daily action in the world is in the church in mission to the world. The quality of their relation with other persons is the measure of the church's fidelity.
>
> Each member is the church in the world, endowed by the spirit with some gift of ministry and is responsible for the integrity of his or her witness in each particular situation. The member is entitled to the guidance and support of the Christian community and is subject to its advice and correction. Each, in turn, in his or her own competence, helps to guide the church.[35]

The overall narrowing of vocation to mean occupation was examined at length in a substantial UPC study, *The Church, the Christian and Work*, also completed in 1967, which sought to clarify the frequently "cartooned" Protestant ethic. That study built on the National Council of Churches' *Series of The Ethics and Economics of Society*, and affirmed the policy commitment to full employment, while also arguing for *good* employment. The core of the study certainly still holds:

> In . . . our contemporary economic situation obedience to the covenant demands the exercise of our imagination in the creation of new modes of work, the assertion of human worth as grounded in community rather than employment, the reminder that unemployment is essentially a problem of community, and the reaffirmation of vocation over occupation as the mark of (hu)man's faithfulness to God.[36]

In contemporary discussions, the concept of vocation involves seeing work as service to a community of which the church is a part, and
fulfilling only in "a political, social and ultimately covenantal context."[37] Lee McDonald poses the vocation question in terms of a
harmony, if not unity, of instrumental and more ultimate virtues.[38]
By vocation he means an integration of personal and communal
values in work that is intrinsically worthwhile. Ultimately, he means a
harmony of both occupation and leisure, production and consumption, in which lifestyle would be oriented by neighbors' needs and
calculated to minimize their envy. This is certainly a good basis for a
contemporary ethic of sufficiency as well as vocation.

The questions our tradition poses to social policy have to do with
both the narrowing of the idea of vocation to the ministry, to the
professions or to middle class occupations, and with the question of
integrating conflicting occupational values. Some of the church's
statements on industrial relations and unionization have addressed
this 'narrowing' and the problems with blue collar job and work
quality. A long PCUSA statement from 1944 went so far as to credit
unions with a "spiritual" function that helped compensate for the
limiting character of much labor.[39]

In the 1980's the General Assembly and its agencies have dealt
more with the question involving value conflicts within corporate life.
Is the church articulating values that can be integrated into the lives
of those who must live in the marketplace? And if the church's values
and claims seem inconsistent with some pursuits, what happens?

This value and identity conflict between the church and business
was the chief focus of *The Church and Transnational Corporations*. This
report reflected on the church's criticism of corporate involvement
with South Africa, toxic chemicals, the arms race, plant closings and
many other issues. The TNC executives on the task force wanted to
have their vocation understood, if not respected. Rather than "the
guidance and support of the Christian community," called for in *The
Confession of 1967*, what they felt they were getting was only "its advice
and correction," at least on the General Assembly level. Was the
church really implying that nuclear weapons manufacture or investment in South Africa could not be considered part of a Christian
vocation? If the corporation were "demon(ized)," would its officials be
classed with torturers, drug dealers, and others whose jobs do not
serve the common good? The report urged a more balanced view,
saw tension on economic issues as inevitable, and asked the church to
look at itself more critically.

Indeed, if this is done with regard to the vocation of ministry, the papers on compensation may suggest that the institutional church is a mirror of society as a whole: a free market system with high unemployment in some sectors, relocation difficulties, limited collegiality, increasing wage differentials, arcane and inefficient work rules such as Hebrew and Greek requirements, plant closings and surplus capacity, and eroding competitive position with other religious groups. And while job sharing is given consideration by clergy couples, there is usually a hierarchical model for multiple staff situations. With regard to the ordained ministry itself, then, is the church modeling a transferable and worthy image of vocation?[40]

The 1985 study paper, *Toward a Just, Caring and Dynamic Political Economy,* does look at the church realistically, in terms of the social location of its membership, while also trying to expand people's sense of power and responsibility for the economy. "Responsibility," in fact, is the paper's chief vocational norm, closely related to participation. "Productive justice," for example, deals with "how employees are able to cooperate in the productive process and have opportunities to contribute to the limits of their abilities," as well as "with the inclusion of all members in economic activity and economic decisions."[41] The study notes that greater equity in compensation has a good effect on motivation, but by downplaying public or worker ownership it does not suggest the full range of worker responsibilities. The study reaffirms the goals of full employment and growth with equity, but calls for "the use of spiritual and social incentives"—i.e. non-monetary ones, and a "re-think(ing of) the very meaning of work," particularly in light of women's work at home and in the marketplace.[42] The vocational question is also raised implicitly in the call for opportunities for the handicapped and elderly.

In comparison to the many good recommendations for structural changes made in the paper, there is much less about why and how a more 'just, caring and dynamic political economy' would be a more fulfilling one vocationally.

Without a renewed vision of vocation it will be hard to develop any alternative economics in church and society, and without any initial alternative communities, it will be hard to develop vocational commitments to greater communal solidarity. What the church might wisely push for is a greater equalization of income and wealth for the bulk of the U.S. population, which has a far less equal distribution than other developed nations. The church may also go beyond the terms of the "industrial policy debate," with its emphasis on teamwork and collective entrepreneurialism. In one direction, the church may note that worker control in enterprises does build a powerful motivation, however threatening it may be to managers, while at the same time the church must celebrate non-financial motivation, the shared nature of empowerment, even an ethics of relinquishment.

Covenant and Community: Women and Racial Ethnic Participation

In contemporary church usage, "covenant" appears to mean a longlasting, voluntary but mutually binding collective agreement, which may or may not be periodically re-established. In our usual baptismal formula, the congregation is asked to welcome "a child of the covenant," with the implication that the church continues the ancient covenant with Israel. In other usage, the idea of covenant is related to our creation in God's image, and to the establishment of faithful relationship. Part of the human side of the covenant's mutual responsibilities includes care for the creation. Looking forward, the covenant relationship is also to model the Realm of God, and be a forerunner of the fully reconciled eschatological community of all humanity.

The problematic side of Reformed thinking on covenant and community can be seen when one looks at those who are excluded from among the elect. The early Puritans clearly saw the covenant in terms of an "in group" that did not include the native inhabitants of the land. The 1976 *Economic Justice Within Environmental Limits* study, which affirmed ". . . justice is the basic civil covenant . . ." also noted that "Governments . . . are made by sinful people. They often express a covenant which favors some people and denies others their rights."[43] Preston Williams in this volume questions whether the church, as "holy community," can faithfully and accurately speak to government and economic institutions without real inclusiveness. Since the mid-1960's, the church's commitment at the General Assembly level to equal employment opportunity and affirmative action seems to indicate that inclusiveness has become one of the marks of a "true church."

On the positive side, Williams invokes the Reformed tradition's assertion of God's sovereignty as the basis for equality across group boundaries. Jane Dempsey Douglass relates the notion of equality to our common creation in God's image, to the ideas of mutual communication of goods and "mutual subjection" between the sexes, and to our eventual equality in the Realm of God, despite the placement of men over women and various other inequalities under the present order of creation.[44] By extension, all significant inequities, of race, gender, and sexual preference are legacies of the Fall, and are not to be the pretext for further discrimination.

Historically the Presbyterian churches had different attitudes toward slavery, from toleration in the South, to firm abolitionism in much of the North. Differences over slavery had a significant role in the New School/Old School split. There are stories of some Presbyterians boycotting slave-made goods, a strategy used by a number of Quaker groups.[45] Yet the economic aspects of racism were not of very explicit policy concern until the 1960's, when many began to see them as the hardest barriers of all.

In an overview of Racial Ethnic Ministry Policies in the United Presbyterian Church, Archie Crouch summarizes the trend from 1919 to 1977:

> During this period the church's ministry to racial and cultural groups shifted rapidly from an attempt to convert and to 'civilize' to an emphasis on advocacy and the transformation of unjust attitudes and structures in the church and nation. . . . After WWII . . . the Church decides it will be a fully integrated community of believers with a mission to transform its social milieu into an integrated society . . . toward that end it will foster self-determination and self-development for all racial and cultural minorities.[46]

Frequently the work of the church was paternalistic, as in the founding of churches and schools, stressing vocational education on a separate and unequal basis. To get a flavor of the ethos, one need only look at the General Assembly reports at the beginning of Crouch's period of post-war change. Despite its 1903 claim that "in this work our church with its marked anti-slavery history, should hold no second place," a 1919 UPNA Freedmen's Board report quoted a common attitude as one of its goals, "not to make the negro smart, but to make him good."[47] That same year a PCUS Report on Home Missions denounced lynching, but noted that "unfortunately, race prejudice is mutual. . . ," and suggsted that "If Bolshevism, the labor question and the race problem should form a coalition, Christian civilization itself will tremble in the balance." Part of the "race problem" with the Negro was due to "leaving him entirely to the tuition and philanthropy of the North."[48]

There was also considerable pride taken in the Freedmen's missions, which were seen as models of what the whole nation including the South should have done after the evil of slavery was ended. In the UPNA, the concept of slavery was applied to prohibition (drink-slavery, 1906), to prostitution (white-slavery, 1914 in particular), and even the slavery of working on the Sabbath (1911). Black membership gains were also reported with emphasis. In the years after the black boards had been reorganized into the national, American or home mission boards, the church's tokenism had an element of affirmative action to it. In 1946, for example, the membership of the newly formed Council on Christian Relations (PCUS) was to include at least one negro and one woman.[49]

It may be helpful to put the church's attitudes towards the Freedman in the context of views on other groups. The UPNA General Assemblies were more than frank, for example, on the Irish-British conflict (1918–21), 'popery' in general, mormonism-polygamy, and secret societies such as Masons, subjecting all to almost the same condemnation as the alcohol trade ('bludgeon of death,' 'god of filth,' modern Beelzebub,' etc.). The statements about the Irish reveal fairly clear prejudice, while the other groups are all evil in some way due to their being separate and alien communities outside the American covenant. At the same time, while native Americans and blacks might be patronized, they were not seen as enemies.

The statements by the denominations in the 1940's and '50's focus on opening opportunity, on redressing inequality in education, housing, and other areas of the economy, and on desegregating the church itself. The statements of the PCUS General Assembly in 1954–55, favoring desegregation, stirred up the church as few statements have. The 1960's statements link racism more clearly to poverty. The formation of national program units on church and race in the mid-1960's in both the Northern and Southern churches marked a new institutional seriousness about the problems. Support for the United Farm Workers' grape and lettuce boycotts and the more recent concern for the Farm Labor Organizing Committee (FLOC) in the Midwest were also signs of economic opposition to racism.

In the early seventies, however, Dieter Hessel noted a shift in focus, from the strong social witness of the 1960's toward a concentration on the church's internal inclusiveness and staffing policies.[50] This may reflect the splitting off of racial and women's concerns from the overall social witness machinery, and the organizational efforts to set up the Presbyterian Economic Development corporation (PEDCO),

Self-Development of People (SDOP), Project Equality and other agencies of social empowerment. This internal focus may also by the consequence of controversies: the reparations demands of James Foreman and others in 1969, the organized criticism of the Angela Davis legal defense grant in 1971, and on-going opposition to grants by the World Council of Churches' Programme to Combat Racism.

One exception to this internal focus would be the very substantial study and policy on Mexican-American relations done in 1981, which looked closely at the economics of dependency and migration in both Mexico and the United States. There has also been attention to the decline in black farm ownership in the Southeast and to the situation of the mostly black Southern woodcutters.

Currently the question of whether to have separate Black organizations affects the church's Creative Investment program, a lower than market rate of return, affirmative investment program operated by MRTI since 1976. It seems time to link the self-development funds to the social investment stream represented by MRTI. The alternative and minority economic ventures at some point will also need to be linked to transformative efforts aimed at the whole economy, such as through local or regional development banks that would re-channel personal savings to community needs on a much larger scale.[51]

As for women and economic life in the Church, the best study of women's political and economic power remains Elizabeth H. Verdesi's *In But Still Out* (1973, 76).[52] Looking at the Presbyterian Church in the USA, Verdesi charts the rise in the 1870's and fall in the 1920's of formal women's organizations when the Women's Board of Home Missions was absorbed in restructure. This was paralleled by the rise and fall of organizational power in the 1950's when the largely female body of commissioned Christian educators yielded influence to male leadership. But her real story is about the pervasiveness of inequality, despite the decisions on eldership (1930) and ministry (1956). Here the lack of separate structures as well as their marginalization is part of the explanation. This lack of separate structures was even more pronounced in the Presbyterian Church, U.S., which authorized a superintendent for Women's Work only in 1912 and did not let her speak to the full General Assembly until fifteen years later. Ordination as elders, deacons, and ministers in the PCUS came in 1965, beginning the end of what Lois A. Boyd and R. Douglas Brackenridge term an "auxiliary type" of status for their women's groups.[53]

The more comprehensive Boyd and Brackenridge study, *Presbyterian Women in America,* also provides considerable information on the gap between procedural and actual equality. After discussing the supportive role of Stated Clerk Eugene Carson Blake in the 1950's debates over ordination, for example, they note that once ordination was approved, he saw no need "to lift a hand beyond that." For them, his position illustrated an ambivalence among men who supported women's equal rights in the church on a procedural basis, but "offered no strategy to alleviate . . . basic inequality."[54] This ambivalence was eliminated on a policy basis in the UPCUSA during the 1970's, culminating with a 1979 decision mandating women elders and deacons in all congregations. The placement and relocation difficulties facing ordained clergywomen illustrate the remaining inequality of women within the church.

With this background it is understandable that General Assembly study and policy on the economic place of women has been limited to the 1970's and 1980's. In 1969, following a major report on The Status of Women in Society and in the Church, United Presbyterian Women and the Office of Church and Society created a Task Force on Women, which led to the Council on Women in the Church (COWAC) in 1973. Working with UPW and other women's organizations, COWAC helped the church focus on specific economic problems such as discrimination against women in employment, the welfare system, the feminization of poverty, and comparable worth. In the process COWAC developed a work book and conferences on Economic Justice for Women.

UPW led the denomination in making the elimination of global hunger a "major mission priority" in 1975, and successfully recommended the endorsement of the Nestle Boycott in 1979. This boycott had been endorsed by the PCUS General Assembly a year earlier. Elder Patricia Young, a past President of UPW and leader in both efforts, went on to serve as first Director of World Food Day, while the hunger emphasis became institutionalized in the Presbyterian Hunger Program.

Despite a recent General Assembly study on feminist theology, there has been relatively little use of feminist perspectives in the policy making and implementation processes of the church. For example, the Committee on MRTI, which had economic justice for women added to its mandate by the General Assembly in 1974, has had few strategies focused on economic discrimination against women. On the positive side, covenant concepts consistent with feminist perspectives have been used in the areas where women play a prominent role, such as the social policy on family, sexuality, and abortion. One example would be the 1983 study, Covenant of Life and the Caring Community, which looked at a spectrum of bio-ethics issues from in vitro fertilization to euthanasia. Women have also been involved in the bio-medical ethics questions examined by the Presbyterian Board of Pensions.

The trend toward formation of exclusive communities and informally restrictive covenants seems likely to continue in our society and stands to be reinforced by economic inequality. If the Church begins to see itself more self-consciously as a faith-based minority group, on the model of Stanley Hauerwas perhaps, or a cognitive minority as with George Lindbeck, then the practical consequences of this may make it even more difficult for the mainline church to be an inclusive body in an inclusive society.[55] Yet the church's distinctive culture and ethos may not be barriers to inclusiveness if our social and economic witness makes clear a commitment to liberation and transformation within our community. In such a church, integration would not simply be the incorporation of diverse individuals, but the movement of a body seeking wholeness and justice, not simply in fair treatment but in full empowerment and participation.

Eco-Justice, the Market, and the Common Good

Lucien Richard, outlining Calvin's inclusive view of the realm of God, asserts: "For Calvin the fulfillment of the kingdom included within it the renovation of the world, the restoration of the created order. At the very core of Calvin's eschatology was the belief that the coming of God's [realm] transforms the created world."[56]

The strong linkage between the common good and environmental concern has led some to favor more effective government problem-solving rather than reliance on the free market. Considerable work on this linkage has been done by Presbyterians William Gibson and Richard Austin under the eco-justice rubric.[57] They argue, for example, that energy, timber and mineral corporations have tended to push short-term resource development at the expense of long term stewardship. Accurate as the 'public' versus 'industry' viewpoint in the church's environmental policy may be, government's fulfillment of the public trust must also be evaluated. Some have proposed new approaches to regulation, and others stress the linkage of environmental degradation to poverty. Thus it may help to examine the relation of liberation to creation with an eye to new regulatory structures.

Extended United Presbyterian policy treatment of ecological concerns began in 1971, in a separate statement and in the estabishment of policy for the committee on Mission Responsibility Through Investment. In 1974 it came up again in relation to the energy crisis and population growth. Then, as the title of the 1976 study, *Economic Justice Within Environmental Limits,* indicates, ecological concern was combined with anxiety about limits to growth. That 1976 study also mentions wilderness, never specifically addressed by the General Assembly, asking, "What is a wilderness worth?"[58] In 1980 a PCUS General Assembly condemned toxic chemical pollution.

In 1981 both predecessor churches joined in a comprehensive energy policy statement, "The Power to Speak Truth to Power,"[59] which provides a solid value basis for on-going work on eco-justice in the church. Building on work by the World and National Councils of Churches, that policy statement proposed three ethical norms to guide an inevitable transition to renewable energy use. These were Justice, Sustainable Sufficiency, and Participation, followed by a longer set of "middle axioms" and a concrete set of specific recommendations critical of both nuclear power and coal, and advocating renewable forms of energy and conservation as the first objectives of public policy.

These themes were more or less ignored in the work of the Just Political Economy committee, although it considered Herman Daly's work in "steady state economics." Perhaps this reflects the fact that the shift to renewable energy seems further away than ever.[60] Environmental stewardship may need more attention again, but declining standards of living, intractable unemployment, and problems with international competition have seemed more pressing. Given the likelihood of serious resource depletion in the twenty first century, this should change as we strive to develop ethics not only of taxation and government assistance, but also ethics for rationing, and even for choosing national and international sacrifice areas.

The implications of an eco-justice model or a "sustainable sufficiency" concept involve changes in thinking about economic development, both at home and abroad. Self-sufficiency, appropriate technology, decentralization, recycling, and community lifestyle changes, including population practices, have become parts of the General Assembly's conceptual reponse to debt crisis overseas and the farming crisis in middle America. On the personal level there is promise that increased understanding of eco-justice approaches will help in renewing the links between work and co-creation, expanding our pictures of vocation and the common good.

Conclusion

In each section, this paper has suggested potential future directions for policy-program work by institutions of the church. In summary, these are:

A. Role of Government and Economic Powers: Consider a clearer statement of economic rights, in light of the need to achieve greater economic democracy. Outline the public, private and church actions necessary to reconceive and renegotiate the basic responsibilities of business, government, and non-profit institutions in a genuinely transnational framework.

B. Poverty, Equality, and Stewardship: Develop a stronger analysis of equality and empowerment to move stewardship away from paternalism and toward solidarity with the world's poor. Show how the church can use its resources, long-range vision, and renewing energy to help communities provide sustenance, shelter and good work (a koinonia economics).

C. Protestant Ethic, Vocation, and Work: Because vocation and common good are not seriously part of our political-economic discourse the church should help develop economically self-sustaining alternative communities that can model meaningful work, a more egalitarian incentive structure, and cooperative or solidarity-based organization. Such renewed communities may help renew the work-enriching, community connection necessary to vocation. Full employment with good jobs remains the untried policy goal.

D. Covenant and Community: Racial Ethnic Groups and Women: Explore new forms of connectedness and the church as an intentional yet inclusive community. Make the church a stronger agent of racial and gender justice in society at large.

E. Eco-Justice, the Market, and the Common Good: Clarify a better approach to governmental stewardship of the environment, wilderness, and the non-market properties of nature. Redirect economic and investment priorities along the lines of the 1981 Presbyterian energy policy and the eco-justice perspective more generally. Develop an "eco-industrial policy" to coordinate needed, affordable economic growth with the phase-out of the unsustainable.

Endnotes

1. The important distinction between General Assembly *policy*, binding on agencies of the church, and *studies*, of a more advisory nature, reflects some of the organizational genius of Dean H. Lewis, Director of the Advisory Council on Church and Society in the United Presbyterian Church and Presbyterian Church (USA) from 1972–88. A special 1977 study on "Social Policy Formation" explains the difference in detail. See *Minutes of the General Assembly of the United Presbyterian Church in the U.S.A.* (New York: General Assembly UPC 1977, I.), p. 323ff.

2. Helpful treatments of the church's economic positions can be found in:

—Dale T. Irvin and Dean H. Lewis, ed., "Social Witness Policies—An Historical Overview" and Richard Poethig, "Urban Metro Mission Policies—An Historical Overview" in *The Journal of Presbyterian History*, Fall 1979 (Vol. 57, No. 3).

—Dieter T. Hessel *Reconciliation and Conflict* (Philadelphia: The Westminster Press, 1969).

—George Chauncey and Y. Jacqueline Rhoades, eds. *Social Pronouncements of the Presbyterian Church in the U.S. (1960–69)*, (Atlanta: General Assembly Mission Board, 1970)

—George Chauncey and Belle Miller McMaster, eds. *A Presbyterian Witness to the Nation (PCUS 1965–79)*, (Atlanta: General Assembly Mission Board, 1980).

3. Jane Dempsey Douglass, "Calvin's Relation to Social and Economic Change," in Christian T. Iosso, ed. *The Church and Transnational Corporations*, The Report of the Task Force on Review of Policies, Strategies and Programs of the United Presbyterian Church Related to Transnational Corporations, with appendices and study guide. A special issue of *Church & Society*, March–April 1984 (Vol. LXXIV, No. 4).

4. *Minutes of the General Assembly of the Presbyterian Church (USA)* (New York: General Assembly, 1985), pp. 335–337. The Report of the Committee on a Just Political Economy of the Advisory Council on Church and Society entitled, *Toward a Just, Caring and Dynamic Political Economy*, is also available separately from the Committee on Social Witness Policy, Presbyterian Church USA, 100 Witherspoon, St. Louisville, KY 40202.

5. James Beumler and Dieter T. Hessel, ed. *Social Teachings of the Presbyterian Church*. A special issue of *Church & Society*, Nov.–Dec. 1984 (Vol. LXXV, No. 2), p. 57.

6. W. Fred Graham, *The Constructive Revolutionary: John Calvin & HIs Socio-Economic Impact* (Atlanta: The John Knox Press, 1971).

7. This distinction is described in David Little, *Religion, Order and Law* (Chicago: University of Chicago Press, 1984; New York: Harper & Row, 1969).

8. A chronological chart of major policy and program measures, theological movements and economic trends is available from Christian Iosso OC Box 2 Union Seminary 3041 Broadway, NYC 10027.

9. The historical summary in this section is dependent on *The Church and Transnational Corporations,* op. cit., pp. 17–37 and 82–102, which includes the cited chapter. This study made nine recommendations for changes in the church's work with TNC's, and was received by a close vote with the recommendation that it be printed with critiques from labor and Third World perspectives.

10. *Minutes of the General Assembly of the Presbyterian Church in the U.S.A.* (Philadelphia: General Assembly, 1910), p. 230–31. Eight of the thirteen "principles" listed closely resemble points from the thirteen point Federal Council document, which was adopted on Dec. 4, 1908. The "Social Creed," though formally a committee document, was largely written by the Methodist Harry F. Ward. The book he edited, *The Social Creed of the Churches* (Nashville: Abingdon Press, 1912), remains its best explication.

11. Charles Stelzle, *A Son of the Bowery* (New York: Geo. Doran & Co., 1926) is both autobiography and apologia. His disappointment with the Presbyterian Churches overall slights some of their (and his) achievements. For example, it was partly his own visit to the UPNS Assembly that led to their acceptance of the Social Creed in 1912, yet he mourns their conservatism.

12 *Minutes* (New York: General Assembly (UPC), 1972), p. 512. "The Church's Witness in Society" pamphlet form, with appendices, can be obtained in photocopy from the Committee on Social Witness Policy.

13. *The Series on the Ethics and Economics of Society* begins with John C. Bennett, et al. *Christian Values in Economic Life* (New York: Harper & Row, 1954) and ends with Victor Obenhaus, *Ethics for an Industrial Age* (New York: Harper & Row, 1965).

14. David Taylor, "A History of PCUS Program Structures," (Atlanta: General Assembly Mission Board, 1980).

15. *The Presbyterian Outlook,* June 23, 1980 (Vol. 162, No. 25), p. 3, provides the initial and final wordings.

16. The Mission Responsibility Through Investment (MRTI) work has been studied not only by the TNCTF, but by the MRTI Committee itself. Notable resources are the "Investment Policy Guidelines" *Minutes* (UPC, 1971), pp. 596–629, *Minutes* (PCUS, 1976), pp. 513–18, the "Creative Investment Policy" *Minutes* (UPC, 1975), pp. 445–6 the "Resolution on Military-Related Investment Guidelines (*Minutes,* UPC, 1982, pp. 259–264 and updated annually), "The Divestment Strategy: Ethical and Institutional Context" (*Minutes,* 1984, pp. 193–206) and "Divestment for South Africa: An

Investment in Hope" (*Minutes*, 1985, pp. 209–232). All are available from the MRTI Office in Louisville.

17. *Minutes* (UPC, 1979) pp. 250–57. In pamphlet form, *Boycotts: Policy Analysis and Criteria* is available from the Committee on Social Witness Policy. It reviews boycotts and selective patronage related to "liquor traffic" (1910 ff.), Sabbath commerce (1910), "suggestive and unclean" films (1922), child labor products (1937; also implied in 1910 Social Principles), goods and services of discriminating employers (1956, 1960), selective investing for racial justice (1964, 1966) and the first General Assembly call for South Africa-linked divestment (1967).

18. "Economic Justice Within Environmental Limits: The Need for A New Economic Ethics," a 1976 United Presbyterian General Assembly study, printed with appendices in *Church & Society*, Sept.–Oct., 1976 (Vol. LXVII, No. 1), p. 15.

19. *Ibid.*, pp. 38, 43, 39–40. One of the authors of the report has recently restated the issues of corporate responsibility and corporate accountability. See Walter Owensby, *Economics for Prophets* (Grand Rapids: William B. Eerdmans, 1988).

20. On the question of rights, see pp. 33–35; for example, "Individual freedom often becomes a private right that controls the destiny and restricts the freedom of others," p. 33.

21. *The Church and Transnational Corporations*, p. 41.

22. *Christian Faith and Economic Life* (A Study Paper Contributing to a Pronouncement for the Seventeenth General Synod of the United Church of Christ) Audrey C. Smock, ed., is available from Hunger Action Office, United Church Board for World Ministries, 475 Riverside Dr., New York, NY 10115.

23. A strong 1978 statement insists, for example, in the "right" to "basic necessities," (*Minutes*, PCUS, p. 186) but is silent on other rights of participants in the economy.

24. Samuel Bowles, David M. Gordon and Thomas Weisskopf in *Beyond the Wasteland* (New York: Vintage, 1983) provide an extensive argument for economic rights with an economic democracy goal.

25. Andre Bieler, *The Social Humanism of John Calvin* (Richmond: John Knox Press, 1964), p. 62. This is a short version of the untranslated *La Pensee Economique et Sociale de Calvin* (Geneve: Georg & Cie, 1961).

26. The inclusive language version of *The Confession of 1967* appears in *The Journal* of Presbyterian History, Spring 1983 (61:1).

27. *A Declaration of Faith* (Atlanta: General Assembly, PCUS, 1977).

28. "Economic Justice Within Environmental Limits," pp. 33, 29.

29. *A Study of the Theology of Compensation* contains "Theological and Ethical Reflections on Compensation" (*Minutes*, UPC, 1976, pp. 645–656), and reports from UPC Compensation task force and PCUS Mission Board (*Minutes*, PCUSA, 1983, pp. 499–501, 683–794), along with the Brueggemann paper and is available from the Office of the General Assembly.

30. *Minutes* (PCUSA, 1984), p. 397 *Christian Faith and Economic Justice*, in booklet form, is available from the Office of the General Assembly.

31. *Ibid.*, p. 383. The work of philosopher John Rawls is cited as a source. Note that "radical inequalities" are criticized. *Toward a Just, Caring and Dynamic Political Economy* has a similar view, p. 10.

32. J. Philip Wogaman, *Economics and Ethics* (Philadelphia: Fortress Press, 1986), pp. 72–3.

33. *The Church and Transnational Corporations*, p. 51.

34. I follow the basic argument in David Little's *Religion, Order and Law* that broadens the "Protestant Ethic" from Weber's focus on individual salvation anxiety to a larger concern for public righteousness, grounded not simply in election and predestination but in the whole structure of Calvinist beliefs. Thus he sees the Protestant Ethic of the Puritans and other Reformed groups as a "highly ambivalent attitude toward economic life," encouraging individual achievement and "private profitableness," while also remembering the fate of the larger community. This helps explain how the doctrine of vocation could link the social transformation characteristic of Reformed believers with the liberation of economic drives. This suggests that the Reformed doctrine of vocation had greater social impact than Calvin's loosening the reins on usury.

35. *The Confession of 1967*, sections 9.37 and 9.38.

36. *The Church, the Christian and Work* (Philadelphia: UPC Board of Christian Education, 1967), p. 34.

37. Charles Rawlings, "New Forms of Worker Organization and the Churches," an unpublished paper.

38. See Lee McDonald's essay elsewhere in this volume.

39. *Minutes*, (PCUSA, 1944), p. 204.

40. Consideration of church vocational life needs to be linked not only to compensation policies, but ministry studies that expressed indirectly views about work and vocation. Notable are *The Church and its Changing Ministry* in 1961, and *Model for Ministry* in 1970.

41. *Toward a Just, Caring and Dynamic Political Economy*, pp. 35, 10.

42. *Ibid.*, pp. 23, 30.

43. *Economic Justice Within Environmental Limits*, p. 23.

44. Jane Dempsey Douglass, "Calvin's Relation to Social and Economic Change," in *The Church and Transnational Corporations*, p. 75.

45. See Aileen S. Kraditor, *Means and Ends in American Abolitionism* (New York: Vintage, 1967), pp. 217–220, 232–34 on slave products and stocks.

46. Archie R. Crouch, "The United Presbyterian Church in Mission: An Historical Overview," *The Journal of Presbyterian History*, Fall 1979 (Vol. 57, No. 3), pp. 301–2. An excellent book-length study is Andrew Murray, *Presbyterian and the Negro—A History* (Philadelphia: Presbyterian Historical Society, 1966). Inez M. Parker, *The Rise and Decline of the Program of Education for Black Presbyterians of the United Presbyterian Church 1865–1970* (San Antonio: Trinity University Press, 1977) underlines the impact of the more than 125 high schools operated by the two Northern churches until the 'great depression.'

47. *Minutes* (UPNA, 1919), p. 761.

48. *Minutes* (PCUS, 1919), pp. 88, 94–5.

49. *Minutes* (PCUS, 1946), p. 81.

50. Dietar T. Hessel, "Prophecy and Politics: The Church and Society Stewardship" (New York: Advisory Council on Church and Society, June 12, 1975).

51. The South Shore Bank in Chicago represents one such profitable, yet socially conscious bank devoted to community development.

52. Elizabeth Howell Verdesi, *In But Still Out* (Philadelphia: The Westminster Press, 1973, 76).

53. Lois A. Boyd & R. Douglas Brackenridge, *Presbyterian Women in America* (Westport, CT: Greenwood Press/Presbyterian Historical Society, 1983), p. 224.

54. *Ibid.*, p. 154.

55. Stanley Hauerwas, *A Community of Character* (Notre Dame, IN: Notre Dame University Press, 1981) and George Lindbeck, *The Nature of Doctrine* (Philadelphia: The Westminster Press, 1983), present in different ways visions of the church as a separated community, with distinctive ethics and self-understanding. To some degree these views may help the church hold and even gain ground, but they also may reinforce impulses for retrenchment.

56. Lucien J. Richard, *The Spirituality of John Calvin* (Atlanta: John Knox Press, 1974), p. 175. Cited in Jane Dempsey Douglass, *Women, Freedom and Calvin* (Philadelphia: The Westminster Press, 1985), p. 39.

57. See William Gibson's essay elsewhere in this volume. Richard C. Austin is the former Chair of the Coalition of American Energy Consumers and has written a number of books on environmental ethics, aesthetics and theology.

58. *Economic Justice within Environmental Limits*, p. 41.

59. *Minutes* (PCUS, 1981), pp. 408–20; *Minutes* (UPC, 1981), 293–306. "The Power to Speak Truth to Power" is also available in a booklet from the CSWP. Robert Stivers, the policy's chief author, expands on its "sustainability" ethic in *Hunger, Technology & Limits to Growth* (Minneapolis: Augsburg Press, 1984).

60. As this was written in mid-summer 1987, U.S. warships were protecting tankers in the Persian Gulf, the speed limit had been raised to 65 miles per hour on many interstate highways, acid rain legislation had been stalled for seven years, and the Price Anderson Act cap on nuclear liability had been extended.

61. "Rural Community in Crisis," *Minutes*, (PC(USA), 1985), pp. 386–401; "Who Will Farm?" *Minutes*, (UPC, 1978), p. 271; *Minutes*, (PCUS, 1977, p. 182.